PERGAMON INTERNATIONAL LIBRARY

of Science, Technology, Engineering and Social Studies

*The 1000-volume original paperback library in aid of education,
industrial training and the enjoyment of leisure*

Publisher: Robert Maxwell, M.C.

COASTAL VEGETATION

SECOND EDITION

THE PERGAMON TEXTBOOK
INSPECTION COPY SERVICE

An inspection copy of any book published in the Pergamon International Library will gladly
be sent to academic staff without obligation for their consideration for course adoption or
recommendation. Copies may be retained for a period of 60 days from receipt and returned
if not suitable. When a particular title is adopted or recommended for adoption for class use
and the recommendation results in a sale of 12 or more copies, the inspection copy may
be retained with our compliments. The Publishers will be pleased to receive suggestions for
revised editions and new titles to be published in this important International Library.

Other Pergamon Press Titles of Interest

FAEGRI and VAN DER PIJL: *Principles of Pollination Ecology*

FAHN: *Plant Anatomy*

GOODWIN and MERCER: *An Introduction to Plant Biochemistry*

GOSS: *Physiology of Plants and Their Cells*

JAMIESON and REYNOLDS: *Tropical Plant Types*

LESHEM: *The Molecular and Hormonal Basis of Plant Growth Regulation*

PARSONS and TAKAHASHI: *Biological Oceanographic Processes*

PERCIVAL: *Floral Biology*

STREET and COCKBURN: *Plant Metabolism*

WAREING and PHILLIPS: *The Control of Growth and Differentiation in Plants*

DAVIES and SUNDERLAND: *Perspectives in Experimental Biology (Botany)*

MAYER and POLJAKOFF-MAYBER: *The Germination of Seeds*

COASTAL VEGETATION

by

V. J. CHAPMAN M.A., Ph.D., F.L.S.

Professor of Botany, Auckland University

SECOND EDITION

PERGAMON PRESS

OXFORD · NEW YORK · TORONTO · SYDNEY · PARIS · FRANKFURT

U.K.	Pergamon Press Ltd., Headington Hill Hall, Oxford OX3 0BW, England
U.S.A.	Pergamon Press Inc., Maxwell House, Fairview Park, Elmsford, New York 10523, U.S.A.
CANADA	Pergamon of Canada Ltd., 75 The East Mall, Toronto, Ontario, Canada
AUSTRALIA	Pergamon Press (Aust.) Pty. Ltd., 19a Boundary Street, Rushcutters Bay, N.S.W. 2011, Australia
FRANCE	Pergamon Press SARL, 24 rue des Ecoles, 75240 Paris, Cedex 05, France
FEDERAL REPUBLIC OF GERMANY	Pergamon Press GmbH, 6242 Kronberg-Taunus, Pferdstrasse 1, Federal Republic of Germany

First edition 1976

Reprinted 1978

Library of Congress Cataloging in Publication Data

Chapman, Valentine Jackson.
Coastal vegetation.
2nd edition
Includes bibliographies and index.
1. Coastal flora. 2. Coastal flora—North Atlantic region. I. Title.
QK938.C6C5 1976   581.9'09'821   76-5805

ISBN 0-08-020896-7 Hardcover
ISBN 0-08-019687-x Flexicover

In order to make this volume available as economically and rapidly as possible the author's typescript has been reproduced in its original form. This method unfortunately has its typographical limitations but it is hoped that they in no way distract the reader.

Printed in Great Britain by Biddles Ltd., Guildford, Surrey

CONTENTS

Preface to First Edition   vii

Preface to Second Edition   viii

Chapter 1.   Basic Ecological Principles   1

2.   Littoral Vegetation   18

3.   Algal Vegetation--the Environment   54

4.   Salt Marshes   87

5.   The Salt Marsh Environment   121

6.   Sand Dune Vegetation   150

7.   Sand Dunes--the Environment   184

8.   Mangrove Swamps   217

9.   Shingle Beaches   234

10.   Coastal Cliff Vegetation   253

Index   274

PREFACE TO FIRST EDITION

THIS book is one of a series designed to give a general account of the ecology
of types of British vegetation. Coastal vegetation differs greatly in various
parts of the world and an author can be faced with the problem of how far a-
field he should wander. Bearing in mind the purpose of this volume, the text
has been restricted almost wholly to the ecology of British vegetation. This
has not proved difficult in the descriptive sections, but when dealing with
the factors of the habitat it might be thought more reference should have been
made to studies outside of Great Britain. This could have involved different
climatic regions and the inevitable occasional reference to vegetation
unfamiliar to residents of Great Britain, and so it has been omitted.
Because it is hoped that one result of this book will be to encourage Sixth
Formers and First Year undergraduates to read accounts of the local
vegetation whenever it is available, every effort has been made to include at
the end of each chapter all known references to specific works on that
particular aspect of British coastal vegetation, whether it is referred to in
the text or not.

No book of this nature could be prepared without advice and critical comment
from those who have particularly worked on coastal areas. I wish, therefore,
to express my sincere thanks to Professor J. A. Steers for comments on the
salt marsh and shingle beach chapters, to Dr D. S. Ranwell for criticism of
the salt marsh and sand dune chapters, to Dr M. Gillham for helpful advice on
the coastal cliff chapter, and to Mr D. J. Chapman for comments on the
chapters dealing with the littoral. I am also most grateful to my colleague,
Professor J. E. Morton, for reading the whole manuscript and for valuable
discussions with him on problems of the littoral. Finally, there is my
deep appreciation of the advice and help given me by the series editor,
Professor G. F. Asprey, and Dr A. G. Lyon of his staff. Their comments and
help have undoubtedly improved the final product, though I must remain
responsible for opinions expressed and the general accuracy of statements.

Permission to reproduce the following figures is gratefully acknowledged:
figs. 1.1, 1.2, 7.8 - Heffer & Son; 4.1-4.4, 4.6, 4.8 - Leonard Hill & Co.;

7.4, 7.10, 7.12 - Bell & Co.; 7.15, 8.1 - Cambridge University Press.

Auckland   V. J. CHAPMAN

PREFACE TO SECOND EDITION

THIS new edition has been enlarged in order to include comparable types of coastal vegetation on the eastern shores of the U.S.A. as well as vegetation of the northern European Atlantic shores. Recent work in all fields of coastal vegetation has been drawn upon in compiling this new edition and the bibliography has been considerably extended. This new edition no longer deals exclusively with British coastal vegetation but with the coastal vegetation of the North Atlantic. It is hoped that this new edition will be of use to University students in Great Britain, northern Europe and the eastern U.S.A.

Auckland   V. J. CHAPMAN

CHAPTER 1

BASIC ECOLOGICAL PRINCIPLES

In this book coastal vegetation will be regarded as comprising (a) the marine
algal vegetation of the littoral and sublittoral, (b) the phanerogamic and
algal vegetation of salt and brackish marshes, (c) the vegetation of sand
dunes together with that of their "slacks", (d) the specialised vegetation
associated with the drift-line, (e) the vegetation of shingle beaches, (f)
the plants found on coastal cliffs and (g) mangrove (Florida).

These habitats are specialised and well defined so that they readily lend
themselves to ecological study. Furthermore, such environments possess
specific features that are reflected in the type of plants found growing
there, so that they are of especial interest. Moreover, within at least five
of these habitats one can find excellent examples of the phenomenon of
vegetation *zonation*. Such zonation is invariably associated with a gradation
in one or more of the environmental factors, and one of the major functions of
any ecological study is to establish those factors responsible for any zonation that can be observed.

ZONATION

When any particular habitat has been selected for study, the first procedure
is to become familiar with, and identify, all the plants that can be found.
The next step is to determine the exact nature of any zonation that can be
observed and to list the various species that are apparently typical of each
zone or belt. A consideration of the habitat should then indicate whether the
zoning is permanent (static) or whether it is in a state of flux (dynamic).
Thus zoning of the vegetation of the littoral, of shingle beaches and less
obviously, often possibly non-existent, of coastal cliffs, will be of a static
nature, not changing unless there is a variation in land-sea-level relationships or a large scale change induced by a major cliff-fall or slump. The
zoning of the vegetation of salt marshes, mangroves and sand dunes will be
dynamic or developmental, so that in any one spot on a salt marsh or mangrove
swamp, as more mud is deposited and the land level rises with consequent

environmental changes, the flora also gradually changes. A similar story can
likewise be observed on sand dunes as successive ridges form on the shore, the
oldest dunes with the most mature vegetation being to the landward, while the
youngest dunes with relatively few species and incompletely colonised are to
the seaward.

The communities associated with static zonation represent what some schools of
ecology term *climax* communities. There are those who believe that only one
kind of climax, the climatic climax, is represented in any one area. There
are others who consider that there may be more than one kind of climax in an
area. In the case of the littoral and of shingle beaches it can be argued
that the physiography determines the zonation, and therefore the communities
represent a physiographic climax. Whilst the idea of climax vegetation, or
vegetation in equilibrium with the environment, may commend itself to many,
there are those who argue that there is no such thing as a climax. Until one
has had an opportunity of studying and comparing many stands of vegetation
from comparable habitats, it is premature to discuss the validity or otherwise
of the climax concept. In the meantime, however, it is convenient for us to
accept the climax as a useful concept.

SUCCESSION

Developmental or dynamic zonation is more commonly called plant succession,
because starting from bare ground one can observe a series of communities that
succeed one another until the final or climax community is attained. When the
succession commences on bare ground not previously colonised it is known as a
prisere. The successions that are to be observed on sand dunes, salt marshes
and mangrove swamps are good examples of priseres (see Chapters 4, 6 and 8).
Should an area of dune that has developed to forest become destroyed by
burning a new succession would arise, but this would be known as a *subsere*.

Subseres in coastal habitats are of rare occurrence, and the student can
generally be assured that he is dealing with a prisere. Under certain conditions the succession may be halted, or it may revert to a previous stage or
it may deviate through another series of communities. The advent of a dense
population of browsing animals can result in the next stage of the succession
not developing. Thus it is probable that excessive grazing of some of the

west coast grass marshes (see p. 108) and former hay cutting of marsh grass on
Atlantic East Coast marshes has delayed or prevented the advent of the rush
or *Juncus* stage. Excessive grazing on salt marsh may damage the soil surface
to such an extent that the closed herb cover disappears and is replaced by
annual *Salicornia* (Saltwort) or *Suaeda* (Seablite), both generally representative of an earlier stage. Over-grazing of coastal cliffs brings about
replacement of Creeping fescue (*Festuca rubra*) by Sea pink (*Armeria maritima*)
or Sea plantain (*Plantago maritima*) (see p. 257). Deviation of a succession
is not common with coastal vegetation, but it has been recorded on Nova
Scotian salt marshes where it was produced as a result of persistent mowing
for hay grass.

Sand dunes, especially their damp valleys ("slacks"), can provide examples of
another ecological phenomenon, namely, *cyclic change*. This is sometimes known
as pattern and process. In this there is a build-up to a vegetation covering
which then becomes destroyed, either as a result of smothering by lichens or
mosses or through damage from animals or man, resulting ultimately in the
complete removal of the vegetation with a new bare surface on which the succession starts afresh (see p. 176). This process differs from a halted or
deflected succession in that there is a regular continuing sequence, whereas
in the others the induced stages only exist so long as the factor, e.g.
grazing, cutting, persists.

During the normal course of a succession, the early stages can be regarded as
far removed from equilibrium with the environment or habitat, successive
communities becoming more and more in harmony with it, so that when the climax
state is attained the final community is in equilibrium with the habitat.
During the course of a succession, each successive community adds to what may
be called the habitat potential, or the degree to which the habitat is
increasingly capable of accepting a new and perhaps wider range of plant
species. This concept is illustrated schematically in Fig. 1.1, where it will
be noted that each community of the succession is marked by a pioneer or
invasion stage (P), a Building stage (B), and a mature (M) stage which is
eventually invaded by the pioneers of the next community.

Because the study of salt marshes, mangroves and sand dunes involves the
study of successions, it is perhaps worth while to make brief reference to
what may be called the nature of the succession.

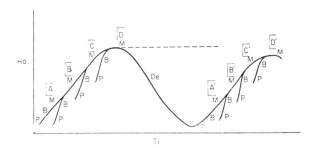

FIG 1.1. *Build-up through successive communities to a climax.*
Each community passes through a pioneer (P), *building* (B) *and*
mature (M) *phase. This development is plotted in terms of build-*
up of habitat potential (Ha) *with time* (Ti). *When degradation*
(De) *takes place the process is repeated (after Chapman).*

The first stage is the existence of the bare ground which arises as deposited
mud in the case of salt marshes and mangroves or as blown sand in the case of
dunes. The bare ground then becomes invaded by the first colonists.
Invasion depends on a variety of factors and again it is the function of the
ecologist to try and determine these factors and analyse their importance.
Such factors include proximity of potential seed parents, method of seed
dispersal (i.e. wind, animals or sea) or whether by vegetation fragments (as
may be the case with *Spartina townsendii*, see p. 145) when the direction and
strength of long-shore currents must be very important.

The arrival of the seeds is followed by the next stage, which is often called
ecesis. This involves the successful germination of the seed (and the existence, therefore, of suitable temperatures and water supply and the absence of
predators), successful growth of the plant to maturity (determined and controlled by the factors of the environment or habitat), flowering and the
setting of seed so that the community is perpetuated.

The advent of the plants brings about changes in the habitat. Thus organic
matter from dead plants is added to the soil, in the case of salt marshes and
sand dunes the presence of the plants results in the former case in increased
silt deposition, and in the second case in fixation of the sand so that it is
no longer so mobile. The plants also bring about changes in the soil
nutrients and soil water supply, and these changes may be further reflected in

the soil microflora and fauna (see p. 208). If the plants happen to be of
some size, they will also bring about changes in the micro-climate, e.g. air
movement, surface evaporation and relative humidity, and these changes may
determine the nature of other species that subsequently invade the community.
All these changes and effects upon the habitat can collectively be termed
reaction.

Invasion and reaction result in more plants entering the former area, and
usually at quite an early stage *competition* for soil nutrients, soil water
and even light may become important features of the community. This
competition is likely to reach its maximum for any species just around the
period of flowering, when plants generally make their greatest demand on the
habitat. A community could therefore be regarded as more successful if the
flowering periods of its principal species do not all occur at the same time.

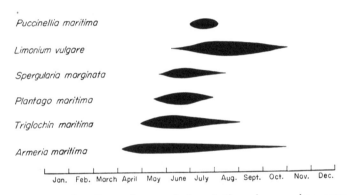

FIG. 1.2. *The flowering periods of the six species comprising the
General Salt Marsh community at Scolt Head (after Chapman).*

In the case of the General Salt Marsh community (see p. 108) where there are a
number of co-dominant species, the flowering times are staggered (Fig. 1.2).
This is one aspect of coastal ecology that merits much more attention, not
only in respect of actual flowering periods, but in determining the demands
made by the principal species at different stages of their life history.

The final stage in the succession is *stabilisation,* when the climax community
is reached, and with it comes dominance of the principal life-form. Earlier
stages will have exhibited the phenomenon of dominance of one or more species
as such, but in the climax community one has not only dominance of species
but also of a particular life-form (see p. 8), which under normal, non-
extreme climatic conditions is generally trees.

COMMUNITY ANALYSIS

Whether one is dealing with a static zonation, and hence climax communities, or a developmental zonation (succession), it is important to be able to describe the communities in such a way that they can be compared with similar communities elsewhere. One also needs to know the extent of variation within any given community.

One way of doing this after recognition of the community, which is generally possible by eye, is to prepare a list of the species, including if at all possible the animals. However, a species list is not of itself sufficient. We must know something of the relative frequency or abundance. This has been done by making use of terms such as dominant, abundant, frequent, occasional, rare, local, etc., but it is evident that such terms are subject to individual interpretation. Analysis of the community is therefore much more satisfactory if this kind of interpretation can be eliminated.

Some communities are very large, and whilst it may be easy to prepare a species list, detailed analysis of the entire community would take far too long. Use is made instead of samples, these being commonly contained within a square area known as a quadrat. The size of the quadrat must be such that it yields a fair statistical sample of the community. There are various ways of determining the minimal area that will give a fair sample of a particular type of community, and for those interested reference should be made to standard ecological texts (2,9,10). Generally speaking, on sand dunes, shingle beaches and salt marshes, one square metre is likely to be sufficient, and at least ten such quadrats should be used for each community. On the rocky sea coast smaller areas may be adequate for the seaweed vegetation. In the case of a mangrove swamp quadrats should be at least a hundred square metres, but a ten metre wide belt transect from sea front to upland is almost better. Traditionally the quadrat is a square, but under certain conditions a rectangle with sides in the ratio 1 : 16 may be better, or a belt transect of one or two metres wide can be employed. In the succeeding chapters reference will be made to investigations that have involved use of all these variants.

With low vegetation it is also possible to make use of what is known as the "point method" where a long pin is repeatedly stuck in the ground and the species physically touched are listed. For the use of this technique,

reference should be made to works by Goodall(8) and Greig-Smith (9). With quadrats, which should normally be located at random, one can provide lists of
species occurring, numbers of individuals of species, or one can map the quadrat showing the species spatially distributed. So long as the quadrats are
all located in the same community, one can determine what is known as
frequency, density, abundance and percentage cover:

$$\text{frequency} = \frac{\text{No. of occupied quadrats}}{\text{Total no. of quadrats}} \times 100$$

$$\text{density} = \frac{\text{Total no. of individual plants}}{\text{Total no. of quadrats}}$$

$$\text{abundance} = \frac{\text{Total no. of individual plants}}{\text{No. of occupied quadrats}} \times 100 \quad \frac{\text{density}}{\text{frequency}}$$

Cover percentage = percentage of ground covered in the quadrats by a perpend-
icular projection of the aerial parts of the individual plants on to the quadrat.

This is not the place to enter into a discussion of the relative value and
significance of the figures for frequency, abundance, density and cover, but
before any of them are used, reference should be made to Greig-Smith (9).

Biological material is notoriously variable and any field method is also subject to experimental error. The increasing application of mathematical
methods in ecology is designed to overcome these problems. Presentation of
the results of mathematical analysis in the form of histogram and scatter diagrams etc. is also desirable. Most mathematical ecological analyses involve
the use of variance, standard error, linear regression, t test and χ^2
test for association and the use of probability tables. All these techniques
will be found in the relevant text books (2,10).

Use can be made of some of the data in order to arrive at what is often known
as a *coefficient of similarity* or *coefficient of community*, whereby two
different or two apparently similar communities can be compared. There are
various ways of arriving at such coefficients, and those interested should

consult Greig-Smith(9). Comparisons of this nature are only justified if one
can really recognise distinct communities that are capable of analysis, and
even then the methods employed are open to some criticism. Recent work has
tended to throw doubt on the reality of many plant communities, and ecologists are talking today in terms of a vegetation continuum, or of a kaleido-
scope of smaller patterns that make up the apparent community (6).

Considerable attention is being given at the present time to methods of analysis of *continua* or of vegetation patterns, and it may be that the objective
approach will differ in the future. Analysis of communities is, however, only
a means to an end, and provided it effectively delineates the community and
enables it to be compared with another analysed by the same technique, the
ecologist has a useful tool in his hand.

Quadrats are not the only means by which communities can be analysed. Life-
form can and has been used successfully, and indeed can give a valuable clue
to lines of further profitable study. Life-form analysis generally involves
use of Raunkaier's life-form classification(13), the principal coastal life-
forms being:

Phanerophytes (Ph)	Trees or shrubs with buds more than 25 cm above soil surface, e.g. Sea Buckthorn (*Hippophäe rhamnoides*), Red mangrove (*Rhizophora mangle*).
Chamaephytes (Ch)	Perennating buds above soil surface to 25 cm, e.g. Creeping willow (*Salix repens, Pluchea camphorata*).
Hemicryptophytes (H)	Plants with perennating organ at soil surface, e.g. Sea plantain (*Plantago maritima*).
Geophytes (G)	Perennating organ below soil surface, e.g. Cord grass (*Spartina* spp.).
Hydro-helophytes (Hh)	Water plants with perennating buds in water or in mud below the water, e.g. Eel grass (*Zostera marina*).
Therophytes (Th)	Annuals, e.g. Sea rocket (*Cakile maritima*).

When the various species have been allocated to their life-form, a biological
spectrum (life-forms expressed as a percentage of the total number of species
in the community) can be produced. It is desirable to make allowance for the
phenomenon of dominance and so the life-form is best calculated on the frequency figures, e.g.

species a (Hemicryptophyte)   97 percent frequency = 97 points

species b (Geophyte)   13 percent frequency = 13 points

An example of the results that can be obtained from life-form spectra is
provided in Table 1.1 and also in Table 4.3, p.97.

TABLE 1.1

*Life-form Spectra of Salt Marshes in different parts of the World (from
Chapman (6))*

Area	Ph.	Ch.	H.	G	Hh.	Th.	P.
California	-	14	31	9	-	43	3
Massachusetts	3.5	3.5	60.5	11	7	14.5	-
Argentine	-	2	37.5	20	1	39.5	-
New Zealand	8	4	56	8	8	16	-
Europe	-	10	40	10	10	30	-
Hungarian inland saline marsh	-	5	40	12	5	38	-

There is no generally recognised life-form system for the algae, so that comparable work on a rocky shore has not been carried out. For those who might
be interested in analysing seaweed communities in this fashion, the system
that seems most workable at present is that of Feldmann, which can be found
summarised in Chapman and Chapman (6). Recently Chapman and Chapman (7) have
proposed a new system of life forms for the algae which results in significant
biological spectral differences as between salt marsh and rocky shore (Table
1.2).

On the Continent, another system of vegetation analysis is employed. This is
based essentially on floristics, and in particular upon groups of species
which are termed the "faithful" species because they are regarded as characteristic of the community (1). Consideration is also given to other ecological
features, but association of characteristic species, and in certain cases
other groups which are known as differential species, is the main basis of the
system. The floristic composition, both qualitative and quantitative, is

TABLE 1.2

Percentage of Life-forms in Total Floras (after Chapman and Chapman (7))

Area	Cp.	Lp.	Gp.	Mp.	Msp.	Chp.	Dp.	Tp.	Ep.	Enp.	Lip.	Ppt.
Scolt SM	0.7	28.9	8.0	0	16.0	0	24.8	12.7	5.3	3.4	0.7	0
Lynn SM	0	54.7	13.3	0	3.9	0	3.4	14.6	7.8	1.3	0	0
Iceland	5.77	1.4	1.4	0	24.5	4.2	1.4	37.0	11.0	6.4	1.9	0
NEN USA	5.07	3.0	1.84	0.26	34.2	6.33	3.0	10.2	26.8	7.44	1.32	0.5
Dry Tortugas	19.5	5.5	0.25	0	55.6	3.75	8.25	2.75	8.25	0.5	0.75	2.0

SM	= salt marsh flora	Cp	= Calciphykes
Lp	= Eleutherophykes	Gp	= Geophykes
Mp	= Megaphykes	Msp	= Mesophykes
Chp	= Chamaephykes	Dp	= Deciduiphykes
Tp	= Therophykes	Ep	= Epiphykes
Enp	= Endophykes	Lip	= Lithophykes
Ppt	= Planktophykes		

regarded as the indicator of the specific environment. The vegetation is sampled in order to determine the faithful species, and at least ten samples should be taken. No size for the sample is set, and as the samples are selected as being representative rather than at random, the system is more subjective than one in which quadrats of a standard size are employed. In each sample every species is given a value for its cover degree-abundance and another for its sociability, and from these values a synthetic list is prepared headed by the "faithful" species.

One value of this system is that any community is based, like a taxonomic species, upon a specific example which takes the name of its original author. Subsequent workers can, if necessary, visit the "type" community in the same way as the taxonomist can study the "type" specimen of a given species. However, it does not always follow that the "type" community will remain in its original condition, because if it is part of a succession it will inevitably undergo change. Listing the "type" community is therefore really only of value in a climax or stable community (details can be found in Braun-Blanquet

(1) and in Poore (11,12) or Whittaker (16).

The present author believes that in specialised habitats such as salt marshes, mangrove swamps and sand dunes, where the number of species is limited by their tolerance to the specific environmental conditions, the Continental system has much to commend it, and a universal classification can be worked out (for details see Chapman (4,5)).

In general it can be suggested that no system of analysis is without its flaws and great interest and value can be derived by the use of more than one system to describe the same piece of vegetation.

TERMINOLOGY

When the vegetation has been analysed, there is still the problem of how it should be classified and what terminology should be used. In this book, the ecological terms will be used in the same sense as by Tansley (14). It is, however, important to note that the same terms have been given rather different meanings by other schools of ecology. In a climax community, regarded by Tansley as a community of relative stability, the *association* is a major plant community dominated by distinctive species and distinctive life-forms. It is convenient to recognise such communities by use of the termination -etum. Thus for a community dominated by species of *Juncus* one refers to the Juncetum. The same procedure can also be used for the next smaller unit, e.g. the Juncetum gerardii is a community dominated by a single species, *J. gerardi.*

Within the association one may find *consociations*, each dominated by a single species, and within the consociation there can be *societies* each dominated by subsidiary species. The *associes*, *consocies* and *socies* are their equivalents in a sere (succession). It is clear, therefore, that analysis of communities should be aimed at classifying the community into one of the groups mentioned above. In carrying out such analysis, it is important to remember that the use of any of these terms can be in either of two senses. They can be used in the concrete sense to refer to a particular community, e.g. the General Salt Marsh associes of Scolt Head Island in Norfolk, or they can be used in the abstract sense, i.e. the concept of the General Salt Marsh associes, based

upon a consideration of numerous samples from a very wide variety of salt
marshes.

The concepts of continua or of vegetation patterns in the study of communities
makes classification much more difficult, and theoretically it may turn out
that the terms used above may cease to be valid. Nevertheless they have
served a very useful purpose in the past, and there is no doubt that at present they can continue to do so.

THE ENVIRONMENT

After the basic steps of recognising, analysing and classifying the communities have been carried out, attention must be directed to the habitat or
environment. Here it is important to be clear from the outset what is being
investigated. In the case of a community (*communal habitat*) it is possible to
make measurements of the environmental features at a given date - in this
case we deal with a *partial habitat*. This picture is obviously inadequate and
a clearer idea will be secured by measurements obtained throughout the year.
These figures can be left as they are or mean values can be calculated, and if
this is then continued over a series of years it is possible to arrive at what
is termed the *successional habitat*. This kind of study can be extended from a
single community to include the habitat of two or more like communities. If
the data is again averaged out, we shall be presented with an abstract concept
of the habitat characterising that particular community. In cases where
attention is being given to the ecology of a single species (*individual
habitat*) one may have the same approach - i.e. the habitat of a single individual of the species at one given moment, the habitat of the same individual
over a long period, or the characteristic habitat derived from a study of the
habitats of a number of individuals.

When the kind of habitat it is proposed to investigate has been determined, it
will be found that the study falls into four major sections:

    (a)   climate   (c)   soil

    (b)   physiography (including tides)   (d)   biota

In the case of the littoral beach, drift-line, mangrove swamp and salt marsh, the tidal factor is of very great importance, and climate is less important. Even so, however, there are extensive periods when the vegetation is not submerged and is therefore subject to the normal climatic factors of the region. It is necessary in these three cases and also with sand dunes, coastal cliffs and shingle beaches to secure as much information as possible about the major regional climate.*

It is also highly desirable to obtain detailed information about the microclimate, that is the climate immediately above and within the community, because this usually plays a part in determining what species may be associated with the dominants. This information can be of particular importance with tall vegetation, e.g. Marram grass, *Juncus maritimus* marsh, *Spartina* marsh, mangrove swamp.

The principal variables that require study within the community are (a) maximum and minimum temperatures, (b) precipitation (this can be done by setting up a rain gauge and taking weekly readings), (c) relative humidity (this can be carried out by using a whirling psychrometer, which gives a wet and dry bulb thermometer reading, and the R.H. is then read off from tables), (d) evaporating power of the air (achieved quite easily by the use of a simple atmometer - see Fig. 1.3), (e) wind velocity (simple portable anemometers are available for this purpose), (f) light intensity (comparative, but *not* absolute values can be obtained by the use of suitable photographic exposure meters).

Study of the tides, which is essential with littoral, mangrove and salt marsh vegetation, really demands the use of a tide gauge. This is rarely available but in default useful information can be obtained by the use of a tide pole. This is a pole clearly marked in feet and inches, which is set up firmly in a sheltered spot and then the height of the tide at different times recorded from it. Such records are obtained on as many calm days as possible and preferably over a full tidal cycle. The tide pole can be related by levelling to a bench mark and hence to ordnance datum, or the help of the Navy hydrographic office can be invoked to relate the information to the nearest port of

* This can be obtained from the Meteorological Office, UK or Department of Civil Aviation (USA).

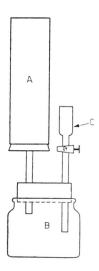

FIG. 1.3. *Simple type of atmometer.* A, *porous clay cylinder;*
B, *water reservoir;* C, *place for addition of water. At start the*
whole apparatus must be full of water. The amount lost over a
given period is measured by the volume of water that has to be
added to bring the water up to the tap.

reference. In either case it will then become possible to use predicted tide
curves, if wanted, from the nearest place with an official tide gauge.

Communities of sand dunes, salt marshes, mangrove swamp, shingle beach and
coastal cliff require that some attention be given to the nature of the soil
or substratum in which the plants grow. The features that are of greatest
importance can be listed as follows:

> A. *Physical*
>> Pore space
>>
>> Aeration
>>
>> Temperature
>>
>> Water table movement
>
> B. *Chemical*
>> Organic matter
>>
>> Carbonate content
>>
>> Salinity

Iron ⎫
Nitrogen ⎪
Potash ⎬ content
Phosphate ⎪
Water ⎭

c. *Biological*

      macro-organisms, e.g. crabs, worms

      micro-organisms (mainly fungi and bacteria)

The significance of these various factors is dealt with in any book on ecological principles and reference will be made here only to those that can conveniently be studied in a simple fashion. Aeration in the soils of a salt marsh is an important feature and can be demonstrated readily (see p. 130). Soil thermometers are available commercially and very interesting results can be secured, especially on sand dunes (see p. 189) and shingle beaches.

In all four habitats, movement of the water table may be of very great importance. In shingle beaches and sand dunes, simple pits will yield valuable information (see p. 249), but on salt marshes and in mangroves another type of approach is necessary (see p. 129). In all cases, one should look for any evidence that suggests movements are determined by tidal phenomena.

After a soil has been dried in an oven at 105°C the organic matter can be determined by the loss on ignition, when the sample is heated red hot in a crucible. Very interesting results have been obtained for certain dune areas in relation to age (see p. 205) and this could be extended to other dune systems.

In coastal vegetation, salinity is of paramount importance, because there is evidence that it plays a major part in controlling some of the zonation. In this respect, the ecologist is concerned with the salinity of the soil water table and the salinity of the soil itself. Thus, with dunes and shingle beaches it is likely that a fresh water table will be found floating on a salt water one (p. 195). Samples of the water can be removed and the salinity determined by titration against standard silver nitrate (see p. 132). In the absence of any soil water table, the salinity of the soil can be determined by leaching with a known volume of distilled water and again titrating. An approximation of the nitrogen, phosphorus, iron and potassium content of the

soil can be obtained by simple spot test methods, e.g. Morgan spot tests,*
which are based upon colours that are compared with standard colour charts.
The iron content has been neglected in the past but the need of some plants
for iron (e.g. *Spartina* spp.) suggests that this element could be important.

The extent to which the biota is of importance varies with the community.
Before the advent of myxomatosis the rabbit population of sand dunes and
coastal cliffs in Europe was an important factor, and in some cases, at least,
determined the stability of the dune system. On coastal cliffs the bird population can be highly significant, especially if the area is used for nesting,
because of the excessive trampling and the great enrichment by nitrogenous
material. On salt marshes and mangrove swamps burrowing crabs, mollusca and
annelids undoubtedly assist in aeration of the soil. The littoral, however,
is the principal coastal habitat in which animals play as important a part as
do the plants, so much so that the communities are in fact biomes in which
sometimes animals are the dominants and sometimes plants.

AUTECOLOGY

We have concerned ourselves so far with communities. This represents what is
known as *synecology*. Communities are comprised of individual species, and
each species can be studied in detail. Such studies represent *autecology*,
and they involve not only the same kinds of investigation outlined for the
communities, but additional work as well. First of all, a taxonomic study is
essential, in order to determine whether there is any evidence of ecological
variation. If there is, the plants need to be grown under uniform conditions
to ascertain whether such variations are "fixed" or not. Germination studies
are essential, especially in relation to degrees of salinity and water content.
In fact, the plant must be followed through its entire life history in relation to every possible variation in the habitat. In addition, any peculiar
morphological features, e.g. existence of aerenchyma (tissue with air spaces)
or succulence, should be investigated in relation to the peculiar conditions
of the habitats. The species has to be studied not only under natural conditions, but it must be grown experimentally under controlled conditions. The

* Cf. Morgan Soil Testing System. *Bull. Connect. Agric. Expt.
Station,* 541.

objective in each case should be the production of an account of the type
appearing in the *Biological Flora of the British Isles* (3).

Because it has been rather easier to carry out, most of the work in the past
has been of a synecological nature. There is abundant scope at present for
autecological studies, especially among species restricted to coastal communities.

REFERENCES

1   BRAUN-BLANQUET J., *Pflanzensoziologie*. 2nd Ed. Vienna (1951).

2   CAMPBELL R.C., *Statistics for Biologists*. Camb. Univ. Press (1967).

3   CHAPMAN V.J., *Suaeda fruticosa* (L.) Forsk. in *Biological Flora of the
     British Isles*. *J. Ecol.*, 35, 303 (1947).

4   CHAPMAN V.J., *Salt Marshes and Salt Deserts of the World*. 2nd Ed. Cramer
     (1974).

5   CHAPMAN V.J., *Mangrove Vegetation*. Cramer (1975).

6   CHAPMAN V.J. and D.J., *The Algae*. 2nd Ed. Macmillan (1974).

7   CHAPMAN V.J. and D.J., Life-form in the Algae. *Bot. Mar.* (in press).

8   GOODALL D.W., Some considerations in the use of point quadrats for the
     analysis of vegetation. *Aust. J. Sci. Res.*, Ser. B, 5, 1-41 (1952).

9   GREIG-SMITH P., *Quantitative Plant Ecology*. Butterworths (1957).

10   KERSHAW K.A., *Quantitative and Dynamic Ecology*. Arnold, Lond. (1964).

11   POORE M.E.D., The use of phytosociological methods in ecological investi-
     gations, I-III. *J. Ecol.* 43, 226, 606 (1955).

12   POORE M.E.D., The use of phytosociological methods in ecological investi-
     gations, IV. *J. Ecol.*, 44, 28 (1956).

13   RAUNKAIER C., The Life-forms of Plants and Statistical Plant Geography.
     (Translation) Oxford Univ. Press (1934).

14   TANSLEY A.G., *The British Islands and their Vegetation*. Camb. Univ. Press
     (1949).

15   WATT A.S., Pattern and Process in the Plant Community. *J. Ecol.*, 35(1),
     1-22 (1947).

16   WHITTAKER R.H., Classification of natural communities. *Bot. Rev.*, 28(1),
     1-160 (1962).

CHAPTER 2

LITTORAL VEGETATION

ALGAL COMMUNITIES

Algal communities are readily studied wherever there is an accessible rocky
coast. A beach of small boulders or pebbles is generally too mobile to carry
any extensive vegetation unless in a very sheltered locality, though even then
the range of species to be found will be restricted. Estuaries with rocky
shores, such as parts of the Bristol Channel or Chesapeake Bay, are not so
rich floristically as the open coast, because the lowered salinity eliminates
some algae. The silt brought down by a river and deposited continuously near
the mouth probably eliminates other species, not only through the actual
deposition, but also because of the greatly lowered light intensity. In the
case of Chesapeake Bay silt is brought down by a number of large rivers.

Ecologically the algal communities of the sea-shore lend themselves admirably
to detailed study. The principal species, together with certain marine
animals, form well-marked belts on the shore and the phenomenon is not confined to any one region, but is more or less universal, though the component
species obviously vary in different parts of the world. If a variety of
localities is readily available, it will be found that there is a variation
both in number of species and abundance of individuals, as between a rocky
coast and an exposed one. Comparisons of the type suggested are well worth
making, since they provide information about species absent respectively from
the different types of coast (Figs. 2.1 and 2.2).

LITTORAL (Rocky Shores)

On the coast the algal vegetation can be divided into that of the littoral and
that of the sublittoral. We shall have to consider very briefly what is meant
by the littoral, as considerable debate has taken place concerning its limits.
There are two possible criteria that can be used in defining it. One is
purely physical and based upon tidal phenomena. Thus it is possible to
regard the littoral as extending from mean high water (M.H.W.) to mean low

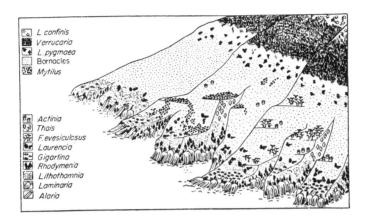

Legend:
L. confinis
Verrucaria
L. pygmaea
Barnacles
Mytilus

Actinia
Thais
F. evesiculosus
Laurencia
Gigartina
Rhodymenia
Lithothamnia
Laminaria
Alaria

FIG. 2.1. *Diagrammatic representation of types of exposed shores around Anglesey. The slope on the left represents a simple extremely exposed shore with few species superimposed upon the barnacles. The other slopes show slightly less exposed shores and indicate the influence of ledges and clefts upon the distribution of* Mytilus, Fucus *var.* evesiculosus *and* Thais. *Although shown separately* Mytilus *and* Fucus *often occur together. The depth of the black zone has been considerably reduced: on these shores it would probably be at least twice as deep as the barnacle zone. Note that* Patella, Littorina neritoides, L. rudis *and* Porphyra *would also be abundant but are not shown (after Lewis).*

water mark (M.L.W.); alternatively, it can be defined as reaching from extreme high water mark (E.H.W.M.) to extreme low water mark (E.L.W.M.). Most of the early ecological work is based upon one of these two definitions. More recently, ecologists have come to realise that the problem is not so simple, because the zones of dominant plants and animals that are so characteristic of the littoral vary according to the influence of factors such as exposure, aspect, latitude and topography, and the tide is not necessarily paramount. For this reason, Lewis(43) urges that it would be far better to employ a biological definition based upon the distribution of major organisms. The biological criteria that he proposes are essentially founded upon the views of the Stephensons(59), which in turn were derived from surveys conducted in many parts of the world. For the moment biological criteria are probably best and whether a tidal basis can be used remains to be seen. It is probable that zonation is primarily an interspecific biological competition(15) phenomenon. In the end it is likely that both biotic and abiotic factors are involved and the relative contribution of each has yet to be worked out. The Stephensons recognised three major belts, the supra-littoral fringe, the mid-littoral and

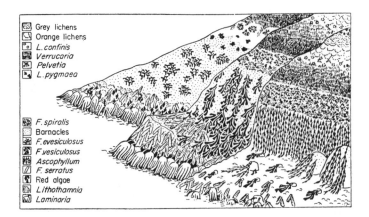

FIG. 2.2. *Diagrammatic representation of one semi-exposed and two sheltered shores around Anglesey, wave action decreasing from left to right. On the sheltered shores the influence of slope and substratum upon the large algae is shown. No attempt has been made to include animals other than barnacles (after Lewis).*

the sublittoral fringe (sometimes called infra-littoral). The Stephensons used the term "zone" for these belts, but since "zone" has a latitudinal or geographical connotation, it is better replaced, as here, by the word "belt". The limits of these belts were determined by certain dominant groups. Thus the upper limit of the supra-littoral fringe was set by the upper limit of periwinkles (*Littorina* spp.); the boundary between this belt and the mid-littoral was determined by the upper limit of barnacles (*Balanus, Chthalamus*), whilst the lower limit of the mid-littoral was marked by the upper limit of the oarweeds (*Laminaria* spp.). The Stephensons used extreme high and low water marks as their limits of the littoral so that their belts did not co-incide with average tidal levels, the supra-littoral fringe straddling extreme high water mark, and the sublittoral fringe straddling extreme low water mark. Lewis(43)suggests that it would be much better to determine the upper limit of what he calls the *littoral zone* by the upper limit of either the *Littorina* or black lichen (*Verrucaria*)/Myxophyceae belt, whichever happens to be uppermost. The lower limit of the littoral zone he regards as the boundary between the oarweeds and the barnacles and Fucaceae (Fig. 2.3). Above the littoral zone is the maritime zone occupied by orange and grey lichens, whilst below it is the sublittoral zone. The Stephensons supra-littoral fringe is termed the littoral fringe, and their mid-littoral becomes the eulittoral zone.

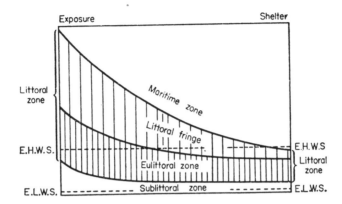

FIG. 2.3. *The proportions and positions of the littoral zones proposed as they may occur around British rocky coasts. Greater variation does exist, however, for on sheltered shores with a large tide range the eulittoral zone may be several times deeper than the littoral fringe, while on exposed shores with a very small tide range or under conditions of greater exposure on mild, northern coasts, the littoral fringe may be several times deeper than the eulittoral zone. Under special, local conditions the upper limit of the sublittoral zone may rise more steeply than that of the eulittoral (after Lewis).*

The existence of the sublittoral fringe has been questioned by some workers, but it is quite clear that there are certain algae, and perhaps also some animals, that occupy a belt just below the eulittoral which, on sheltered coasts, straddles extreme low water mark. Whether one regards this fringe as a subdivision of the sublittoral, in the same way as different belts can be recognised within the eulittoral, or as a belt equivalent to the littoral fringe, must be a matter of opinion. In any case, it is clear that further work is necessary before it can be said that the sublittoral fringe belt is as universal as the eulittoral and littoral fringe.

In the present state of our knowledge, it would seem that the system proposed by Lewis has great merit and is the one that should be adopted. It avoids difficulties over the definition of the littoral proper and the universality of the principal demarcating organisms makes for easy recognition of the belts. It will be observed (Fig. 2.3) that the relationships between these belts and the tide marks varies depending upon the degree of exposure. On very exposed coasts the swash of the waves raises the sublittoral well above extreme low water mark of spring tides.

So far as algae are concerned, the sublittoral will extend downwards to the point where algae cease to grow. This depth varies in different parts of the world and is greatest in the clearer waters of the world, e.g. 250 m in the Adriatic, 180 m off the Balearic Isles.

Within the littoral zone one can generally find rock pools of varying size and depth. These can contain a very rich vegetation and it is well worth examining the deeper pools to see if a micro-zonation is present or not. The environmental conditions are very different from those on the rocks around and because they represent compact, self-contained units rock pools are ideal for study. It will be found that the vegetation varies with height of the pool on the shore, so that when pools are selected for study their height in relation to the tide heights must be determined at an early stage.

It will be evident that certain marine animals are equally important as dominant organisms of recognisable belts. Indeed the marine rocky coast communities are ideally biotic communities or biomes in the sense that often a plant and animal species are co-dominant. Study of such communities therefore emphasises the importance of both kingdoms in nature.

Within the major divisions outlined above, the belts of the different communities can be recognised. The actual number of different communities or belts may vary from place to place and some of the variations in the published literature almost certainly reflect the opinions of the different authors. Whilst the zonation is essentially a static one and the dominants are to be found at all times of the year, some of the associated species may be seasonal so that a full descriptive account requires observations made over at least twelve months. One of the major issues is the problem of how the communities comprising the belts shall be named. Should one use the terminology of terrestrial ecology as applied to static or climax communities (e.g. Formation, Association, Consociation, Society), or should a completely new set of terms be formulated? Thus it has been suggested that a group of belts that follow one another vertically should be termed an "association complex", which automatically assumes that each belt has the status of an Association as defined in terrestrial ecology. A belt may be broken horizontally by another community, especially in places where fresh water trickles over the rocks, or where there are couloirs.* The interrupting community can be termed as Association fragment. At present most marine ecologists are using the terminology of terrestrial ecology, no other alternative so far proposed having proved satisfactory. If it is considered difficult to determine the status of the belts, then one can use the non-committal term of "Community".

BELT ANALYSIS

Although it is generally easy to recognise a dominant or dominants within any belt, and hence to name the belts according to the dominants, nevertheless the belts can also be analysed in terms of the Continental or Montpellier system (see p. 9).

In the past, analysis of belts has generally been carried out by listing the species that occur, and often, in addition, making an estimate by inspection of their relative frequency. If the Montpellier system is used, not only are the species listed but they are given the usual two-figure values.

Apart from the existence of the algal belts that lie within one of the major belts as delineated by Lewis or the Stephensons, the algal communities would appear capable of classification either according to their dominant(s) or on the basis of the "faithful" species, without the necessity of introducing a completely new terminology.

So far very little attempt has been made by marine botanists to use the traditional quadrat techniques of the terrestrial ecologist. In 1953 quadrats had been used with some success in Norway (2), especially in connection with littoral vegetation. From the quadrats the density of the brown rockweed *Ascophyllum*, in terms of fresh weight per quadrat, was obtained and the percentage occurrence (= frequency) of *Ascophyllum*, *Fucus vesiculosus*, *F. serratus* and *Codium* determined in six areas. In view of the great variation in fresh weight that can occur in algae, depending mainly upon the time after exposure, the density would have been better expressed in terms of dry weight. Quadrats should normally be located at random, but in the Norwegian study it was considered best to lay out ½ m transects vertical to the shore-line at

*A deep cleft between the rocks.

intervals of 5 m. Each transect was divided into metre lengths, and all quadrats containing *Ascophyllum* were sampled from the topmost one on the shore down to the lowest. As may be expected the percentage occurrence (frequency) increases with increasing size of quadrat. Mathematically the increase is not so great as it should be if the species were randomly dispersed. The conclusion therefore reached is that the plants are over-dispersed or aggregated into clumps. This raises an interesting problem because in the case of land plants, where seeds may drop to the ground around the parent plant, one can see how over-dispersion may arise; in the case of the fucoids, fertilisation takes place in the water and one would have expected the fertilised eggs to settle randomly, though this possibility would be affected by the presence of other plants and local water movements.

For those who wish to try the use of quadrats, and there is no doubt that a great deal of very valuable information can be obtained from them, it is worth noting that the $\frac{1}{2}$ m^2 quadrat was found to be the best size. Quadrats very often may not do more than confirm the field observations but they have the advantage of expressing the results quite objectively. Thus in the Norwegian study the *Ascophyllum* density was less on stony shores than on rocky ones, but there was no maximum density in the middle of the zone. *Ascophyllum* and *Fucus serratus* were more frequent on rocky shores but *F. vesiculosus* was more frequent on stony ones. It also emerged that on the shores sampled, *Ascophyllum* (Fig. 2.4) and *Fucus vesiculosus* were more frequent in the upper half of the zone whereas *F. serratus* and *Codium* were more frequent in the lower half. The quadrats were also used to demonstrate the effect of shore physiography upon species frequency. With a large number of quadrats it is possible to determine the degree of association between pairs of species. There are various ways of doing this and for those who are so minded they will be found in any good book on statistics. The calculations in this particular case showed that there was a significant positive association between *Codium* and *Fucus vesiculosus* (i.e. they were likely to occur together), a negative association between *Codium* and the other two fucoids, similarly between *Fucus serratus* and *F. vesiculosus*, whilst the distribution of *Ascophyllum* was found to be independent of both *Fucus* species.

Using single transects on five different types of shore in the Isle of Wight and 25 cm^2 quadrats, Kain(32) determined the levels and occurrence of 65 macroscopic algae and 25 diatoms. This particular study was of interest because

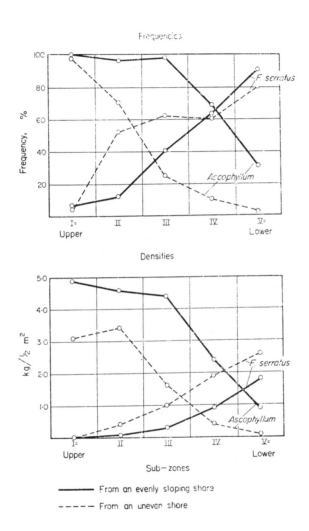

FIG. 2.4. *Frequencies and densities of* Ascophyllum *and* Fucus serratus *on two kinds of rocky shore (after Baardseth).*

the original survey was made in April and then repeated in July. The results
showed that the vertical distribution of the common species showed little
change, but the existence of the fucoid belts was clearly dependent upon the
slope of the substratum where fucoids are greatly restricted (Fig. 2.5). The
use of quadrats, coupled with the exclusion of the sea urchin, *Echinus*
esculentus, successfully demonstrated that grazing by these animals on sporelings of *Laminaria hyperborea* effectively determined the lower limit of the
belt.

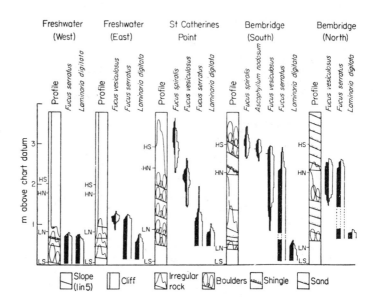

FIG. 2.5. *Diagram of the summarised profiles in five localities on*
the Isle of Wight, together with the limits to which the fucoids
and Laminaria *extended, in April and July.* HS, HN, *mean high water*
springs and neaps; LN, LS, *mean low water neaps and springs (after*
Kain).

There is no doubt that the use of quadrats can be greatly extended on the sea-
shore, not only on the littoral but also in the sublittoral (see p. 40). It
has been pointed out (p. 8) that terrestrial ecologists are moving towards
the view that any piece of vegetation is either a mosaic or else part of a
continuum with gradual variation in all directions towards other patterns. So
far no attempt has been made to determine whether the vegetation patterns to
be observed on the sea-shore should be interpreted as mosaics or continua, or
whether the limits of the belts are so distinct that neither of these concepts

is necessary.

We have seen that the ecologist can study the vegetation of the sea-shore by observation, recording his results either according to the Anglo-American system or to the Continental one. The belts can be analysed in more detail by the use of transects and quadrats when the frequency and density of species can be determined. The dry weight of the algae in a quadrat represents the algal biomass at that place at the time of sampling, so that sampling by cropping and weighing can give a picture of the vegetation. In recent years the productivity of marine crops has also been estimated in terms of the chlorophyll a content. This method was first applied in the marine environment to the floating phytoplankton, but more recently it has been applied to the attached or benthic algae. The gross productivity of a belt is of considerable interest, particularly when it appears that the density and occurrence of the principal species can vary so greatly in a vertical direction. Generally, very little work of this nature seems to have been done, but a study on the coast of Massachusetts [25] gives an indication of the kind of results that can be obtained. Areas of 25 cm^2 were sampled on the shore in

TABLE 2.1

Average Chlorophyll a *in Four Intertidal Belts*

Belt		No. of samples	Mean g/m^2	Standard deviation
1.	*Littorina* ("Black") belt. 100 percent cover *Calothrix crustacea,*	25	0.80 ± .009	0.48
	63 percent cover *Calothrix crustacea*	25	0.50	
2.	Barnacle belt (+ *Gomontia* and *Rivularia* (100 percent cover).	52	0.27 ± .001	0.19
3.	*Fucus vesiculosus, Balanus* 100 percent cover.	50	1.47 ± .051	0.86
4.	"Algae" 100 percent cover (*Chondrus, Polysiphonia, Ceramium, Dasya*)	50	1.04 ± .009	0.68

mean 0.82

four different belts, the samples ground up, extracted with acetone, which
was then filtered and centrifuged, and the chlorophyll a determined spectro-
photometrically. The results are given in Table 2.1.

Rather surprisingly it will be seen that under comparable conditions of cover
Calothrix in the "Black" belt contains over half the chlorophyll a content of
the *Fucus* and "algal" belts. Although there are differences in chlorophyll
content, they may not be ecologically significant, but a final answer to this
problem will not be forthcoming until physiological studies have been undertaken on the principal algae during submergence and exposure (see p. 59).

PHYSIOGRAPHIC FEATURES

Rock Pools

We have been directing our attention up to the present to the main ecological
features of the vegetation that can be observed on rocky and boulder shores,
whether exposed, sheltered or estuarine. On the shore there are other physiographic features that lend themselves to ecological study, and which merit
further comment. Such features comprise the rock pools, couloirs and caves.

Rock pools may conveniently be grouped into three major categories: those of
the lower eutlittoral (often never uncovered during neap-tide periods), the
pools of the middle eulittoral (covered once or twice every day) and the pools
of the upper eulittoral and littoral fringe, which may remain exposed for
several successive days during neap-tide periods. In these upper pools the
conditions of temperature and salinity can become extreme, particularly in
summer. These pools have an interesting counterpart in the pans of the salt
marshes (see p. 48), and, providing both are accessible, comparisons could
prove extremely interesting. The elements comprising the flora of rock pools
can be grouped as follows: (a) species characteristic of the sublittoral, (b)
species from the sublittoral fringe or lower eulittoral that reach their upper
limit on the shore in the pools, (c) eulittoral species, (d) species wholly
confined to pools. Any study made of rock pools should, therefore be related
to the position of the pools on the shore, and the analysis of the vegetation
should be considered in relation to the occurrence of the species elsewhere.
It is also obvious that algae inhabiting high pools must be capable of

tolerating rapid changes of salinity and temperature. The flora is conse-
quently predominantly Cyanophyceae, Chlorophyceae and diatoms. It is probably because of this type of algal response that Gustavsson (28) classified
rock pools on the Swedish west coast into (a) Phaeophyta-Rhodophyta pools,
(b) Chlorophyta pools, (c) Cyanophyta pools.

Caves and Couloirs

Some shores are characterised by deep couloirs and caves. Both these physiographic features provide environments that are very different to the open
rock surface and, as such, are worthy of independent study. In the case of
caves the principal phenomenon is the change in vegetation with diminishing
light intensity. It is now quite easy to make simple light measurements and
the vegetation of a cave or couloir can be plotted in relation to the light
intensities (Fig. 2.6). In doing such work it must be remembered that the
intensity of light will vary with the time and kind of day and also with the
season of the year, so that extended observations are essential if they are
to mean anything. It may safely be assumed that those species which penetrate
into caves and occur low down in couloirs are fundamentally "shade" species,

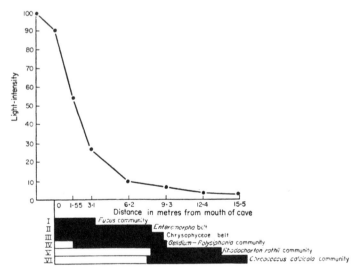

FIG. 2.6. *Graph showing the relation between light intensity and
the distribution of algal communities in a long cave at various
distances from the opening. The shaded areas indicate the extent
of the various communities inside the cave (after Anand).*

whereas those that occur on open rock surfaces are "sun" species. In a cave
on Stronsay, Sinclair (34) recorded on walls or in pools, *Odonthalia dentata*,
Lithothamnion (two species), *Plumaria elegans*, *Lomentaria articulata*, *Cryptopleura variosum* and *Rhodochorton purpureum*. The same or similar species were
recorded (50) for cave vegetation at Lough Ine in Ireland. *Plumaria elegans*
appears capable of the deepest penetration, whilst other cave species not
recorded at Stronsay were *Phyllophora epiphylla* and *Hildenbrandtia*. Sixteen
species are listed from the sublittoral of the cave.

Couloirs have been but little studied and this is unfortunate because the
ecology presents an interesting response to wave surge and also to light
since both sides receive less light than the adjacent flat rocks. A study of
such couloirs would serve to show whether there are any algae more or less
restricted to such a habitat.

BIOTIC RELATIONS

Another feature that lends itself to study on the sea-shore is the relationship between certain animals and plants. One can, for example, make a study
of the algae that occur on the shells of some of the larger mollusca or on
barnacles. This is a field that has not been greatly investigated and would
well repay investigation. The algal population on barnacles has been
described by den Hoek (30) and studies have been undertaken (18,56) in respect of
the browsing habits of limpets (*Patella*) in relation to the presence of algae.
Fucus, *Ascophyllum* and *Pelvetia* are commonly absent or scarce on exposed
coasts and these two facts have in the past been regarded as related. The
common limpet (*Patella vulgata*) is very frequent on exposed shores and it now
appears that the absence of the fucoids may be closely related to the limpet
population. Clearing areas completely of algae and limpets resulted in a
colonisation sequence of diatoms - filamentous algae - sheet algae (*Porphyra*,
Ulva) - fucoids. Within two years a dense growth of algae develops but
underneath limpets can be found, often in great numbers. With their appearance, there is little further successful establishment of algae and old plants
begin to disappear. With the gradual elimination of the algae the limpet food
supply becomes reduced and they too decrease and the bare area becomes colonised by barnacles (Fig. 2.7). It will be observed that the limpet maximum
occurs a year behind that of the *Fucus* maximum. Further work of this nature

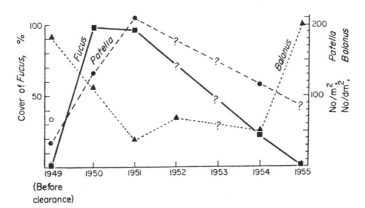

FIG. 2.7. *Fluctuations in the abundance of* Fucus vesiculosus, Balanus balanoides *and* Patella vulgata *at Mean Tide Level on the area cleared of limpets in 1949 (after Southward).*

is greatly to be desired because there are almost certainly other local factors that can become involved.

VEGETATION PATTERN

Rocky Shores

We are now in a position to outline the general pattern of algal vegetation to be found on the rocky shores of Europe and U.S.A., and it is convenient to commence with the upper sublittoral (= sublittoral fringe). In the North Sea and on the colder Atlantic shores of Europe the upper limit of the fringe is generally set by the upper limit of the laminarian zone. In most parts *Laminaria digitata* or *L. cloustoni* (*L. hyperborea*) are the species involved, but on exposed coasts, they are replaced by *Alaria esculenta* with its characteristic mid-rib and lateral reproductive appendages (31). Where rock and sand are mingled or in quieter localities *Laminaria saccharina* may be the principal species (54) whilst in south and west Ireland and south-west England *Saccorhiza polyschides* with its bulbous base and twisted stipe mingles with the other laminarians or may be the sole dominant. As Lewis (41) has pointed out, there are two types of locality in which it may be difficult to recognise the upper limit of the sublittoral. One is where there is excessive exposure, when no laminarian is present and its place is taken by the encrusting red

Lithothamnia, but since these are capable of extending into the eulittoral
they do not provide a means of demarcating the sublittoral. Accessible
shores of this type are very rare but they clearly merit further study.

The second case is provided by sheltered bays and lochs where the substratum
changes to pebbles or gravel. In such places there is sufficient water movement from time to time to move the stones with the large laminarians so they
are replaced by a great variety of smaller algae. The composition of this
algal population varies with turbidity and water movement. In the south-west,
species of *Cystoseira* may dominate, in other places *Stilophora*, *Spermatochnus*
and *Laurencia obtusa* form the major components. Where the stones are so small
as to be regarded as shingle, *Rhodochorton* and *Cladophora* may be the predominant algae. Transitional floras on more stable stones can include *Laminaria*
saccharina and *Lithothamnia* with fucoids (*Himanthalia*, *Halidrys*) mixed with
Codium and *Chorda*. From accounts that have been published for different parts
of the world, it is evident that small algae, albeit different species, behave
in a similar manner elsewhere, though such shores cannot be regarded as wholly
typical, at least in the Northern Hemisphere. The transition to estuarine
conditions can be marked by the replacement of laminarians by *Ulva* spp.

The lower limit of this fringe belt is not at present well understood. It
would seem that there are certain species which are limited to a region just
above and below extreme low water mark. Until these species have been listed
for the different types of coastline, it will not be possible to set any lower
limit, nor is it possible to say whether the lower limit will be set by organisms or by reduction in light quantity or quality. The use of the aqualung
(p. 40) will undoubtedly facilitate research in this particular field.

The lower eulittoral is commonly occupied by *Fucus serratus*, with which is
often associated *Himanthalia*, though in exposed places these disappear and
are replaced by red algae, such as *Chondrus* and *Corallina*. Above *Fucus serr-*
atus one finds *F. vesiculosus* and *Ascophyllum nodosum*. Sometimes *Fucus ves-*
iculosus occurs below the *Ascophyllum* whilst in other places the situation is
reversed, and there are also regions where both species occur mixed together.
On the Norwegian coast *Fucus distichus* spp. *anceps* replaces *F. vesiculosus*
and *Ascophyllum* (31). On exposed coasts these algae disappear and the belt is
essentially demarcated by the barnacles. The upper limit of the barnacles was
postulated by the Stephensons (59) as representing the upper limit of the

eulittoral (mid-littoral). This upper limit may be set by either *Balanus bal-anoides* or by *Chthalamus stellatus*. One complexity that arises by making use of these two indicator species is that *Chthalamus* generally rises to a slightly higher level on the shore than *Balanus*. As a result, depending on which genus is present, the upper limit of the eulittoral can change its level from one part of the British Isles to another. Furthermore since *Pelvetia canaliculata* commonly grows above the uppermost *Balanus* but below the upper limit of *Chthalamus*, it will belong to the littoral fringe in the former case and to the eulittoral in the latter. It is evident that the upper limit of the barnacles is not an absolutely constant feature because it fluctuates (41) within a narrow belt located approximately between high water of spring and neap tides.

The typical *Balanus* type of zonation (found mostly around the North Sea and in parts of the Irish Sea) is depicted in Fig. 2.1, where it will be seen that in sheltered places it or the *Ascophyllum/Fucus vesiculosus* belt gives way to *F. spiralis* and *Pelvetia* of the littoral fringe plus, in places, *Catenella*, *Bostrychia* and *Calothrix*. With increasing exposure these algae gradually disappear, and are replaced by the black lichen *Lichina pygmaea* and the red laver, *Porphyra umbilicalis*, both of which, together with the Littorinids, lie astride the upper barnacle limit.

In Caithness and to some extent also in Northern Norway (31), a modification of this zoning has been recorded (39) on exposed shores where the balanoid belt gives way to a growth of *Porphyra*, *Enteromorpha*, *Fucus inflatus*, *F. distichus* and *F. spiralis* f. *nana* (Fig. 2.8).

The *Chthalamus* (barnacle) type of zonation as it is found on exposed coasts of west Scotland and Ireland contains *Balanus* as well, though the latter occurs essentially below the upper limit of the *Chthalamus*. Exposure is generally too severe for *Pelvetia* to occur and, because of the higher level attained by *Chthalamus* in relation to *Balanus*, the lichen *Lichina* lies wholly within the barnacle zone and is therefore a mid-littoral plant. In south-west England, *Balanus* is less common and in sheltered places *Pelvetia* and *Chthalamus* jointly provide the upper limit (Fig. 2.9). With extreme shelter the barnacle limit descends farther together with the *Fucus spiralis* belt.

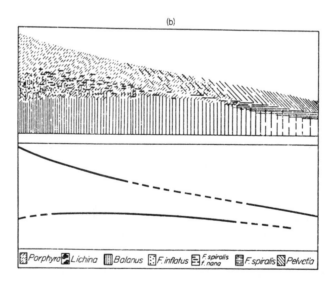

FIG. 2.8. *(See opposite)*.

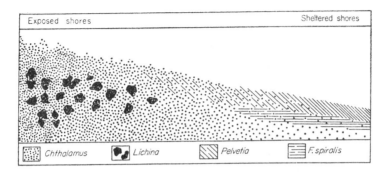

Exposed shores   Sheltered shores

| ▒ Chthalamus | ● Lichina | ⧄ Pelvetia | ≡ F. spiralis |

FIG. 2.9. *The* Chthalamus *pattern of zonation as it usually occurs in south-west England.* In south-west Ireland, Porphyra *and* Fucus spiralis *f.* nana *frequently mingle with or lie just above the uppermost patches of* Lichina *(after Lewis).*

Between the two types of zonation described above (*Balanus* and *Chthalamus*) it is only to be expected that varying degrees of transition will exist. The essential feature of these transitional zonations is the existence of a well-marked *Balanus* upper limit with, in exposed places, *Chthalamus* above. The latter species is found either just below or in the *Pelvetia* belt, but with increasing exposure it extends farther up the shore. In places there may even be a gap of some inches between the two barnacle belts. As Lewis (41) points out, the first appearance of the *Chthalamus* may be gradual or it may occur quite suddenly. On such transitional shores, the upper limit of *Chthalamus* (where present) must be regarded as the limit of the eulittoral, leading in more sheltered places to a lower limit that is demarcated by *Balanus*. In estuaries, with the advent of fresh water, *Fucus edentatus* replaces other fucoids and *Ascophyllum* and *Balanus* is replaced by *Enteromorpha* and *Mytilus edulis* (Söderstrom, 1965 at Göteburg (54)).

FIG. 2.8. *The* Balanus *pattern of zonation,* (a) *shows the typical pattern, while* (b) *shows the modified form which occurs on the exposed shores in Caithness. The upper part of each figure shows the distribution of important species, and the lower part shows the position of the most conspicuous landmarks (clear upper limits) of the upper shore. On some Caithness shores* Fucus spiralis *and* F. spiralis *f.* nana *are linked by intermediate forms, while on others two distinct communities exist.* Enteromorpha, *which is usually mixed with the* Porphyra, *has been omitted from the diagram. (N.B. To avoid confusion the Littorinae have been omitted from this and the succeeding figure, and no attempt has been made to show the* Mytilus, Fucoids *or* Rhodophyceae *which may overlie the barnacles to a greater or lesser extent) (after Lewis, 1955).*

In sheltered places the littoral fringe is occupied at its lower levels by
Pelvetia, Fucus spiralis, accompanied perhaps by *Catenella, Bostrychia* and
Myxophyceae (*Calothrix*). Above this is a zone of black lichens dominated by
Verrucaria marina and *V. maura.* Still higher it may be possible to recognise
orange and grey lichen zones. Some workers regard these as still within the
littoral fringe, but others, including the present writer, regard them as
outside but in a maritime zone (p. 21) becuase the littorinids do not penetrate them under normal conditions. With increasing exposure the fucoids are
replaced by *Porphyra* and *Lichina* and the littorinids increase in number (39).
The black lichen zone also may increase in importance (Fig. 2.1). With
increasing brackish conditions the lichens are often replaced by *Ulothrix,*
Urospora and *Phormidium corium.* The presence of brackish conditions generally
results in a reduced flora such as that reported for the Baltic Sea east of
Darsser Schwelle (48).

It will be found that the general arrangement of the principal algal belts
around the rocky shores of the North Sea and temperate Atlantic Europe will
fit into the broad framework that has been outlined above. In any given area
there will be other seaweed species that are sufficiently prominent to
justify inclusion in a local schema. Thus around the shores of north and west
Scotland *Rhodymenia, Gigartina, Laurencia, Corallina, Leathesia, Cladophora,*
may all become significant. Where fresh water runs down the shore or where
streams spread out over the shingle *Fucus spiralis* is generally replaced by
F. ceranoides and there is an abundant growth of green algae such as *Entero-*
morpha intestinalis, Monostroma grevillei and *Cladophora rupestris.* Where
slopes become very steep and there is considerable water movement the usual
algae may be more or less completely absent, being replaced by small turfy
algae, which are better enabled to find lodgement in the small cracks and
crevices and with small thalli are better able to withstand the conditions.

Once the principal belts have been recognised, further detailed study may lead
to the recognition of smaller, less extensive, secondary communities. A
number of such communities have been recognised from different areas: they
include the *Enteromorpha intestinalis* community, *Porphyra-Urospora-Ulothrix*
community, *Laurencia* community or association, *Gigartina-Cladophora* community,
Ulva linza community, *Porphyra* association, *Bangia-Urospora* society, *Cal-*
lithamnion-Ceramium association, *Nemalion* society, *Gigartina* association,
Lomentaria society and so on. From the nomenclature that has been used by

different workers and repeated above, it is clear that a wide divergence of
opinion exists as to the status of the particular communities. For general
work it is almost certainly better not to apply status to these smaller
groups and the non-committal name of community meets the circumstances
admirably.

What has been said so far essentially concerns the large benthic (attached)
algae. Beneath them or growing on substrate not occupied by other algae one
can find growths of diatoms. A study of these (1) has shown that the communities vary with substrate (concrete piles, rocky reef or pool) and also with
the geological nature of the substrate, whether calcareous or otherwise
(Table 2.2). There is, as may be expected, very much more variation in seasonal aspect than with the larger algae. These communities can be sought for
and after collection examined under the microscope.

Although diatom taxonomy is a difficult field it is clear that it presents a
worth while field of study.

TABLE 2.2

Diatom communities, south of England

	On concrete	On chalk
Supra-littoral	Achnanthes-Cyanophyceae	Amphora-Nitzschia
Eulittoral	Fragilaria-Melosira	Melosira-barnacles Synedra-Pylaiella
Sub-littoral fringe		Schizonema ramosissima Schizonema grevillei Rhabdonema-Licmophora

On the western North Atlantic temperate shores algal belts occur in which
Ascophyllum and *Fucus* play an important eulittoral part but in general, the
algal flora is much poorer than in Europe (60).   In Nova Scotia and Prince
Edward Island (44,61) there is a narrow supra-littoral fringe dominated by
littorinids and Cyanophyta, especially *Rivularia*. The upper and mid-
eulittoral barnacles, *Fucus vesiculosus* and *Ascophyllum* are abundant. In the
lower eulittoral they are replaced by *Chordaria* and *Syctosiphon* in protected

areas and *Chorda* and *Chondrus* where there is more exposure. The Laminarian zone is not well represented on Prince Edward Island but on the Atlantic shores of Nova Scotia Mann (44) recognises four Laminatian zones occupying the sub-littoral fringe and sub-littoral. The principal components of the fringe are *Laminaria digitata* and *L. longicruris*.

Farther south in Maine the supra-littoral fringe remains essentially the same and also the upper and mid-eulittoral. The lower eulittoral has changed in that *Rhodymenia* and *Spongomorpha* form the small algal component. The sub-littoral fringe has also changed in that *Laminaria* spp. have been replaced by the brown *Alaria* and the red *Halosaccion*.

Farther south the two great bays of Delaware and Chesapeake have generally soft friable shores and algal vegetation is not very extensive. In Rehoboth Bay, Delaware, Orris and Taylor (46) recorded 59 species of which three, *Agardhiella tenera, Gracilaria verrucosa* and *Ulva lactuca* occurred year round and formed three distinct aggregations each with a number of species of smaller algae. The spatial distribution of these three aggregations was closely correlated with sediment distribution and this suggests that water movements are a significant ecological factor. The same three algal species also play a major role in Chesapeake Bay. It is clear that both Chesapeake and Delaware Bays offer a splendid opportunity for research. A survey of past work on the benthic macro-algae of Chesapeake Bay reveals a dismal lack of information (37, 47).

Still farther south in North Carolina (60) the supra-littoral fringe is dominated by *Calothrix* (Cyanophyta) and *Enteromorpha*. In the eulittoral barnacles still remain but the water is too warm for *Fucus* and *Ascophyllum* and instead there is a successive zoning of *Modiolus* (mussel), *Porphyra* (red algae), *Gelidium-Polysiphonia*, *Rhodymenia* and at the base of the eulittoral *Ostrea-Padina* (oyster-phaeophyte). In the sublittoral fringe the water has become too warm for Laminarians and their place is taken by the brown *Sargassum* spp., *Dictopteris* and *Grateloupia* (74). From here, south to Florida the shore-line is essentially sandy with numerous sand-built off-shore sea islands so that the algal flora is essentially that associated with salt marshes and mangrove swamps (see pp. 46-49).

As may be expected there is a substantial change of vegetation when tropical

waters are reached. An example from the eastern Atlantic is provided by the
zonation at Teneriffe (Canary Island) (38). Here the supra-littoral fringe is
dominated by *Littorina neritoides,* and the upper limit of the eulittoral by
the barnacle *Chthalamus stellatus.* Characteristic of tropical shores the
lower part of the eulittoral carries only turf-like algae. There is an upper
belt of the red *Caulacanthus ustulatus* with *Ulva* and a lower belt of
Corallines and the green *Valonia.* The sublittoral fringe is typified by the
red algae *Gelidium arbuscula* and *G. cartilagineum.*

Western Atlantic tropical shores are exemplified by the zonations to be seen
on the coral of the Florida keys. Here the supra-littoral fringe may have
three belts: (a) upper bare, (b) grey belt of *Bostrychia,* (c) black belt of
Cyanophyta. The eulittoral carries an upper mixed algal turf and a lower
belt of Corallines and *Valonia* (as at Teneriffe). The sublittoral fringe is
almost non-existent because of the small tidal range and specific algae
associated with it have not been recognised.

SUBLITTORAL

The sublittoral fringe where present may be represented by a specialised group
of algae (see p. 32) which occupy a narrow belt around mean low water mark of
spring tides. Below this belt, and extending down to a varying depth, there
is a collection of algae which comprise the sublittoral flora proper. The
principal components of this flora around most of the European shores are the
oarweeds *Laminaria cloustoni* (*L. hyperborea*) and *L. digitata* (34). The First-
named species is often very heavily epiphytised and on one plant washed
ashore at Stronsay (53) no less than 14 other species of algae were attached.
Indeed, a study of the epiphytic flora of *L. digitata, L. cloustoni* and
species of *Fucus* would form an admirable ecological exercise, because it would
be concerned not only with the species that occur but also with attempting to
determine the conditions under which they are found.

On cold temperate western Atlantic shores the sublittoral is dominated by
Laminarians. Three belts have been recognised in Nova Scotia (44) characterised
respectively by *Laminaria longicruris, L. longicruris* and *Agarum cribrosum,*
Agarum cribrosum and *Ptilota serrata,* the last-named reaching a lower limit
around 20-30 m. In the middle belt the two main components formed about 83%

of the total biomass.

In the warm waters of the Canary Isles Lawson and Norton (38) reported that the sublittoral was characterised by a mixed flora of *Cystoseira abies-marina*, *Padina pavonia*, *Lobophora variegata* and *Halopteris scoparia*. In comparable warm waters around the Florida keys calcareous red algae, *Sargassum*, *Caulerpa* spp. and Codiaceae (*Avrainvillea, Halimeda, Penicillus*) form the main components (15).

Up to fairly recently the only effective method of securing information about the sublittoral was by means of standard zoological trawls. Since the war, however, new techniques have been developed, but whilst all these may not be readily available the potentialities are now much greater. Among these newer techniques is the combination of aerial photography, grab sampling and the echo-sounder as a means of mapping entire submarine beds and recording the composition of the major species (Fig. 2.10).

Another means of studying the sublittoral is by use of the aqualung, which enables the investigator to collect carefully and to observe the distribution of the various species (Fig. 2.11). This technique is likely to be used with increasing success and value because one can then employ traditional ecological sampling methods such as the transect and quadrat. It is also possible, if water and light conditions are suitable, to secure photographs of the vegetation being studied. The aqualung should not, however, be used except by persons who have undergone a course of training in it.

Further refinements are provided by small submersibles of one kind or another, and the time is not far distant when under-water laboratories will be established (29,49).

The detailed survey of the Scottish submarine beds (11,62-72) covered 80,000 acres, and was carried out over a period of seven years so that sampling included seasonal and perennial changes. The survey was mainly restricted to the zone between low water mark and 10 fathoms, the dominant species being *Laminaria cloustoni* (*L. hyperborea*), *L. digitata* and *L. saccharina*. At the conclusion of the survey the master means (= mean of the means) for 59 surveys were determined for both density (based on wet weight rather than the more desirable dry weight) and cover (Table 2.2).

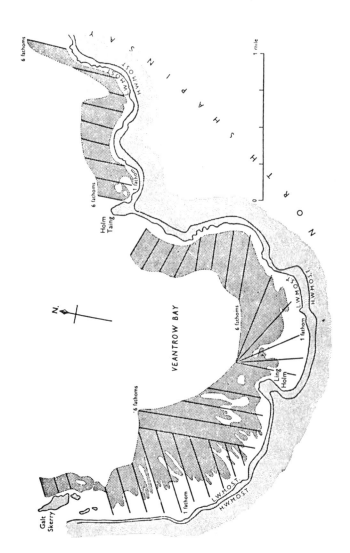

FIG. 2.10. *Correlation of seaweed cover by sampling and aerial photography. Straight lines indicate the measured transects (1–6 fathom) along which sampling was carried out by boat during May 1947, and the shaded areas show the algal cover photographed from the air two years later. The cover was 78 percent by both methods (after Walker).*

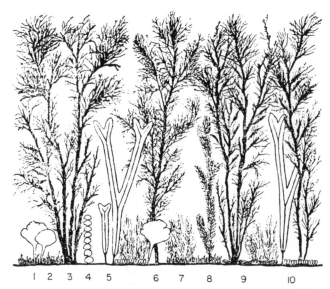

FIG. 2.11. *Profile of a* Cystoseira discors *stand in the Adriatic.*
1, Udotea petiolata. 2, Rytiphlaea tinctoria. 3, Cystoseira
discors. 4, Halimeda tuna. 5, Dictyopteris membranacea. 6, Cystoseira barbata. 7, Cladophora prolifera. 8, Digenea simplex. 9,
Peyssonelia squamaria. 10, Valonia utricularis *(after Ernst).*

TABLE 2.2

Oarweed density and cover in relation to depth

Depth L.W.M.O.S.T (fathoms)	Density lb/yd^2	Cover percent	$\frac{Density}{Cover}$ X 100
1	11.0	76	14.4
2	10.3	72	14.3
3	8.8	65	13.2
4	7.5	57	13.1
5	6.2	48	13.0
6	5.3	44	12.0
7	4.7	35	13.4
8	3.3	28	11.7
9	2.7	21	12.9
10	2.3	18	12.8

It will be seen that the density/cover values approximate to a constant so
that the fresh weight is proportional to the percentage cover. A relationship
was also established between both cover and density, and depth of occurrence,
all of them decreasing exponentially. The decrease in density appears to be
more a result of reduction in the actual number of plants per unit area
rather than in size (or weight). It has been argued from the results that
with increasing depth the total spore production is decreased, dispersion of
spores reduced and also fertilisation reduced and plant cover limited.

Spore production of these algae is colossal, one plant of *L. digitata* producing over eleven million zoospores, so that even if spore production is
reduced there should be more than sufficient spores to provide a deep-water
population. There is no published evidence that fewer gametophytes are produced at greater depths or that fertilisation is reduced. Whilst the results
of this extensive survey cannot be ignored, there may be other hypotheses that
could account for the facts.

The seasonal and perennial changes in beds of this nature can be quite extensive but until we have more information, particularly in relation to gale
incidence and changes of sea temperature, it would be premature to suggest any
causes. As may be expected, the perennial changes exceed the seasonal ones
(Figs. 2.12, 2.13).

A combination of glass-bottomed view box, grab and aqualung has been used to
study the sublittoral algal populations of the Isle of Man (6,33). Two types
of substrate were encountered; continuous rock and sand with shells, or
stones and small boulders. The use of the grab was checked by a diver and it
was found that it did not always give a complete sample of all species in the
area. The use of the aqualung is, in fact, the only effective means of sampling. On the rock surface the large Laminarians form the perennial under-
water forest with smaller algae growing below or as epiphytes on the oarweeds.
On the sandy floor of the bay there was a more or less loose-lying flora dominated by *L. saccharina*, *Saccorhiza polyschides*, *Chorda filum*, and *Desmarestia aculeata*. These algae must all have started life as attached forms and
with increase in size have become detached. Smaller algae such as *Dictyota*
and *Plocamium* were also present in tangled masses. The loose-lying population
is essentially seasonal, occurring during the summer months and decreasing in
winter when much is washed up on to beaches by storms. How far such detached

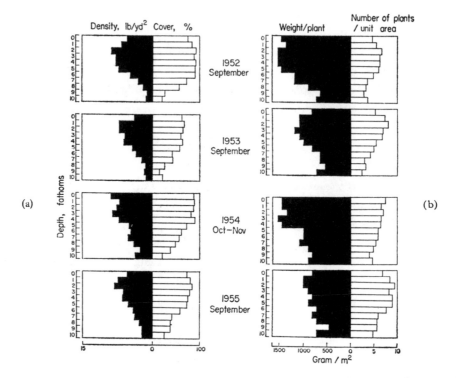

FIG. 2.12. (a), Fraserburgh-Rosehearty. Density (based on quadrats with algae) and cover of Laminariaceae at 1 fathom intervals
of depth. (b), Fraserburgh-Rosehearty. Fresh weight of plants of
Laminaria cloustoni at 1 fathom intervals of depth (after Walker
and Richardson).

algae are effectively living and growing and capable of reproduction, has yet
to be studied.

In muddy bays and estuaries, one can find an association of submerged marine
phanerogams, though such communities are by no means so extensive as they
used to be because of the incidence of an epidemic disease. The principal
plant is Eel-grass, Zostera, but in parts of Europe this may be accompanied
by equally abundant growths of the plant Ruppia maritima. Although such
fields are generally exposed at low water, in some regions they extend into
the sublittoral. Zostera can indeed be regarded as a plant of the sublittoral
fringe. This community also represents one in which the aqualung has been
used as a means of studying the perpetually submerged vegetation. The principal study has been in the Bay of Gdansk (Danzig, Poland) where, in addition
to the marine phanerogams a number of algal communities, e.g. Fucus-

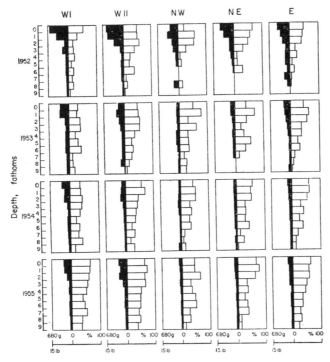

FIG. 2.13. *Seaweed density (black histograms), fresh weight, based on quadrats with Laminariaceae; seaweed cover (white histograms), at fathom intervals of depth in 5 sub-areas, during the winters of 1952, 1953, 1954 and 1955 (after Walker and Richardson).*

Furcellaria, Enteromorpha compressa, have been described. The distribution of the phanerogamic vegetation extends down to about 5 m, but the *Fucus-Furcellaria* community descends even deeper. The distribution appears to depend upon the depth of the water and the degree of exposure to water current. A similar study has been carried out in Denmark (27), where the amount of standing crop has been determined during periods of maximum and minimum growth. Studies of standing crop, in terms of dry weight, for unit areas over the seasons would be extremely valuable and would not be beyond the resources of a school located near a coastline with *Zostera* beds.

In recent years increasing attention has been given to the effects of pollution upon marine algae. There have also been studies associated with notorious oil spills, such as that of the Torrey Canyon. Badly polluted areas such as the Firth of Forth and N.E. England (7) can have the algal communities,

especially sublittoral ones of *L. saccharina*, severely affected. Oil also
has an effect upon the algal belts, but once the oil has been dispersed the
effect is more ephemeral than that of pollution. Schramm (52) has shown that
oil depresses CO_2 uptake in emersed littoral algae but this is temporary.
Mercury is often released in quantities that can be serious but this is only
just beginning to be realised. Boney (5) reports the sub-lethal effect of this
element on marine algae.

The increasing establishment of power stations upon maritime coasts has already raised issues concerning the effect of increased water temperatures
(from emission of cooling water) upon benthic organisms. It is already clear
that there are limits to which temperatures should be raised and that critical
temperatures with the main stresses will be in the summer months (73).

SALT MARSH AND MANGROVE ALGAE

In areas that possess beds of *Zostera* it is likely that there will be salt
marshes (see p. 105). Whilst the main interest of salt marshes will tend to
centre around the phanerogams, nevertheless there is also a distinct algal
vegetation. As one might expect, the nature of the vegetation on salt
marshes and in mangrove swamps is very different to that on rocky coasts. On
the latter we have seen that it is static though there is a well-marked vertical zonation. On the salt marsh and in mangroves the perpetual accretion of
mud brings about a steady rise in soil level so that conditions change and
the vegetation changes (10) (see p. 107). Both phanerogamic and algal vegetation
are therefore dynamic in character, changing with the years, and the changes
may be quite rapid. For this reason, therefore, it is legitimate to use
successional terminology, e.g. associes, consocies. At any given moment in
time, however, a zonation of algae can be observed stretching from the lowest
salt marshes up to the highest, and belts exist, though their existence may
be masked by the vast horizontal extent of the marshes. The distribution of
the communities varies from place to place and is at least partly determined
by the nature of the soil (sand, mud or peat) (see Table 2.3).

On low marshes, at a level below that of the phanerogams, one can find a mat
of green algae (mainly species of *Enteromorpha*, some *Cladophora* and *Vaucheria
sphaerospora*) on the more sandy flats, whilst on mud flats the firmer areas

TABLE 2.3

Salt Marsh and Mangrove Algal Communities
(after Chapman and Chapman)

1	General Chlorophyceae	11	Autumn Cyanophyceae consocies
2	Low sandy Chlorophyceae consocies	12	*Phormidium autumnale* socies
3	Sandy Chlorophyceae consocies	13	*Rivularia-Phaeococcus* socies
4	Muddy Chlorophyceae consocies	14	*Catenella-Bostrychia* consocies
5	Marginal diatom consociation	15	*Pelvetia limicola* consocies
6	Marginal Cyanophyceae consociation	16	*Enteromorpha clathrata* socies
7	Vernal *Ulothrix* socies	17	Limicolous Fucaceae consocies
8	*Enteromorpha nana* socies	18	Pan association
9	Gelatinous Cyanophyceae socies	19	*Vaucheria* consocies
10	Filamentous diatom consocies	20	*Gracilaria* consocies

often bear a green covering of xanthophycean (yellow-green alga) *Vaucheria thuretii*. This alga, particularly, tends to form a community on the banks of creeks at low tidal levels. On the European and western North Atlantic coasts in the *Spartina* (Cord grass) zone one can also see a blue-green soil covering, comprising species of *Lyngbya, Oscillatoria* and *Phormidium* (General Cyanophyceae). With the advent of phanerogamic vegetation, green algae such as *Enteromorpha* (especially *E. prolifera* and *E. prolifera* var. *tubulosa*) and *Lola* persist, but on the plants themselves there is often a green mat of the small *Enteromorpha nana* (= *Blidingia minima*). On the European channel and east coasts of England these low marshes are characterised by a dense covering of the remarkable free-living salt marsh fucoids (3,9,13,45). At the lowest level one finds the spirally twisted thalli of *Fucus vesiculosus* ecad* *volubilis*. Higher up it is replaced by the partially embedded *F. vesiculosus* ecad *caespitosus* whilst around it can be found masses of the free-living *Pelvetia canaliculata* ecad *libera+* with which in places may be associated the red *Bostrychia scorpioides*. These algae are particularly abundant in the Sali-

*Signifies an ecological variant.

+This occurs also on East Lothian marshes in Scotland.

cornietum.

Whilst East Anglia and the Channel and north sea coasts of Europe are rich in these peculiar fucoids they are also to be found on marshes in Wales (e.g. *Pelvetia canaliculata* ecad *radicans*), in Strangford loch in Ireland and also some forms confined to the Baltic (e.g. *F. vesiculosus* ecads *nanus*, *subecostatus* and *filiformis*). All these marsh fucoids probably arose as a result of vegetative budding from cast-up fragments of parent species, though they could also have developed from fertilised ova that became attached to marsh phanerogams (14,15).

Along the creek banks, where *Halimione* predominates, *Catenella repens* and *Bostrychia scorpioides* form a red algal community on the stems (sometimes also on *Spartina*) and extending up on the fringes in Europe to form a mud community beneath bushes of the Shrubby seablite, *Suaeda fruticosa*. In the Spartinetum of the Essex marshes, another free-living fucoid, *Ascophyllum nodosum* ecad *scorpioides* is to be found, and it, together with *A. nodosum* ecad *mackaii*, also occurs on the salt marshes of the western Scottish lochs, Strangford loch and on marshes in eastern North America. South and Hill (55) have especially discussed the distribution of these two forms in Newfoundland. Scattered around Europe a smaller fucoid, *Fucus vesiculosus* ecad *muscoides*, can be found on some of the higher marshes, whilst in East Anglia the General Salt Marsh community and Plantaginetum (see p. 110) bear a green covering dominated by *Enteromorpha clathrata* f. *prostrata*. Most of the marshes have salt pans scattered over them and here, with conditions comparable to those of rock pools (p. 79), one can find an algal flora composed of species from the adjacent marsh together with other species that clearly survive because of the particular environment. Some of these other species may be naturally free-living whilst others are attached to the plants or roots around the edges of the pan, e.g. *Striaria attenuata*, *Sphacelaria radicans* (6,45).

Chlorophyceae form the principal component of pans on lower marshes. With increasing marsh height the Chlorophyceae are gradually replaced by Cyanophyta. Chapman and Chapman (15) point out that two generalisations can be made about pan algae: (a) Some littoral rocky coast species grow at lower levels, usually sublittoral on marsh coasts. This is probably related to lack of solid substrate. (b) Some littoral rocky coast species grow at higher levels on the marshes. Some of these are found in pans or channels. Others grow on the marsh where the phanerogams provide protection from desiccation.

Apart from the salt marsh fuccoids, the algae of the salt marshes are not so spectacular as those of rocky coasts. In addition to the larger algae extensive diatom communities exist in the different habitats but this is a field that has not received much study.

In the tropics, e.g. Florida, mangrove replaces salt marsh. *Bostrychia* and *Catenella* form a dark violet red turf on the pneumatophores and lower parts of the trunks of seaward species (see p.69). At a lower level on the same organs one can find a turf of *Caloglossa* spp., *Murrayella periclados, Polysiphonia, Bryopsis* and *Centroceras clavulatum* with epiphytic *Enteromorpha* spp., *Rhizoclonium* and *Lyngbya*. On the mud between trees *Caulerpa verticillata, C. cupressoides, Gracilaria cornea* and *Batophora oerstedii* form green or red patches, the last named species being often associated with fallen leaves.

Despite the drawbacks, these salt marsh and mangrove algae deserve study, in some ways more so because so much less work has been carried out upon them.

REFERENCES

1   ALEEM A.A., Distribution and ecology of British marine littoral diatoms. *J. Ecol.*, 38(1), 75 (1950).

2   BAARDSETH E., A statistical study of the structure of the *Ascophyllum* zone. *Norsk. Inst. for tang-og tarefons. Rept. II.* 1-34 (1953).

3   BAKER S.M. and BOHLING M.H., On the brown seaweeds of the salt marsh. I. *Jour. Linn. Soc. Bot. Lond.*, 40, 275-291 (1921); II. *Jour. Linn. Soc. Bot. Lond.*, 43, 325-380 (1916).

4   BLACKLER H., An algal survey of Loch Foyle, North Ireland. *Proc. Roy. Irish Acad.*, 54, B, No. 6. 97-139 (1951).

5   BONEY A.D., Sub-lethal effects of Mercury on Marine Algae. *Mar. Pollut. Bull.*, 2(5), 69-71 (1971).

6   BURROWS E.M., Sublittoral algal population in Port Erin Bay, Isle of Man. *J. Mar. Biol. Ass. U.K.*, 37, 687-703 (1958).

7   BURROWS E.M. and PYBUS C., *Laminaria saccharina* and marine pollution in N.E. England. *Mar. Pollut. Bull.*, 2(4), 53-56 (1971).

8   CHAPMAN A.R.O., A critique of prevailing attitudes towards the control of

seaweed zonation on the sea shore. *Bot. Mar.*, 16, 80-82 (1973).

9   CHAPMAN V.J., A revision of the marine algae of Norfolk. *Journ. Linn. Soc. Bot. Lond.*, 51(338), 205-263 (1937).

10   CHAPMAN V.J., Studies in salt marsh ecology. Section IV. *J. Ecol.*, 27(1), 160-201 (1939).

11   CHAPMAN V.J., Seaweed resources along the shores of Great Britain. *Econ. Bot.*, 2(4), 363-378 (1948).

12   CHAPMAN V.J., Studies in salt marsh ecology. Section IX. *J. Ecol.*, 47(2), 619-639 (1959).

13   CHAPMAN V.J., The Plant Ecology in *Scolt Head Island*. Ed. J.A. Steers. 2nd Ed. Cambridge. pp. 85-163 (1960).

14   CHAPMAN V.J., *Salt Marshes and Salt Deserts of the World*. Cramer (1974).

15   CHAPMAN V.J. and D.J., *The Algae*. Macmillan (1973).

16   COTTON A.D., Clare Island survey. 15. Marine algae. *Proc. Roy. Irish Acad.*, 31, 1-171 (1912).

17   DUNN M.D., The marine algal associations of St. Andrews district. I: the dominant associations of the spray and littoral regions. *Trans. Bot. Soc. Edin.*, 33(2), 83-93 (1941).

18   EBLING F.J., SLEIGH M.A., SLOANE J.F. and KITCHING J.A., The ecology of Lough Ine. *J. Ecol.*, 48(1), 29-54 (1960).

19   EVANS R.G., The inter-tidal ecology of Cardigan Bay. *J. Ecol.*, 34, 273-309 (1947).

20   EVANS R.G., The inter-tidal ecology of selected localities in the Plymouth neighbourhood. *J. Mar. Bio. Assoc. U.K.*, 27, 173-218 (1947).

21   EVANS R.G., The inter-tidal ecology of rocky shores in south Pembrokeshire. *J. Ecol.*, 37, 120-139 (1949).

22   GIBB D.C., The marine algal communities of Castledown Bay, Isle of Man. *J. Ecol.*, 26, 96-117 (1938).

23   GIBB D.C., Some marine algal communities of Gt. Cumbrae. *J. Ecol.*, 27(2), 364-382 (1939).

24   GIBB D.C., A survey of the commoner fucoid algae on Scottish shores. *J. Ecol.*, 38(2), 253-269 (1950)

25   GIFFORD C.E. and ODUM E.P., Chlorophyll *a* content of intertidal zones on a rocky seashore. *Limn. and Oceanog.*, 6(1), 83-85 (1961).

26   GOULD D.T., BAGENAL T.B. and CONNELL J.H., The marine fauna and flora of St. Kilda, 1952, *Scot. Nat.*, 65, 29 (1953).

27   GRÖNTVED J., Underwater macrovegetation in shallow coastal waters. *J. cons. Intern. L'Expl. Mer.*, 24(1), 32-42 (1958).

28   GUSTAVSSON U., A proposal for a classification of marine rock pools on
     the Swedish west coast. *Bot. Mar.*, 15, 210-14 (1972).

29   HELGOLAND MEERESUNTER., 24 1/4 (1973). Entire volume devoted to under-
     water habitats.

30   HOEK C. VAN DEN, The algal microvegetation in and on barnacle shells,
     collected along the Dutch and French coasts. *Blumea*, 9(1), 206-214
     (1958).

31   JORDE I., Algal associations of a coastal area south of Bergen, Norway.
     Sarsia, 23, 1-52 (1966).

32   KAIN J.M., Observations on the littoral algae of the Isle of Wight.
     J. Mar. Biol. Ass. U.K., 37, 769-780 (1958).

33   KAIN J.M. Direct observations on some Manx sublittoral algae. *J. Mar.
     Biol. Ass. U.K.*, 39, 609-630 (1960).

34   KAIN J.M., The biology of *Laminaria hyperborea*. VI. Some Norwegian popu-
     lations. *J. Mar. Biol. Ass. U.K.*, 51, 387-408 (1970).

35   KITCHING J.A., An introduction to the ecology of inter-tidal rock
     surfaces on the coast of Argyll. *Trans. Roy. Soc. Edin.*, 58, 351 (1935).

36   KORNAS J., Sea bottom vegetation of the Bay of Gdansk off Rewa. *Bull.
     Acad. Pol. Sci., Cl. II.*, 7(1), 5-10 (1959).

37   KRAUSS R.W. and ORRIS O., Benthic macroalgae of the Maryland portion of
     the Chesapeake Bay. *Ches. Sci. 13 Supp.* 81-83.

38   LAWSON G.W. and NORTON T.A., Some observations on littoral and sub-
     littoral zonation at Teneriffe (Canary Isles). *Bot. Mar.*, 14, 116-26
     (1971).

39   LEWIS J.R., The ecology of rocky shores around Anglesey. *Proc. Zool. Soc.
     London*, 123(3), 481-549 (1953).

40   LEWIS J.R., The ecology of exposed rocky shores of Caithness. *J. Ecol.*,
     62(3), 695-723 (1954).

41   LEWIS J.R., The mode of occurrence of the universal inter-tidal zones in
     Great Britain. *J. Ecol.*, 43(1), 270-290 (1955).

42   LEWIS J.R., Inter-tidal communities of the northern and western coasts of
     Scotland. *Trans. Roy. Soc. Edin.*, 63(1), 185-220 (1957).

43   LEWIS J.R., The littoral zone on rocky shores - a biological or physical
     entity? *Oikos, Fasc.* 11, 12, 280-301 (1961).

44   MANN K.H., Ecological energetics of the seaweed zone in a marine bay on
     the Atlantic coast of Canada. I. Zonation and biomass of seaweeds. *Mar.
     Biol.*, 12, 1-10 (1972).

45   NIENHUIS P.H., The benthic algal communities of flats and salt marshes in

the Grevelingen, a sea arm in the S.W. Netherlands. *Nether. J. Sea Res.*, 5(1), 20-49 (1970).

46 ORRIS R.K. and TAYLOR J.E., A floristic and ecological survey. The benthic macroalgae of Rehoboth Bay, Delaware. *Bot. Mar.*, 16, 180-92 (1973).

47 OTT F.D., Macroalgae of the Chesapeake Bay. *Chesapeake Sci.*, 13 (Suppl.) 83, 84 (1972).

48 OVERBEEK J., Die Meeresalgen und ihre Gesellschaften an der Küsten der Insel Hiddensee (Ostsee). *Bot. Mar.*, 8, 218-33 (1965).

49 PERES J.M., Le rôle de la prospection sous-marine autonome dans les récherches de biologie marine et d'oceanographic biologique. *Experientia*, 22, 417-24 (1966).

50 REES T.K., The marine algae of Lough Ine. *J. Ecol.*, 23(1), 70-133 (1935).

51 ROUND F.E., The diatom flora of a salt marsh on the River Dee. *New Phyt.*, 59, 332-348 (1960).

52 SCHRAMM W., Investigations on the influence of oil pollutions on marine algae. I. *Mar. Biol.*, 14(3), 188-198 (1972).

53 SINCLAIR J., The marine algae of Stronsay. *Notes Roy. Bot. Gard. Edin.*, 20, No. 99, 160-179 (1949).

54 SÖDERSTROM J., Vertical zonation of littoral algae in Bohuslan. *Act. Phytogeog. Suec.*, 50, 85-91 (1965).

55 SOUTH G.R. and HILL R.D., Studies on marine algae of Newfoundland. I. *Can. J. Bot.*, 48, 1697-1701 (1970).

56 SOUTHWARD A.J., The population balance between limpets and seaweeds on wave-beaten rocky shores. *Rep. Mar. Biol. Sta. Port Erin.*, 68, 20 (1952).

57 SOUTHWARD A.J., The ecology of some rocky shores in the south of the Isle of Man. *Proc. & Trans. Liverp. Biol. Soc.*, 59, 1-45 (1953).

58 SOUTHWARD A.J. and ORTON J.H., The effects of wave action on the distribution and numbers of the commoner plants and animals living on the Plymouth Breakwater. *J. Mar. Biol. Ass. U.K.*, 33, 1 (1953).

59 STEPHENSON T.A. and STEPHENSON A., The universal features of zonation between tidemarks on rocky coasts. *J. Ecol.*, 37, 289-305 (1949).

60 STEPHENSON T.A. and STEPHENSON A., Life between tide marks in North America. II. Northern Florida and the Carolinas. *J. Ecol.*, 40, 1-49 (1952).

61 STEPHENSON T.A. and STEPHENSON A., Life between tide marks in North America. III. Nova Scotia and Prince Edward Island. *J. Ecol.*, 42, 14-70 (1954).

62 WALKER F.T., Sublittoral seaweed survey. *J. Ecol.*, 35(1), 166-185 (1947).

63 WALKER F.T., Sublittoral seaweed survey of the Orkney Islands. *J. Ecol.*, 38(1), 140-165 (1950).

64 WALKER F.T., Sublittoral seaweed survey: Dunbar to Fast Castle, East Scotland. *J. Ecol.*, 40(1), 74-83 (1952).

65 WALKER F.T., Distribution of Laminariaceae around Scotland. *J. Cons. Intern. L'Expl. Mer.*, 20(2), 160-166 (1954).

66 WALKER F.T., A sublittoral survey of the Laminariaceae of Little Loch Broom. *Trans. Proc. Bot. Soc. Edin.*, 36(4), 305-308 (1955).

67 WALKER F.T., The Laminaria cycle. *Rev. Algol. N.S.*, 3, 179-181 (1956).

68 WALKER F.T. and RICHARDSON W.D., The Laminariaceae off North Shapinsay; changes from 1947-1953. *Ann. Bot. N.S.*, 18(72), 483-494 (1954).

69 WALKER F.T. and RICHARDSON W.D., An ecological investigation of *Laminaria cloustoni* Edin. (*L. hyperborea* Fosl.) around Scotland. *J. Ecol.*, 43(1), 26-38 (1955).

70 WALKER F.T. and RICHARDSON W.D., The Laminariaceae of North Shapinsay, Orkney Is., changes from 1947-1955. *J. Mar. Res.*, 15(2), 123-133 (1956).

71 WALKER F.T. and RICHARDSON W.D., Survey of the Laminariaceae off the Island of Arran: changes from 1952-1955. *J. Ecol.*, 45(2), 225-232 (1957).

72 WALKER F.T. and RICHARDSON W.D., Perennial changes of *Laminaria cloustoni* on the coasts of Scotland. *J. Cons. Intern. L'Expl. Mer.*, 22(3), 298-308 (1957).

73 WARINNER R.J.E and BREHMER M.L., The effects of thermal effluents on marine organisms. *Air Water Pollut.*, 10(4), 277-89 (1966).

74 WILLIAMS L.G., Marine algal ecology at Cape Lookout, North Carolina. *Bull. Furman Univ.*, 31, No. 5 (1949).

CHAPTER 3

ALGAL VEGETATION-THE ENVIRONMENT

In the previous chapter we have seen that on most coasts it is possible to observe a zonation of plants and animals. Certain indicator species dominate the different belts and it is only natural to ask what are the factors (3,12 , 13,17) that determine the upper and lower limits of the major belt-demarcating species. Once these have been established, then the same question can be asked for other seaweeds that occur on the shore. In trying to arrive at an answer to the problem it should be realised that more than one factor may be involved, though it is not unlikely that at one time of the year or at a certain phase in the life history of the alga, one factor may be paramount. The factors may act directly or indirectly insofar as they may affect biological competition. We shall see that the environmental factors must exercise an influence upon the physiological behaviour of the plants, and therefore a full understanding cannot be achieved without a study of algal physiology accompanied by the necessary experimentation. In fact, proof that any particular factor determines either the upper or lower limit of a species must depend ultimately upon experiment.

GEOGRAPHICAL DISTRIBUTION

The geographical distribution of any species is probably determined by the temperature of the sea water, though in many cases we do not know whether it is the mean temperature, the maximum summer temperature or the minimum winter temperature. It must be this factor that controls the northern limit of Mediterranean plants, e.g. species of *Cystoseira*, that reach the shores of Great Britain and species such as *Batophora oerstedii* in eastern U.S.A. More recently, however, evidence has come forward to show that another factor may operate, namely day-length or photoperiodism. A very large body of information about this phenomenon is available for terrestrial plants but practically nothing is known for the algae. There is, however, sufficient to show that some algae are long-day plants (requiring 16 hr or more) and others are short-day plants (8-10 hr). Thus sporelings of some *Enteromorpha* species are essentially long-day whereas those of some *Monostroma* species grow best under

54

short-day conditions (13). In Europe the Northern *Ulva lactuca* is reported (39)
to be a long-day plant whilst the southern *U. thuretii* is a short-day plant.
Certain algae may then be limited to particular latitudes where the correct
day-length or photoperiod will be available for some of the year at least.
The failure of species of *Laminaria* to penetrate the warmer waters of the
globe has usually been regarded as a temperature phenomenon, but it may turn
out to be one of photoperiodism, growth of the adult plants being dependent
upon long-day conditions. It is already known that light determines largely
the production of gametes in *Laminaria* (32). Here then is a whole new field
awaiting urgent investigation. Green algae such as *Enteromorpha* and *Ulva*
are not difficult to culture in the laboratory and it should be quite possible
using fluorescent lights, to grow such plants under different day-lengths and
determine rates of growth.

FACTORS

Some years ago I suggested (12) that the environmental factors operating on the
sea-shore could be divided into those that are (1) causal, i.e. directly
responsible for determining the upper and lower limits of species, (2) presence or absence factors that determine whether a species shall be present or
not in the area provided it is within its geographical range, (3) modificatory.
This last group comprises those factors that result in an elevation or depression of the upper or lower limits of species, such as heavy spray, much shade,
etc. Any study of the shore should therefore aim at trying to evaluate the
factors into these three groups. In addition it is also convenient to divide
the environmental factors into four main categories, (1) physiographic, (2)
physical, including the regional climate, (3) chemical, (4) biological. In
the following pages it is proposed to consider these one by one, indicating
their behaviour in controlling the limits of species.

PHYSIOGRAPHIC FACTORS

The Tides

The principal physiographic factor is the tide, though it operates in a
number of directions. Tides differ from place to place and in any study of
zonation it is important to acquire a knowledge of the kind of tide in the
area. If there is only one high and one low water per 24 hr the tide is said
to be diurnal. In most places there are two high and low waters and such
tides are called semi-diurnal. In the case of semi-diurnal tides, if successive high and low waters are different in height the tides are said to be
mixed. In a few localities, where there are two separate entrances, such as
Southampton Water, one can have four high and low waters in every 24 hr.
Figure 3.1 illustrates some of these different tides and it will be noticed
that over a neap- and spring-tide cycle the nature of the tide may change.

Information about the tides can be obtained from simple float gauges or from
pressure gauges. If such are not available, useful though not extensive
information can be secured from marked tide poles (see p. 13). The main dis-
advantage of tide poles is the necessity to have records of tides over spring-
and neap-tide cycles at different times of the year, and securing this information is laborious.

Submergence and Exposure

One of the most important effects of the tides relates to submergence and
exposure, which in turn have a profound influence upon the physiological activities of algae (see p. 71). Two kinds of exposure exist insofar as effects
on algae are concerned. There is first the exposure that occurs between two
successive semi-diurnal or diurnal tides: the second is the exposure at upper
levels that occurs during neap tides. The former is of relatively short
duration, but in this time excessive water loss or a major effect upon photosynthesis, which in some seaweeds falls to zero soon after exposure, or upon
respiration, may operate as a causal factor (see p. 62). During the period
of exposure the seaweeds are subject to ordinary climatic conditions and
these may be so severe as to restrict their extension upwards on the shore.
The high temperatures of the midday tropics probably prevent most algae from

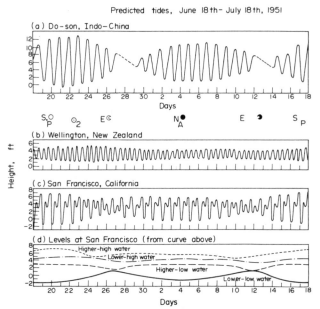

FIG. 3.1. *Predicted tides of different types plotted for 30-day periods at the designated localities. Compiled from the U.S.C. and G.S. tide tables (after Doty).*

occupying the littoral, whilst the high humidities of many higher latitude regions may well enable algae to extend high up on the shore because water loss is reduced. Higher humidities on salt marshes and mangrove swamps must enable some algae to occupy higher levels than on the open coast. At the other extreme very low temperatures can result in the death of algae, whilst the formation of ice can bring about a complete clearing of rocks when the ice is torn bodily from the rock at the time of spring melt (see p. 69).

The inter-tidal exposure also affects conditions in the tide pools, partic-ularly those at higher levels. In the summer the temperature of the water in the shallow upper pools may rise considerably: increased evaporation then takes place and salinity will also change. It can be seen from Fig. 3.1, curve C, that a very slight change in elevation can result in the inter-tidal exposure being doubled, e.g. above and below the lower high tide mark of a pair. At low-tide levels exposure is replaced by submergence, and whilst it may be very difficult to separate the two phenomena, nevertheless there are levels below which the submergence period can be trebled. Such changes, which occur between low water mark of neap and spring tides and between high water

mark of neap and spring tides may well determine the existence of certain
critical levels (see p. 80).

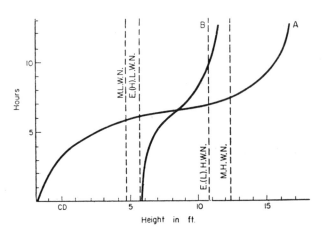

FIG. 3.2. *Hours of exposure during* (A) *spring tides and* (B)
neap tides at Wembury (after Colman).

In Fig. 3.2, which depicts the differences in hours of exposure between neap
and spring tides, it will be seen that above mean high water mark of neap
tides there will be levels that do not get a daily submergence and this period
of continuous exposure (the second kind of exposure) increases in length with
increasing height on the shore. Similarly below low water mark of neap tides
there will be levels that do not become exposed at all during the day and
such periods will be more and more extensive as one descends towards low water
mark of spring tides. These periods of prolonged exposure or submergence over
days will be more profound in their effects than the inter-tidal periods and
equally may determine the existence of critical levels. In particular these
periods have a direct effect upon water loss, thallus temperature and salinity
changes. The periods are probably of greater significance to the sporelings
of the algae than to the adult plants but we possess remarkably little information on this subject. Kain (33) has, however, shown that populations of
Laminaria hyperborea are controlled mainly by factors affecting establishment
rather than factors affecting growth. It is a matter of observation that
fucoid sporelings rarely occur outside the belts the species occupy as adults
and injurious exposure may be responsible. Injurious exposure permits of
various possibilities: in some algae it may be water loss: in the case of at
least one alga (*Hormosira banksii* of New Zealand) it is known that the

respiration rate of the juvenile is affected to such an extent (Fig. 3.3)
that after a few such exposures the plants would surely respire to death: in
other algae it may be the effect upon photosynthesis. In some cases, whilst
not actually killing plants, it may reduce a species powers of competition to
the point where it succumbs. In those cases where there are seasonal changes
of level (particularly tideless seas) the long periods of exposure may result
in the appearance of a special algal community or the development of a bare
zone in the summer.

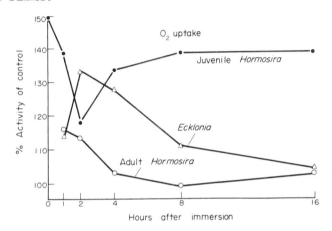

FIG. 3.3. *Respiration rate of juvenile and adult* Hormosira
banksii *and* Ecklonia radiata *after desiccation and reimmersion.*
Note that the adult Hormosira *and* Ecklonia *return to the control*
value (non-dehydrated plants) but the juvenile Hormosira *does*
not (after Bergquist).

Emphasis has been laid upon the changes that take place at different tide
levels, and it might be supposed that algae affected by such changes would
reach their limits (upper or lower) at the same tidal levels in all the
regions where they occur. This does not prove to be entirely the case (Fig.
3.4) thus showing that other local factors may intervene. One of the principal local factors intervening in this manner is the degree of wave action,
which is itself dependent on the degree of physiographic exposure or shelter.
On a very exposed coast the elevation of the algal zones can be quite considerable, e.g. North Gavel on Fair Isle (11) (see p. 64 and Fig. 3.5), whilst
exposure commonly brings about a difference in the composition of the vegetation (see p.34 and Figs. 2.1, 2.2). There is also the effect of latitude,
operating through other factors, such as temperature, humidity, etc., which
may result in the elevation of species on the shore with increase of latitude.

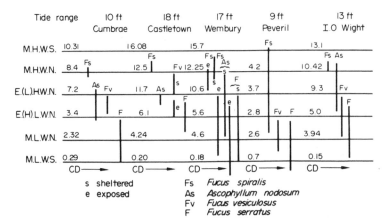

FIG. 3.4. *Showing the relation of the principal known fucoids (at five localities) to the important tidal levels. The tide levels are represented by the horizontal lines. Underneath each locality the vertical extent of the principal fucoid zones is shown by the dark lines. Where exposure or shelter make a difference there are two lines, labelled e and s respectively. On the left of each locality the tide-table level (chart datum) for the six tidal levels is placed opposite the respective line. Above each locality is noted the maximum tidal range (based on Admiralty tide-tables) (after Chapman).*

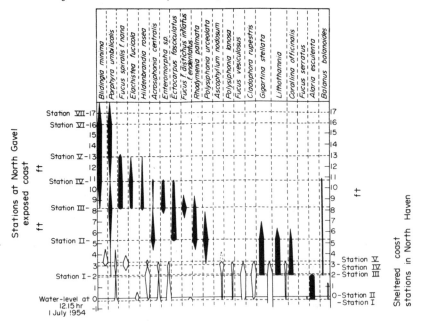

FIG. 3.5. *Comparison of the distribution of inter-tidal algae in relation to tide levels. Fair Isle, June–July 1952. Dark bands for exposed coast, plain for sheltered coast (after Burrows et al.).*

This has been demonstrated for *Fucus serratus* (37) in Great Britain and for some algae in other parts of the world.

Water Loss

The principal phenomenon associated with tidal exposure is that of daily water loss, especially if it occurs during the heat of the day. Various workers (29,30,34,49) have directed their attention to this problem and much of the work has been performed with the fucoids that occur on British shores. In the case of the highest fucoid on the shore *(Pelvetia canaliculata)* the major loss occurs in the first 3-6 hr, whereas with other fucoids (Fig. 3.6) the loss is spread over as much as 18 hr. Figure 3.6 shows that *Fucus spiralis* (= var. *platycarpus*) loses water more slowly than the other three fucoids, and that

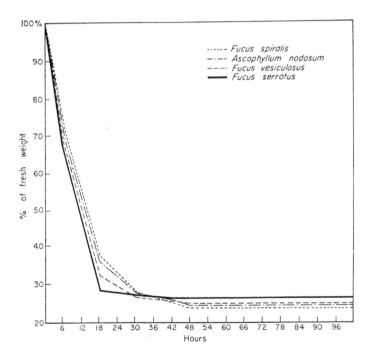

FIG. 3.6. *Loss of water in fucoids during exposure. The curves show the percentages of fresh weight in relation to the time of desiccation. The higher a fucoid is growing the slower it loses its water and the greater is its total percentual water content (after Zaneveld).*

the rate of water loss with the various species increases in relation to
their successively lower positions on the shore. Although *F. spiralis* loses
its water at a slower rate than the other three species, nevertheless it
eventually suffers a greater water loss. Some evidence has been produced (26)
to show that the rate of water loss is related to the fat content, and that
this in turn is related to the thickness of the cell walls (Table 3.1).

TABLE 3.1

Fat Content of some Littoral Fucoids (26)

	% ether extracted fat	% true fat
Pelvetia canaliculata (upper littoral)	4.88	3.6
Ascophyllum nodosum (mid-littoral)	2.87	-
Fucus vesiculosus (mid-littoral)	2.60	1.9
Halidrys siliquosa (low littoral)	2.18	-
Himanthalia lorea (low littoral)	1.21	-
Laminaria digitata (sublittoral)	0.46	0.46

It can be demonstrated that water moves readily out of these cell walls when
they are placed in sea water of increasing concentration. The walls also
decrease in thickness during periods of desiccation, the higher the species is
growing the greater is the ultimate shrinkage. Species which lose water more
slowly take longest to reabsorb it, and, water being necessary for growth,
species highest on the shore (which lose and reabsorb water most slowly) will
have the slowest growth. The rate of water loss in these fucoids must influence their upper limits, though before this could be said with certainty one
would need information on the effect of desiccation on metabolism both during
exposure and on subsequent re-immersion.

A study (15) of the mangrove species *Caloglossa leprieurii* showed that the maximum inter-tidal exposure was about 8.8 hr and in that period it could lose
between 35-40% of its water content. This is about half the lethal water loss
of 70%, so that water loss per se could not be a serious causal factor. On
the other hand it was found that photosynthesis under light of 2000 ft candles

on resubmergence decreased with increasing desiccation up to a limit of 40%
above which photosynthesis became disorganised. In this alga, therefore, the
indirect effect of water loss upon photosynthesis would seem to set the upper
limit.

Water loss in algae cannot be studied without considering the weather conditions. The effect of cloud or unrestricted sunlight upon water loss (and also
assimilation) in *F. serratus* and *F. spiralis* var. *platycarpus* is strikingly
demonstrated in Fig. 3.7. Drying of the thallus may also, in some forms,
affect the respiration rate of the plant. In *F. vesiculosus* the respiration
rate decreases steadily with increasing water loss (34).

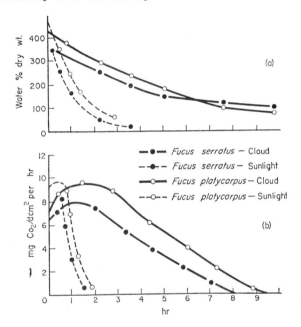

FIG. 3.7.   (a), *water loss, and* (b), *assimilation of* Fucus serratus
and F. spiralis *var.* platycarpus *in relation to exposure (drying)
on sunny and cloudy days (after Stocker and Holdheide).*

It is possible to investigate water loss on other species of algae, particularly those that form mats, such as *Enteromorpha*. In these cases portions of
the mat are cut out and fitted into waterproof paper dishes which are then
replaced in position on the shore. In this way it was found (2) that an *Enteromorpha* mat lost 25 percent of its moisture in the first three hours of exposure as compared with a mat of Chrysophycean (golden-brown) algae that lost
only 8.4 percent. The reduced loss by the latter algae, whether through

evaporation or drainage, is due to the gelatinous nature of the Chrysophycean
algae which aids water retention. In these experiments the evaporating power
of the air over the Chrysophyceae was 1.41 units as against 1.1 over the
Enteromorpha.

Wave Action

Other physiographic factors include the degree of shelter or exposure to
waves. This is essentially a presence or absence factor and the absence of
Ascophyllum on exposed coasts is an example of its operation (3). Extreme
exposure to wave action may operate mechanically in preventing swarmers or
fertilised eggs from becoming attached to the rocks. In the case of successful species one must suppose that attachment is very rapid. We still, however, know very little about this process.

Apart from operating as a presence or absence factor, wave action may also act
as a modifying factor. The important feature of wave action is related to the
mean average height of prevailing waves or the height of storm waves if they
are of any frequency. Big waves commonly result in much splash and spray and
as a result of large waves and spray the upper and lower limits of algae and
animals, mainly of the upper eulittoral and littoral fringe, can be elevated
to a height of many feet. This elevation forms what is known as the *"Splash
zone"*. When the coast is very exposed and waves generally large, the splash
zone can be subdivided into (a) the swash zone, which is the height the actual
waves wash up the rock face (this will, of course, depend upon the slope of
the rocks themselves), (b) the splash zone, which is that part of the shore
actually splashed by the waves (this tends to be greater the more the rocks
are inclined to the vertical), (c) the spray zone which can often be very
extensive, particularly on the west coast of the Outer Hebrides and western
Eire (see Chapter 2, p. 34).

Tidal range acts as a modifying factor because the vertical height of a belt
is related to the maximum tidal range. Even regions with a very small tidal
range, e.g. the Gulf of Mexico and the Caribbean, possess a distinct zonation
of marine organisms. It is true that such shores do not provide the great
variety of rock pools to be found on shores with a large tidal range.

Tide Currents

Strong tidal currents can affect the growth and size of plants. On the east coast of Scotland the strength of the current determines in large measure whether *Laminaria saccharina* or *L. cloustoni* (*L. hyperborea*) is the dominant, the latter occurring with the stronger currents. Currents also tend to vary with the state of the tide. Thus at high and low tide, when one talks of "slack water", there is commonly little or no current, whereas between these periods, when the rise or fall may be rapid, currents tend to be strong. It is interesting to note that high water of neap tides marks the lower limits of *Fucus spiralis* in certain places, e.g. Castleton, Isle of Wight (Fig. 3.4), and low water mark of neap tides is closely associated with the lower limits of *Ascophyllum*, whilst *Fucus vesiculosus* generally lies within this zone of stronger currents. On another type of shore, the salt marsh shore, the strength of the current flowing up and down the creeks largely determines the degree of erosion and upon this depends the extent to which characteristic creek bank communities can develop. In estuaries silt load carried down reduces light intensity and can smother organisms. In such places (e.g. Severn, Chesapeake Bay) species can be eliminated. Occasional excessive loads arising from hurricanes, e.g. Hurricane Agnes in the Chesapeake, can be disastrous and organisms affected for some years afterwards (16).

PHYSICAL FACTORS

Substrate

We can conveniently include here the nature of the substrate, i.e. whether it is rock, boulders, stones, mud or peat. In determining the effectiveness of anchorage, this factor must operate as a presence or absence one. Larger algae obviously cannot grow or survive on stones and small pebbles. Mud demands especial adaptations as shown in the embedded salt marsh fucoids (see p. 47). The angle of slope of rock faces and the presence of cracks and crannies affects the occurrence of some species, and can either operate as a presence or absence factor or as a modifying factor (Fig. 2.5).

Temperature

During the period of tidal exposure temperature affects the algae, high temperatures causing loss of water from the thallus together with the consequent
effect this loss has upon photosynthesis and respiration (see p. 76). It has
already been noted that sea temperatures affect biogeographic distribution
and may set the limits of species. Gradual changes of sea temperatures over
a number of years can bring about the appearance of species from warmer or
colder waters depending upon the direction in which the temperature is changing. Seasonal changes of temperature may even change the composition of the
flora. A classical example here is Cape Lookout in North Carolina where the
winter sea temperatures result in a flora of essentially northern species,
whilst in the summer the temperatures rise to the point that enables a well-
marked group of southern species to appear.

On upper levels of salt marshes where the phanerogamic vegetation may be of
low stature, i.e. General Salt Marsh or Plantaginetum (see pp. 108-10), evaporation may be so severe that salt crystallisation takes place on the soil
and only gelatinous algae, e.g. *Rivularia atra, Phaeococcus adnatus,* can grow
successfully in such places.

Changes of temperature affect the metabolism of algae. In the case of *Fucus
vesiculosus* respiration rate decreases with fall of temperature but is still
measurable at $-15^{\circ}C$ (75) whilst *Enteromorpha nana* (= *Blidingia minima*) still
functions at $-22^{\circ}C$ (9). Seasonal changes of temperature may be equally significant. Thus growth of *Laminaria digitata* in Norway is related to the summer
and winter temperatures as well as to light intensity. Another example of
light meshed with temperature is provided by *L. hyperborea*. At $10^{\circ}C$ water
temperature the minimum light intensity for growth of the gametophytes is 20
lux with a saturating light intensity of 350 lux. At $17^{\circ}C$ the saturating
light intensity is between 1000-2000 lux (32).

The effect of temperature upon algal metabolism needs further study. Temperature changes can affect both photosynthesis and respiration during submergence and exposure. Photosynthetic activity is generally low or absent during
the periods of exposure. A balance sheet between net gain during submergence
and net loss during exposure therefore needs to be compiled.

Some very interesting results have been obtained (34) for the effect of temperature on respiration of *Fucus vesiculosus*, the respiration rate dropping
sharply below 0°C. Very similar results were also found for *Chondrus crispus*
and *Ulva lactuca*. In Europe Ehrke (21) found that for *Delesseris* the optimum
temperature for photosynthesis was 0°C, and that maximum growth took place in
winter and early spring when sea-water temperature was nearest 0°C. For
Fucus and *Enteromorpha*, however, the optimum temperature for assimilation is
17°C, and maximum development occurs in August or September when sea temperatures are around 17°C.

Seaweeds appear to fall into four groups (43) in their temperature responses
during exposure periods:

(1) Algae of the upper littoral of protected bays or of upper tide pools.
     These are resistant to air temperatures up to 35-37°C.
(2) Algae of the upper littoral of open coasts which are resistant to air
     temperatures up to 32°C.
(3) Winter and spring annuals of the upper littoral. These resist air temp-
     eratures up to 30-32°C.
(4) Sublittoral algae which are intolerant to air temperatures above 30°C.

While smaller algae can be studied as a whole, larger algae may need to be
studied organ by organ. Thus the main frond of *Alaria esculenta* probably
behaves very differently to the lateral reproductive leaflets. The same may
be true of the lateral vegetative, fertile, and vesicular appendages of
Ascophyllum. This is certainly the case on the Pacific coast of North
America where the various organs of deep water plants of *Egregia laevigata* (14)
behave quite differently in relation to temperature (Table 3.1).

In the sea itself, changes of temperature can affect both photosynthesis and
respiration. The point at which these two processes exactly balance, and
where oxygen content remains stable, is called the *compensation point*. The
effect of temperature upon the compensation point has been worked out for the
Southern Hemisphere fucoid, *Hormosira banksii* (Fig. 3.8). At temperatures
around 15°C, the compensation point occurs at a much lower depth than it does
at 20°C. The compensation point must set the lower limit to which an alga
descends and this point is not only related primarily to available light but
is also presumably related to the mean sea temperature or possibly to the mean

TABLE 3.1

Photosynthesis (μl. O_2 g dry wt/5 min) of organs of deep water plants of
Egregia laevigata

Organ	$10^{\circ}C$	$15^{\circ}C$	$20^{\circ}C$	$25^{\circ}C$ Temp.
Dissected "leaves"	130	375	1175	630
Juvenile "leaves"	670	725	700	965
Basal "leaves"	530	540	265	145

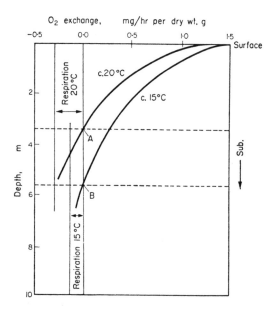

FIG. 3.8. *Variation of compensation point with depth and sea*
temperature in Hormosira banksii *(After Trevarthen).*

summer temperature.

In confined spaces such as rock pools or salt pans (p. 100) temperature fluctuations can bring about considerable changes.

Elevation of the water temperature affects metabolism, and the increase in
salinity through evaporation may be very considerable in pools high up on the

littoral as well as on salt marsh muds. Rise of water temperature probably
does not cause damage at moderate or high latitudes, but daylight respiration
may be so speeded up that the overall metabolism no longer permits growth.
Biebl (6) devoted some time to the study of rock pools on the south coast of
England, and he found that temperature increases up to 26°C over a period of
24 hr had no effect on most red algae and, further, that rapid changes of as
much as 12°C, when the incoming tide flooded a pool after a hot day, could
occur without causing any damage.

In arctic waters very low temperatures are commonplace in winter and algae may
be frozen for many weeks. In *Fucus vesiculosus* as much as 80 percent of the
contained water can be frozen (34), yet upon thawing out there is no impairment
of metabolism. It is partly for this reason, of course, that the algae are
able to survive in the Arctic. Another reason is their capacity to survive
the long Arctic night. This it has been suggested (48) is made possible by a
capacity to be heterotrophic at very low light and low temperatures. Similar
behaviour has been recorded for the cold water plants of *Ascophyllum nodosum*,
Chondrus crispus and *Ulva lactuca*.

Humidity

Humidity may be significant on a rocky coast (see p. 63), and there is no
doubt it is very important on a salt marsh and in a mangrove swamp. Within a
stand of tall plants, such as Sea rush (*Juncus maritimus*) or *Spartina townsendii*, the relative humidity can be high whilst outside it may be much lower.
The same is also true near the mud floors of *Avicennia* or *Rhizophora* forest.

It is possible that certain algae associated with these phanerogams, e.g.
Enteromorpha nana (*Blidingia minima*) on Cord grass (*Spartina*),   *Avicennia*
leaves or Sea purslane (*Halimione*), or *Bostrychia* and *Catenella* under *Halimione* or on mangrove pneumatophores or Shrubby seablite (*Suaeda fruticosa*), are
able to survive at these levels because of the maintenance of high humidities.
Some useful facts on this problem could easily be obtained: thus, wet and dry
bulb thermometers give the relative humidity, and water loss of algae maintained in desiccators over solutions that provide a given humidity should not
prove difficult to measure.

Pressure

An ecological factor that has received very little attention is that of
pressure. Certain species develop bladders which commonly contain a gas (18),
and such bladders are normally regarded as a flotation mechanism. Speculation
as to the function of bladders is complicated in that some have extremely
thick walls; in one species, *Pelagophycus porra*, the gas pressure is less than
1 atmosphere and the gas contains carbon monoxide. In another species,
Egregia laevigata (this and *Pelagophycus* occur in the Pacific) many of the
bladders in deeply submerged plants are full of liquid. In *Ascophyllum* and
Fucus bladder pressure is related to oxygen production and therefore increases
during the day and decreases at night (1).

Light

The most important physical factor is that of light, because of its necessity
for photosynthesis. Light, however, is not an easy factor to measure. There
are also problems with lower littoral algae, connected with daily and seasonal variation in light intensity, the former obviously being related to tide
height provided the tidal range is large (40,42,45). Finally, there are all
the problems associated with the changes of light intensity and the varying
spectral composition of light at different depths (Fig. 3.9). From the point
of view of photosynthetic efficiency, one needs to know not only the quantity
of light reaching any given depth of water, but also its quality (spectral

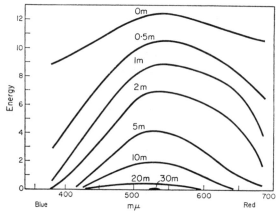

FIG. 3.9. *Spectral distribution of radiant energy (in relative
units) at different depths (after Levring).*

composition). The combination of light intensity and clarity of water will determine the maximum depth to which seaweeds can descend (see p. 22). At such depths, the amount of light penetrating is a very small proportion of the incident surface light. Experiments on a few deep-growing algae have shown that they can be fully light-saturated at very low values, though much more information is needed. We also know that certain algae when submerged, rapidly cease to photosynthesise at a rate in excess of the respiratory rate, and hence their compensation point is quickly reached (36). Such algae obviously cannot descend to any great depth.

The extent to which the incident light is cut down in passing through a body of water depends, among other things, upon water turbidity, which in turn depends on quantity of plankton, "yellow" material and the amount of silt carried. The "yellow" material, which is probably phenolic in nature, is found mainly in coastal waters and derived from algal exudates. Coastal waters are particularly variable in this respect, as may be seen from some data for the Californian coast (13) (Fig 3.10). This variation in absorption coefficient for the different waters will affect the relative photosynthesis of the algae. Again using the data from California, the likely variation in photosynthesis and the resulting variation in depth of the compensation point has been calculated for the dominant sublittoral alga, *Macrocystis pyrifera* (Fig. 3.10).

With the sublittoral algae, especially those near the low tide mark, there are changes in quantity and quality of light with rise and fall of the tide, but with the littoral algae there are in addition the effects of light intensity during the periods of exposure (46). This varies, at least to some extent, with humidity, which itself may be affected by sun and cloud, because the more rapidly the thalli dry up the more rapid is the fall-off in assimilation rate. Under extreme conditions level on the shore does not seem to make much difference, but when the rate of water loss is not so great then an upper belt alga, such as *Fucus platycarpus*, has a slower fall off in assimilation rate than a low level alga such as *F. serratus* (Fig. 3.7). The same kind of effect has been found for the fucoid *Hormosira banksii* in New Zealand, whilst in another New Zealand littoral alga (*Scytothamnus*) it seems likely that net assimilation gain is restricted to the periods of submergence, and this probably sets the upper limit to which the alga can grow.

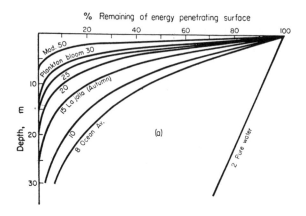

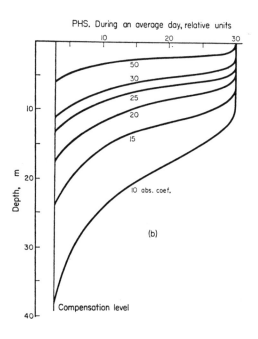

FIG. 3.10. (a), *percent light absorption in sea water of different absorption coefficients*, (b), *relative photosynthesis in* Macrocystis *on an average day in waters of different absorption coefficients (after North)*.

TABLE 3.2

Percentage of Normal Assimilation re-attained on Flooding after Exposure

Level	Species		After 5 hr exposure at 90 percent R.H. and 4 hr after flooding
Upper littoral	*Pelvetia canaliculata*	70-80 percent 9 hr after flooding. 11 days exposure	
Top of mid-littoral	*Fucus spiralis*	49 percent 8-9 hr after flooding. 3 days exposure	97 percent
Mean sea level	*F. vesiculosus*	20 percent 8-9 hr after flooding. 3 days exposure	72 percent
Lower littoral	*F. serratus*	Cannot tolerate 3 days exposure	42 percent
Sublittoral fringe	*Laminaria digitata*		Cannot tolerate 2 hr exposure

When an alga has been exposed, one needs to know how rapidly it returns to
the normal assimilation rate after the reduced exposure rate (8). Delicate
plants such as *Ulva* and *Porphyra* recover very rapidly, while the behaviour of
the tougher fucoids varies with position on the shore (Table 3.2).

With algae that are permanently submerged, the rate of photosynthesis depends,
as we have seen, upon the amount and quality of penetrant light. Apart from
considerations mentioned earlier, this may be affected by the degree of wave
action or choppiness of the water and the angle of the sun (see also p. 63).
Thus Tschudy (47) found that on choppy days maximum photosynthesis occurred at
the surface, but that on calm days it occurred at about 5 m down. With the
brown fucoid *Hormosira* the rate of photosynthesis during exposure and submergence was related to light intensity, and under supra-optimal light conditions
(unclouded sky, midsummer and calm water) maximum photosynthesis took place
at 1 m below the surface (Fig. 3.11).

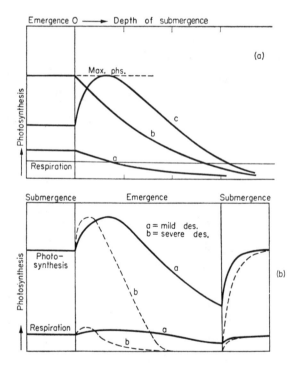

FIG. 3.11. (a), *effect of light intensity upon photosynthesis of
exposed and submerged* Hormosira banksii *in relation to depth.* a,
low light intensity; b, *optimum light intensity;* c, *supra-optimum
light intensity.* (b), *effect of desiccation upon photosynthesis
(full line) and respiration (broken line) of* H. banksii *when
exposed (after Trevarthen).*

When the photosynthesis of algae is studied in relation to different light
intensities, it is found that the littoral algae have an optimum light intensity around 50,000 m candles (= 5000 foot candles), which is in the same
region as that for many terrestrial plants. This is certainly true of *Fucus*,
Ulva linza and *Porphyra atropurpurea*. In the sublittoral alga, *Laminaria
saccharina*, the optimum is much lower (Fig. 3.12). In extra-European waters
where there are algae with distinct appendages the efficiency of the different
organs may vary, particularly with the brown Pacific laminarian *Egregia laevigata* (14), where there are differences between the entire and dissected appendages and the axis. For every sublittoral alga there must be a minimum light

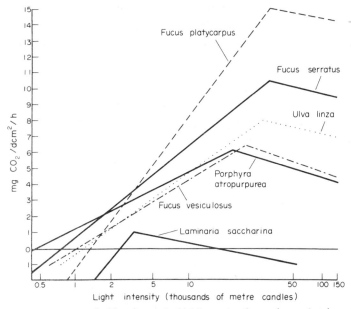

FIG. 3.12. *Assimilation of different algae in relation to light
intensity (after Stocker and Holdheide).*

intensity below which there is no growth. The depth at which this occurs is
known as the compensation point so far as light intensity is concerned (there
is also one for temperature, see p. 67). This minimum light intensity may
sometimes be very low, e.g. at 15°C it is 32 foot candles for *Laminaria saccharina* and 38 foot candles for *Fucus serratus*. An indication of the light
compensation depth can be obtained quite readily by the Winkler technique for
determining oxygen content in water. Round-bottomed flasks are completely
filled with sea water. Some have seaweed added and after being stoppered one
or more of these are covered effectively with black cloth, whilst one or more

remain without seaweed as a control. All are attached to a metal ring and if
several such rings are set up they can be lowered from a boat or wharf to
different depths in the sea for an hour. At the end of the period the oxygen
in the flask water is determined and in the case of littoral algae it is generally not difficult to find a depth above which an oxygen gain is recorded
and below which there is an oxygen loss.

In so far as both temperature and light exert an effect upon assimilation it
is almost desirable to devise experiments involving both factors, as Lampe(39)
has done for *F. serratus* and *Porphyra*. With *Fucus serratus* the assimilation
rate increases in sunlight with increasing temperature; with *Porphyra*, on the
other hand, when the temperature is raised above 15°C the rate of photosynthesis is lowered with low light intensity. Very similar results for *Fucus
serratus* were also obtained by Hyde(28) (Fig. 3.13), except that above temperatures of 25°C there was a decrease in photosynthesis with increasing light
intensity. *F. serratus*, therefore, can be regarded as a *eurythermal* species,
tolerating a wide range of temperature, whilst *Porphyra* would have to be regarded as *stenothermal*, tolerating a much narrower temperature range.

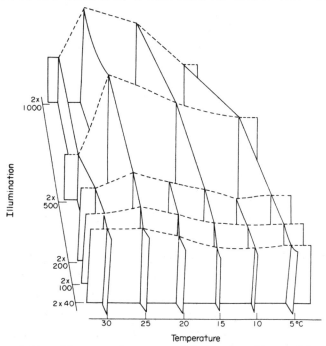

FIG. 3.13. *Diagram of paper model to show the combined effects of
light and temperature on the rate of apparent assimilation of*
Fucus serratus *(after Hyde).*

Most work relating to temperature and assimilation has been carried out with the experimental material submerged in water. Temperature, however, can be very important during the periods of exposure in its effects after re-submersion.

It has been shown (42) that, in general, littoral algae exhibit an increase in photosynthesis on submersion after exposure to high temperatures whereas sublittoral algae show a decrease. Among the algae studied, *Fucus serratus* was the only lower littoral species showing any tolerance towards high temperatures.

Today no really effective work can be carried out on photosynthesis of algae without a consideration of the absorption curves (27) in relation to light of different wave-lengths (Fig. 3.14). Quite a number of years ago the German physiologist Englemann put forward the view that the colour of an alga, particularly those growing in the sea, was complementary to that of the available

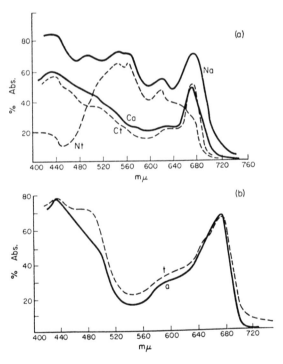

FIG. 3.14. *Absorption* (a) *and action* (t) *spectra of marine algae.* (a), Coilodesme californica (Ca, Ct) *and* Smithora (Porphyra) naiadum (Na, Nt). (b), Ulva taeniata (a, t) *(after Haxo and Blinks).*

light: maximum assimilation in Chlorophyceae occurs in red (long waves) and
blue-green light; as the former are rapidly absorbed such algae generally
grow at the upper levels. This is not invariably true as many Siphonales,
such as *Caulerpa* and *Udotea*, can grow at considerable depths.

In the brown seaweeds, due to the presence of the pigment fucoxanthin, maximum
absorption occurs in the blue and blue-green region which assists them in
growing at medium depths; similarly because of the phycobilins the red algae
with their capacity to absorb light of the short wave-lengths (green-yellow)
can also grow at great depths.

Although the different parts of the light spectrum are absorbed differentially
this does not mean that they are equally efficient in photosynthesis. The
absorption spectrum needs, therefore, to be complemented by the action spectrum (Fig. 3.14) which indicates the degree of efficiency of the different
wave-lengths. Levring (40) has pointed out that for any given species the pig-
ments, which determine absorption and utilisation of light, can vary depending on locality, depth and season. This means that the spectral absorption
and action curves will also vary and that a single determination is not sufficient. He further points out that Englemann's complementary theory is mainly
valid for "shade" or "weak light" algae, whereas with "sun" algae light intensity determines their lower limit, because a shallow depth of water is sufficient to reduce their assimilation rate and this involves very little change
in quality of the light.

CHEMICAL FACTORS

The major factor here is salinity which may be particularly important in estuaries, where red and brown seaweeds tend to disappear. Changes in salinity
may also be very significant in rock pools and salt pans (7). Internal salinity
changes also take place in algae when they are exposed and this can affect
their assimilation rate (29). Biebl (7,10), who has done much work in this field,
believes that algae can be placed in one of three groups according to their
behaviour on exposure:

(1) Deep-growing algae: resistant to a concentration 1.4 times that of sea
     water.

(2) Algae of L.W.M. and lower littoral tide pools: resistant to a concentrat-
     ion of 2.2 times that of sea water.

(3) Littoral algae: resistant to a concentration 3 times that of sea water.

Generally the physical nature of the substrate, i.e. rough or smooth, with
cracks or without, is more important than its chemical composition. A comparison of the algal flora of chalk cliffs, such as those on the south coast
and East Anglian coasts, reveals differences which are probably due to the
excess chalk. This must be regarded as a presence or absence factor.

In rock pools and salt pans pH (acidity or alkalinity) and oxygen can change
very greatly during a day, particularly in summer, but there is no evidence
that such changes inhibit or prevent the growth of algae. Most marine algae
that have been investigated tolerate a wide range of pH. Shade appears to be
a much more important factor in the case of rock pools, where depth of water
and overhang of ledges may determine the type of vegetation that occurs.

With some salt marsh fucoids the existence of thallus twisting has been linked
with stimulus from soil nutrients promoting extra growth in that part of the
thallus that is currently in contact with the soil. In *Ascophyllum nodosum*
ecad *mackaii*, Gibb (24) has shown that its development from normal plants of
A. nodosum is promoted by either darkness or lowered salinity. Nutrient variations in sea water are mainly of concern in the development of plankton and
need not interest us here.

                            BIOLOGICAL FACTORS

Animals may often operate as presence or absence factors, e.g. the presence of
abundant *Patella* (limpets) generally prevents the establishment of *Fucus*
sporelings and the sea urchins, *Paracentrotus lividus* and *Echinus esculentus*
rapidly clear areas of algae (31,35). The mollusc *Helicion pellucidum* is also
responsible for the detachment of plants of *Laminaria saccharina*, whilst on
salt marshes the small snail *Hydrobia ulvae* can damage beds of *Ulva* species.
Grazing by marine animals is a field in which many more observations are
needed, especially at dusk or dawn, and at night.

Plants of course may exhibit host-parasite relations, e.g. the parasite
Harveyella on species of *Rhodomela*, and *Holmsella pachyderma* on *Gracilaria
confervoides*, and host-epiphyte relations where there is some restriction of
host (this may include *Polysiphonia fastigiata* on *Ascophyllum*). In another
direction there is the dependence of *Fucus* sporelings upon the presence of an
existing *Enteromorpha* felt. On salt marshes there is the restriction of
certain algae to the neighbourhood of phanerogamic plants, e.g. *Bostrychia*
and *Catenella* to *Suaeda fruticosa* and the base of *Juncus maritimus* tufts (p.
107). No such restriction appears to exist in the case of mangroves.

SUMMARY

It can be seen that there is a great complex of factors operating on the sea-
shore. Nevertheless there is a remarkable uniformity in the belts to be observed. When the upper and lower limits of algae occurring at different
levels are calculated, it is found that there are certain levels at which
there are more algae reaching their limits than elsewhere. These are termed
critical levels. At these levels there are presumably changes in a factor or
factors that affect a number of organisms. The following critical levels
appear to be fairly general, which suggests that the tidal factor is probably
paramount:

(a)   Around extreme high water mark of neap tides.

(b)   Around mean low water mark of neap tides.

(c)   Between mean and extreme low water marks of spring tides.

Clearly the major belt algae must continue to be investigated in the fullest
possible manner. A prerequisite to any such study is an analysis of the various ecological forms, because all work must be based upon taxonomically properly understood plants. In the Southern Hemisphere, *Hormosira banksii* exists
in a number of forms and statistical methods were used (4) to show that populations could be clearly delimited (Fig. 3.15). In a study of *Egregia laevigata*
on the Pacific coast of North America, I (14) found that there were distinct
deep and shallow water forms.

In a similar detailed study of *Ascophyllum nodosum* Baardseth (3) has shown that
there may be giant and dwarf races. Furthermore, in this seaweed vesicle

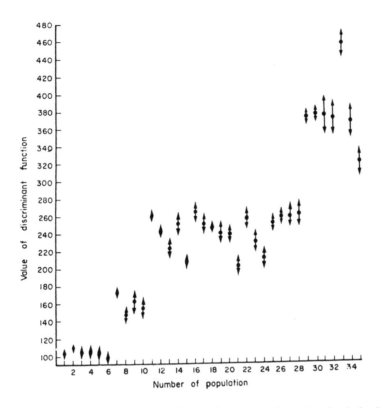

FIG. 3.15. *Plot of discriminant function with standard deviation for all open rock populations of* Hormosira banksii. *The populations fall into five distinct groups (after Bergquist).*

formation takes place at different times of the year in different regions, and varies between basal and lateral shoots. Basal shoot vesicles do not appear in under 1½ years (½ year for lateral shoots) or before they have reached a weight of 50 mg (5 mg for lateral shoots). Such development aspects must always be kept in mind in any detailed study of a major species.

When an alga has been carefully studied, we may attempt a first approximation to understanding its behaviour, and the factors responsible. In *Hormosira banksii* this has been done, and Fig. 3.16 compares the response of plants at the upper and lower limits. Further modification is necessary in order to allow for the additional effect of varying times during the day of high and low water. Fig. 3.17 shows a similar diagram for the small red turfy alga *Caloglossa leprieurii*. These schemas are deficient in neglecting annual temperature variations in sea water, and air temperatures during exposure.

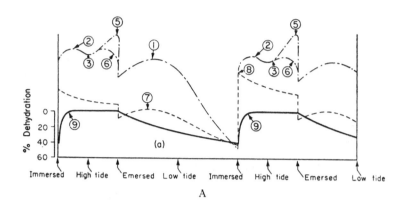

A

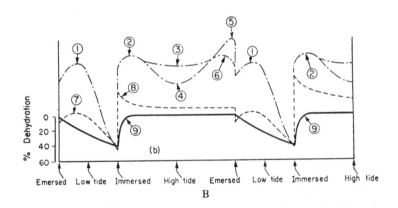

B

FIG. 3.16. *Schematic diagram showing variation in major factors for* Hormosira banksii *at A, its upper limit, B, its lower limit. 1, dehydration photosynthesis rise; 2, reimmersion photosynthesis rise; 3, high tide depression of photosynthesis from reduction of light; 4, further depression under suboptimal light conditions or in presence of turbid water; 5, photosynthetic elation as tide starts to rise on dehydration; 8, enhanced respiration stimulus on reimmersion; 9, tissue rehydration (after Bergquist).*

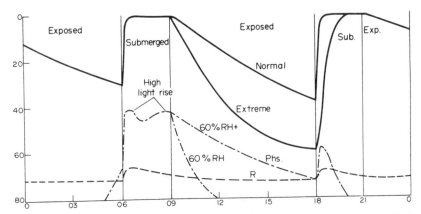

FIG. 3.17. *Summarised behaviour of* Caloglossa leprieurii *during daily period (after Chapman and Chapman).*

In spite of this they point the way in which ecological problems will ultimately have to be attacked on the sea-shore.

REFERENCES

1   ALEEM A.A., Zonation; vesicle pressure and gas composition in *Fucus ves-
     iculosus* and *Ascophyllum nodosum* at Kristeneberg (west coast of Sweden).
     Mar. Biol., 4, 36-43 (1969).

2   ANAND P.L., An ecological study of the algae of the British chalk cliffs.
     J. Ecol., 25, 344-367 (1937).

3   BAARDSETH E., Regrowth of *Ascophyllum nodosum* after harvesting. *Inst. for
     Indust. Res. & Stand. Rept.*, Eire (1955).

4   BAKER S.M., The causes of zoning of brown seaweed. *New Phyt.*, 8, 196-202,
     (1909); 9, 54-67 (1910).

5   BERGQUIST P.L., A statistical approach to the ecology of *Hormosira bank-
     sii*. *Bot. Marina*, 1(1), 22-53 (1959).

6   BIEBL R., Okologische und zell physiologische Studien an Rotalgen der
     engishe sudkuste. *Beih. Bot. Cent.*, 57, 381 (1937).

7   BIEBL R., Trochenresistenz und osmotische Empfindlichkeit der Meeresalgen
     verschieden tiefer standorte. *Jahr. Wiss. Bot.*, 86, 350 (1938).

8   BIEBL R., Lichtresistenz von Meeresalgen. *Protoplasma*, 46, 1/4, 63 (1956).

9   BIEBL R., Temperaturesistenz arktischer Susswasseralgen *in* Raum von
     Barrow, Alaska. *Mikroscopie*, 25, 3-6 (1969).

10   BIEBL R., Vergleichende Untersuchungen zur Temperatur resistenz von
      Meeresalgen entlang der Pazifischen Küste Nordamericas. *Protoplasma*,
      69, 61-83 (1970).

11   CHAPMAN A.R.O., A critique of prevailing attitudes towards the control
      of seaweed zonation on the sea shore. *Bot. Mar.*, 16, 80-82 (1973).

12   CHAPMAN V.J., Zonation of marine algae on the sea-shore. *Proc. Linn. Soc.
      Lond.*, 154, 239-253 (1943).

13   CHAPMAN V.J., A contribution to the autecology of *Egregia laevigata*
      Setch. Parts I-III. *Bot. Marina*, 3, 33-55, 101-122 (1962).

14   CHAPMAN V.J., The physiological ecology of some New Zealand seaweeds.
      Proc. 5th Inter. Seaw. Symp., 29-54 (1966). Pergamon Press.

15   CHAPMAN V.J. and CHAPMAN D.J., *The Algae*. 2nd Ed. Macmillan (1973).

16   CHESAPEAKE RESEARCH CONSORTIUM. Symposium on the effects of Tropical
      Storm Agnes on the Chesapeake Bay estuarine system. *CRC Publ.*, 27 (1974).

17   COLMAN J., The nature of the inter-tidal zonation of plants and animals.
      J. Mar. Biol. Ass. U.K., 18, 435-476 (1933).

18   DAMANT G.C.C., Storage of O_2 in the bladders of the seaweed *Ascophyllum*
      and their adaptation to hydrostatic pressure. *J. Exp. Biol.*, 14, 198
      (1937).

19   DAVID H.M., Studies in the autecology of *Ascophyllum nodosum* (L.). La Jol.
      J. Ecol., 31, 178-198 (1943).

20   DELF E.M., The significance of the exposure factor in relation to zon-
      ation. *Proc. Linn. Soc. Lond.*, 154, 234 (1943).

21   EHRKE G., Uber die Wirkung der Temperatur und des Lichtes auf die Atmung
      und Assimilation einiger Meeres und Süswasser algen. *Planta*, 13, 221
      (1931).

22   EHRKE G., Uber die Assimilation komplementar farbter Meeresalgen in
      Lichte von verschiedenen Wellenlängen. *Planta*, 17, 650 (1935).

23   GESSNER F., *Hydrobotanik*. Vol. 1. Berlin (1955).

24   GIBB D.C., The free-living forms of *Ascophyllum nodosum* (L.) La Jol.
      J. Ecol., 45(1), 49-84 (1957).

25   GRUBB V.M., Marine algal ecology and the exposure factor at Peveril
      Point, Dorset. *J. Ecol.*, 24, 392-423 (1936).

26   HAAS P. and HILL T.G., Observations on the metabolism of certain seaweeds.
      Ann. Bot., 47, 55-67 (1933).

27   HAXO F.T. and BLINKS L.R., Photosynthetic action spectra of marine algae.
      J. Gen. Physiol., 33, 389-422 (1950).

28   HYDE M.B., The effect of temperature and light intensity on the rate of

apparent assimilation in *Fucus serratus*. *J. Ecol.*, 26, 118-143 (1938).

29 ISAAC W.E., Some observations and experiments on the drought resistance of *Pelvetia canaliculata*. *Ann. Bot.*, 47, 343-348 (1933).

30 ISAAC W.E., A preliminary study of the water loss of *Laminaria digitata* during inter-tidal exposure. *Ann. Bot.*, 49, 109-117 (1935).

31 JONES N.S. and KAIN J.M., Sub-tidal algal colonisation following the removal of *Echinus*. *Helgoland. Meeresunt.*, 15, 460-88 (1967).

32 KAIN J.M., The role of light in the ecology of *Laminaria hyperborea*. *in* Light as an Ecological Factor. pp. 319-334. Oxford (1966).

33 KAIN J.M., Populations of *Laminaria hyperborea* at various latitudes. *Helgoland. Meeresunt.*, 15, 489-499 (1967).

34 KANWISHER J., Freezing and drying in inter-tidal algae. *Biol. Bull.*, 113(2), 275-285 (1957).

35 KITCHING J.A. and EBLING F.J., The ecology of Lough Ine. XI. *J. Anim. Ecol.*, 30(2), 373-383 (1962).

36 KLUGH B. and MARTIN J.R., The growth rate of certain marine algae in relation to depth of submergence. *J. Ecol.*, 8, 221 (1927).

37 KNIGHT M. and PARKE M., A biological study of *Fucus vesiculosus* and *F. serratus*. *J. Mar. Biol. Ass. U.K.*, 29, 439-514 (1950).

38 LAMI R., Sur les conditions d'éclairement de quelques algues vivant dans les grottes et anfractuosites littorales de la région malouine. *C.R. Acad. Sci. Paris*, 208, 764 (1939).

39 LAMPE R.H., Die Temperatureeinstellung des Stoffgewinns bei Meeresalgen als plasmatische Anpassung. *Protoplasma*, 23, 534 (1935).

40 LEVRING R., Submarines licht und die Algenvegetation. *Bot Marina.*, I(3/4), 67-73 (1960).

41 MACFARLANE C. and BELL H.P., The effect of salinity of water on algal assimilation. *Proc. Trans. Nova Scotia Inst. Sci.*, 18, 27 (1932).

42 MONTFORT C., Assimilation und Stoffgewinn der Meeresalgen bei Aussung und Rüchversalzung. *Ber. Deut. Bot. Gesell.*, 55, 85 (1937).

43 MONTFORT C., RIED A. and RIED I., Abstufeungen der funktionellen Warm-resistenz bei meeresalgen in ihren Bezeihungen zu Umvelt und Erbgut. *Biol. Zentrl.*, 76(3), 257 (1957).

44 NICHOL E.A.T., The ecology of a salt marsh. *J. Mar. Biol. Ass. U.K.*, 20, 203-261 (1935).

45 SEYBOLD A., Uber die Lichtenergiebalanz submerser Wasserpflanzen, vorne-hmlich der Meeresalgen. *Jahr. Wiss. Bot.*, 79, 593 (1934).

46 STOCKER O. and HOLDHEIDE W., Die assimilation Helgoländer Gezeitenalgen

ährend die Ebbezeit. *Zeit. Bot.*, 32 (1) (1938).

47 TSCHUDY R.H., Depth studies on photosynthesis of the red algae. *Amer. J. Bot.*, 21, 546-566 (1934).

48 WILCE R.T., Heterotrophy in Arctic sublittoral seaweeds: an hypothesis. *Bot. Mar.*, 10, 185-197 (1966/67).

49 ZANEVELD J., The littoral zonation of some Fucaceae in relation to desiccation. *J. Ecol.*, 25, 431-468 (1937).

CHAPTER 4

SALT MARSHES

Salt marshes are tracts of land covered with phanerogamic vegetation and subject to periodic flooding by the sea. During the flooding mud is deposited
on the marsh as the water movement slows down. Salt marsh areas can be
either coastal or inland, but the latter have little or no mud deposition and
are of no consequence in Great Britain. Areas such as the Neuseidlersee
exist in Europe and in the western U.S.A. there are extensive areas. These,
however, are not coastal marshes and hence will not be considered further.

OCCURRENCE

Maritime salt marshes are found on coastlines that are stable, sinking or
rising, though on submerging coasts they will form only if the rate of sedimentation is greater than that of subsidence. On these coasts marshes can be
found if any one of the following physiographic conditions is fulfilled: the
presence of estuaries, the shelter of spits, off-shore barrier islands, and
large or small protected bays with shallow water. Some of the finest salt
marshes in Great Britain have developed behind Blakeney spit in Norfolk and
in the protection of Scolt Head Island (76) as well as behind the Friesian
islands (3). Extensive estuarine marshes are to be found in the Humber, Solway
Firth, the Thames and estuaries of the English Channel (29) as well as those
farther east, i.e. Scheldt and Elbe. Bay marshes occur in Morecambe Bay and
in the Wash. In this last example although there is some exposure to wave
action nevertheless the off-shore region is so shallow that large destructive
waves are very infrequent.

In the U.S.A. extensive marshes occur in the Gulf of St. Lawrence, in the Bay
of Fundy, Delaware Bay and Chesapeake Bay (65,66), behind spits such as Barnstaple Marsh (63), behind Sandy Neck as well as in the protection of off-shore
islands, such as those in Pamlico Sound and behind the sea islands of
Georgia (27).

All these physiographic situations provide admirable conditions for salt
marsh formation, though the extent of marsh formed depends on the slope of
the land. If it comes down steeply into the sea, as in the Scottish lochs
or Norwegian fjords, the strip of salt marsh will be narrow and generally at
the head. When the slope is gradual and the beach shelves gently, the
marshes can become very wide. In estuaries, where the final fall is also
usually very slight, the rivers which often bring down much silt, are checked
in flow by the estuarine plain and by the tide backing up the water. Silt is

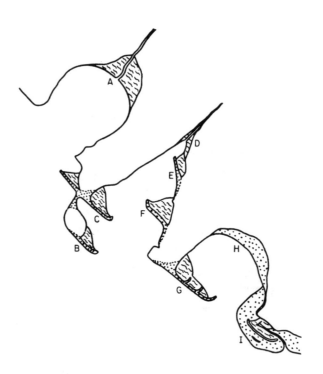

FIG. 4.1. *Diagram illustrating marsh formation behind various
types of spits and bars. Marsh areas are indicated by fillings of
short wavy lines. A, bay estuary marsh; B, marsh behind simple
spit; C, marsh behind bay mouth bar; D, estuary marsh in narrow
valley; E, marsh behind bay head bar; F, marsh behind mid-bay bar;
G, marsh behind complex spit; H, sand beach; I, off-shore barrier
island and marsh.*

hence deposited, the greater its amount the more extensive are the marshes. In estuaries, therefore, the banking up of the tide raises the marsh level from the mouth of the estuary up to the limit of tidal influence. There is a similar lateral rise of level from the banks of the river to the upland on either side.

Spits or barrier islands can be built of many different materials, including shell or shingle, and may be simple, double, recurved or complex. When spits extend across from one headland to another they are known as bars. The various types of spit can be near the mouth, near the centre, or at the head of a bay (Fig. 4.1). Their position and extent is primarily dependent on long-shore movement influenced by currents, the angle of wave approach, and other factors (see p. 235) (28). During the growing period occasional storms may turn the growing point, more or less at right angle, so that the mature structure exhibits a series of laterals (69,76)(Fig. 4.1G).

In other regions, the spit may grow without the formation of numerous later-als, as appears to have occurred at Romney where marsh developed in relation to a cuspate foreland (see Fig, 9.4). Similarly in the early stages of marsh formation behind a small barrier island there is no evidence of any lateral (Fig. 4.1I), and several vegetation zones may develop before the first lateral is formed (Fig. 4.2).

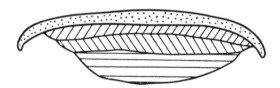

FIG. 4.2. *Diagram showing marsh development behind a small and single off-shore barrier island. Three successive vegetation zones are shown, the oldest being next to the bar (after Chapman).*

Where we have spits or barrier islands with laterals, increasing rise of level of the sand or mud will eventually cause salt marsh to develop between the laterals. At this stage we can recognise two types of marsh (Fig. 4.3): one (a) will have a wide mouth with silt being deposited over a wide area, whilst the other will have a narrow mouth (b) with silt being deposited al-most wholly on the enclosed marsh with the result that growth in height takes place much more rapidly. The former are known as *open marshes* and the latter

as *closed marshes*.   Vegetation change on the former is relatively slow whereas with the latter, because of the rapid rise of land level, vegetation
change is much quicker.

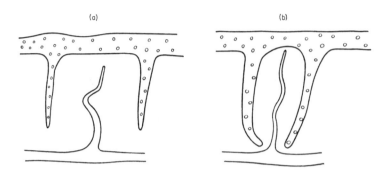

FIG. 4.3.   (a), *open marsh*; (b), *closed marsh. Each is bordered
by shingle laterals on which sand dunes may develop. Note wide
mouth to* (a) *and narrow mouth to* (b) *(after Chapman).*

Where there are a series of laterals, and marshes form between them, the oldest marshes will naturally be those near the proximal end and the youngest,
generally bare mud or sand flats, nearest the distal end (Fig. 4.4), though
closed marshes at any place will upset the general sequence for the reasons
given above. Whilst much valuable information can be gained by investigation
of the area, the full story is only revealed by a study of old maps over a
period of years. Excellent examples of this use of maps can be seen for the
development of the closed marsh at Gore Point in Norfolk (71), Scolt Head
Island and for the Island of Baltrum in Friesia (Fig. 4.5) (see also p. 11).
The changes and growth of the salt marshes in Morecambe Bay between 1845 to
1967 have been documented by Gray (38). During this period erosion and accretion have both occurred resulting in a net increase of marsh acreage from 557
ha in 1845 to 1485 ha in 1967 (Fig. 4.6).

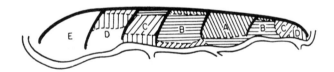

FIG. 4.4.   *Later stages in marsh development behind a complex off-
shore barrier island growing from right to left. The oldest marsh
type is* A. E *is a mud or sand flat as yet uncolonised.* D *represents the youngest marsh association and is the primary colonising
community (after Chapman).*

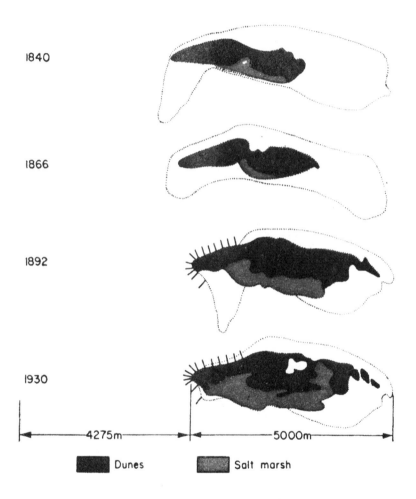

FIG. 4.5. *Stages in the development of Baltrum Island (after Tüxen).*

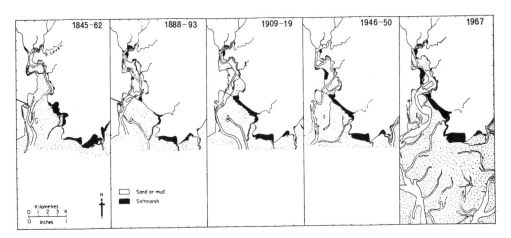

FIG. 4.6. *Changes in the salt marshes of the Leven Estuary in Morecambe Bay (U.K.) between 1845 and 1967 (after Gray).*

Whilst growth of spits or barrier islands takes place laterally, strong on-shore winds from time to time can cause the spit or island to move landward and in that event former salt marsh mud may be exposed from time to time on the fore-shore, e.g. Scolt Head in Norfolk (19), Romney Point near Boston (20).

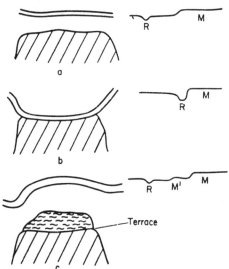

FIG. 4.7. *Diagrams illustrating how changes of river channel could result in the establishment of an erosion cliff and the development of a new marsh, which, if removed by land elevation from tidal influence, will give rise to terraces. Hatching, old marsh; waves, new marsh at lower level (after Chapman).*

As we have pointed out, salt marshes can develop on rising, stable or submerging coastlines. On rising coasts there is usually only a narrow belt of
marsh, unless the sea is extremely shallow so that with elevation a large
area of mud or sandy mud becomes continually exposed. If the rate of rise is
considerable, the upper zones of the salt marsh soon pass into a fresh water
condition which may be reed swamp (p. 111) or grassland (p. 110). It seems
likely that the present salt marshes in Scotland and in Denmark are forming
on an emerging coastline. On the Solway marshes one can generally recognise
two or three distinct terraces, probably a result of land elevation with concurrent changes in the channel of Solway (Fig. 4.7) (45). Other evidence of
elevation is the existence of obvious invasion by glycophytic species at the
higher levels, e.g. White clover (*Trifolium repens*), Tormentil (*Potentilla
erecta*) associated with Sea plantain (*Plantago maritima*) and Sea pink
(*Armeria maritima*), etc. The upper marshes are only flooded by storm tides
so that they are used extensively for grazing. Unexpected storm tides have
on isolated occasions in the past caused stock loss.

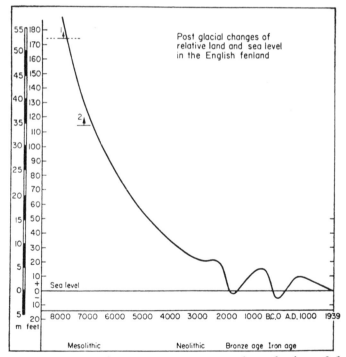

FIG. 4.8. *The thick curve represents the relation of land level
to sea level in the Fenland throughout the period indicated on the
base-line. The diagram is meant to imply nothing of the absolute
movement of land and sea level: sea level has been regarded as
constant only as a convention (modified after Godwin).*

If the level is stable, then the development of salt marsh will be dependent
upon the slope of the fore-shore and the rate of silting. On a sinking coastline marsh will form only if the rate of sedimentation exceeds the rate of
sinking.

In Great Britain the south-east coast marshes and possibly some south coast
marshes are developing upon a subsiding coastline. By making use of pollen
analysis, Godwin (34) has suggested the course of land/sea level changes in
East Anglia since the end of the Ice Age (Fig. 4.8). The successive heights
of the enclosing sea walls (7) of locally reclaimed marches confirm such subsidence, and there is further evidence, despite some doubt that has been cast
upon the conclusions, from the tide gauge and levels at Newlynn in Cornwall
which over the years of operation indicate that subsidence is occurring.

The Atlantic coast of North America has for long been regarded as in the process of subsidence. The earlier evidence for and against the hypothesis has
been fully discussed (20). More recent work, using radio-active carbon techniques to date the peat has served to confirm the subsidence hypothesis.
Barnstaple marsh appears to have commenced formation about 4000 years ago (63).
Over the last 2100 years mean high water level in relation to the land has
risen at an average rate of 3.3×10^{-3} ft. per yr. Prior to that the rate
was 10×10^{-3} ft. In Connecticut a rate of 0.11 to 0.6 ft per century has
been estimated for the years 7000-3000 BP (Before Present) and 0.06 to 0.3 ft
since then. These rates, however, do not seem to fit in with a rate of 3 ft
for New Hampshire (43) and of 1.4-2.0 ft per century for Nova Scotia. Chapman
(20) has suggested that there may have been an increasing rate with increasing
latitude and this hypothesis needs to be investigated.

It should be evident from what has already been said that a knowledge of the
rate of sedimentation is, then, very important in any study of salt marshes.
The sediments may be of silt or of sand blown up from the beach; the latter
can provide complications since it is dependent upon the intensity of prevailing on-shore winds and the incidence of gales.

We may study sedimentation by laying down on the soil a layer of a distinctive
sand (the coloured sands from Alum Bay in the Isle of Wight are very suitable,
brick dust or iron filings). A continuous band may be used or else patches
at measured intervals. The line should be well marked by stout posts. After

twelve months small sections can be removed and the depth of mud above the
marker measured. The method has been used successfully on the Scolt and
Dovey marshes in England and elsewhere (50,64,72). From the observations, the
sedimentation is greatest on the lowest plant-covered marshes, which are the
first to be flooded and also the ones that are flooded most frequently, and
also it is greater nearer the major creeks and decreases with distance from
them. Because more of the material in suspension, particularly the coarser
particles, is deposited along creek banks as the tide spills over, a natural
revetment to the creeks is produced.

Other factors involved in sedimentation include:

(1) Tidal currents during ebb and flood tides, which may be considerable in
     the middle periods (see p. 65), so that the mud may be removed after
     deposition.
(2) Physico-chemical deposition due to the flocculating action of sodium on
     suspended soil colloids.
(3) The physical effect of fresh water overlying salt water.
(4) Vegetation, which slows down water movement so that the burden of silt
     is deposited.

As an example of what has been found, the mean annual accretions on the mud
marshes of East Anglia are given in Table 4.1.

The Welsh marshes are very much more sandy and the rate of growth seems to be
rather less, because although sand can accumulate more rapidly than mud, it
can also be rapidly removed before being fixed by the arrival of plants
(Table 4.2).

Nielsen (50) used the sand technique to obtain information about sedimentation
rates on the Danish Skälling marshes. The average rates that he obtained are
set out in Table 4.3.

These values, though slightly lower than those of Richards are of the same
order of magnitude.

The present author (20) has carried out sedimentation observations on *Spartina*
marshes in Massachusetts. An annual rate of 6.0 mm per yr was found in the

V. J. CHAPMAN

TABLE 4.1

Mean Annual Accretion Rate (1935-1957) on Scolt Head Marshes (after Steers)

Marsh	Vegetation (see p. 108)	261 mths (cm)	141 mths (cm)	45 mths (cm)	Mean ann. (cm)
Missel marsh	Asteretum	18.8	10.6	5.33	0.84
Lower Hut marsh	Halimionetum	12.9	7.5	2.67	0.45
Golf Links marsh	Puccinellio-Halimionetum	-	6.4	2.16	0.57
Aster marsh	Asteretum	-	5.25	1.74	0.45
Upper Hut marsh	Suaedeto-Halimionetum	-	2.8	0.81	0.20

increasing height above sea level

TABLE 4.2

Accretion on Dovey Marshes (after Richards)

Vegetation	Mean annual			
	Line I (mm)	Level (ft)	Line II (mm)	Level (ft)
Puccinellietum	7.8	1.65	4.4	1.15
Puccinellio-Armerietum ecotone	6.6	1.53	8.3	1.64
Armerietum	4.2	2.13	4.8	1.67
Armerio-Festucetum ecotone	2.4	2.85	-	-
Festucetum	2.1	3.24	4.0	2.31
Juncetum	2.4	2.69	2.7	3.0

TABLE 4.3

Accretion on Skälling marshes (after Nielsen)

Vegetation	Ann. increment (cm)
Bare	3.1
Puccinellia-Salicornia	4.7
Puccinellia-Halimione	3.4
Puccinellia-Aster	3.6
Aster-Plantago	2.5
Puccinellia-Plantago	3.4
Festuca-Plantago	1.3

tall *Spartina alterniflora* zone, 1.3 mm in the *Spartina patens* zone and 0.6 mm in the highest *Spartina-Distichlis* zone. On the south of England sedimentation takes place at a greater rate in the *Spartina townsendii* zone where it ranges from 26 to 100 mm per yr (Bridgewater) and 10-20 cm per yr in Poole Harbour. The high rate at Bridgewater can be related to silt brought down by the Severn and it should be noted that the low rate in Massachusetts results in the development of a peat soil composed mainly of *Spartina* roots (20).

If one has in addition to the sedimentation rate information about the vertical range of a community, and also the rate of subsidence or elevation of the land in relation to sea level it is possible to calculate the approximate time taken for different stages. Early attempts (20) at this were not satisfactory because of inadequate land/sea level figures. Based on recent figures the kind of conclusions one can reach are set out in Table 4.4.

If the Juncetum stage is omitted the figures to reach the Juncetum stage in the three areas are 744, 328 and 530 years respectively. Marshes in the first group are solely silt, in the second essentially sand and in the third silt plus organic matter. Further work and measurements are now needed in order to determine the extent to which sediment type may affect the time scale. It may also be observed that the first and third figures are for marshes on subsiding coastlines.

Before considering the vegetation of the marshes there are two important physiographic features which must be described. The first of these are the

V. J. CHAPMAN

TABLE 4.4

Vegetation	Av. vert. range (ft)	Av. time to accumulate mud (yr)	
Salicornietum	1.3 ft	58	
Asteretum	2.2	86	
Late Asteretum	2.8	106	Norfolk marshes
Limonietum	3.2	121	
Armerietum	3.8	172	
Plantaginetum	4.2	201	
		744	
Puccinellietum	39 cm	64	
Armerietum	31.8	70	Dovey marshes
Festucetum	58.2	194	
Juncetum	57.0	228	
Spartina alterniflora	5 ft	330	
Spartina patens-Distichlis	1.5	200	Massachusetts marshes
Juncetum	0.5	100	

creeks. In early stages of marsh development the future course of the creek probably depends on minute irregularities of the ground. As soon as the first channels are formed, they are enlarged by the scouring action of the water as it runs off after each tide. On sandy marshes the head of the creek may also start to erode backwards. The advent of the vegetation increases the rate of deposition along the banks, so that we have a stream becoming deeper simultaneously by scour and by building up of its banks.

Sooner or later the banks reach a height where miniature waterfalls arise as the water pours off a marsh after a flooding tide. The creek thus commences to widen by the erosion of its banks. Erosion of the creek banks leads to undercutting and collapse of the walls (Fig. 4.9c), and often one finds secondary marsh developing at a lower level (Fig. 4.9d,e). On high marshes,

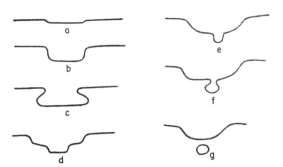

FIG. 4.9. *Stages in the undercutting and collapse of creek walls (a-e), followed by overgrowth of vegetation (f,g) (after Chapman).*

where flooding is not so frequent, the vegetation may succeed in growing over the creek (Fig. 4.9f,g), or else a succession of pans are formed (see below). The earlier stages in creek formation with rapid accretion and head extension with bed deepening is seen in Fig. 4.9a,b.

I have previously (16) classified marsh creek systems into three main groups. On very sandy marshes, the creek system is very simple and drainage channels are not numerous. Such systems are characteristic of the Welsh, Lancashire, Solway and Danish marshes. On more muddy marshes, minor branches are more numerous, and the whole system has a tree-like appearance when seen from the air. This type of drainage system is found in the Humber and Wash marshes. On the south coast of England and eastern U.S.A. where *Spartina* (Cord grass) vegetation is dominant, the growth habit of this plant appears to favour the development of extremely tortuous and intricate drainage creeks.

Tidal range can also be important in relation to creek pattern. Thus in the Bristol Channel (tidal range 40 ft), *Spartina* marshes have simple creek systems like small, branched, parallel creeks running normal to the shore-line. In Poole Harbour (tidal range 6 ft) there are the complex dendritic tree-like creeks referred to above.

The second feature of salt marshes remaining to be described is the *salt pan*. These are the marsh equivalent of rock pools (p. 28) and they may contain an algal vegetation that is quite distinct from that of the adjacent marsh. Pans develop in a variety of ways that were first clearly enumerated by Yapp

et al (85). Most pans fall into the category of *"primary"* pans, which means
that they have developed along with the marsh. In the early stages of primary colonisation, bare areas become cut off and surrounded by vegetation.
When this happens, water can no longer escape after a flooding tide, and this
discourages any plant colonisation. In summer, when the water evaporates,
the area becomes highly saline, which may again inhibit plant growth. Where
a creek cuts back into such a pan, normal drainage is established, and the
bare area rapidly becomes colonised.

On the Solway, Lancashire and Welsh marshes the seaward edges may suffer
erosion and a low cliff then forms. Below and in front of such a cliff, new
secondary marsh may form, not only from new colonists but also from the
spread of plants eroded off from the primary marsh. In such conditions
"secondary" pans may develop. The third type of pan is known as the *"creek"*
pan, and is derived from the tributary ends of older creeks as a result of
vegetation growing across and forming a dam. Such pans tend to be elongate
in shape and are perhaps more frequent on sandy than on muddy marshes because
of the greater preponderance of grasses that can be principal dam formers.
At times a series of dams can give rise to pans so that the former course of
the creek can be readily traced. The fourth type of pan to be found on British and European salt marshes is the *"residual"* pan. This arises from subdivision of any of the other three types of pan, either as a result of colonisation or as a result of vegetation slowly growing across and breaking up
the bare area. This is especially to be found on marshes where the plant
species are grasses and rushes that propagate vegetatively.

On the Atlantic marshes of the U.S.A. from Virginia northwards a further type
of pan has been recognised. This has been called a *"rotten spot"* because it
seems to be produced as a result of vegetation die-off, brought about either
by accumulation of trash that can be found left on marshes after the spring
snow melt or else by continual water-logging due to slow depression of the
soil with no outlet (18). As a result of applying statistical analysis to pan
distribution Pethick (56) found that numbers increased with marsh height. This
increase in number could be the result of the production of *"residual"*,
"creek" or *"trash"* pans.

MARSH ALIENATION

In the past salt marshes have been regarded as areas suitable for reclamation
or for the disposal of urban waste. In recent years considerable concern has
been manifest over the loss of salt marsh areas and their use for industry,
housing, airports and waste disposal. The detritus from salt marsh vegetation decays on the mud and in the creeks and forms the base for an extensive
food chain that culminates in the oyster, estuarine and off-shore fisheries.
In the past marsh grass has been cut on the Atlantic shores of the U.S.A. for
hay and sheep and cattle have been grazed on European salt marshes. Mowing
marsh grass for hay has almost ceased in the U.S.A. but farm animals are
still grazed on marshes in Europe. In Morecambe Bay less than 1% of the
marsh has remained ungrazed over the years and sheep are stocked at an average of between 5-7 sheep per ha. Less than 100 grazing days are lost annually due to spring flooding tides. Mowing or grazing encourages the marsh
grasses at the expense of forbs such as *Limonium* spp., *Suaeda* and *Halimione*
which then become restricted to suitable ungrazed areas (38).

Wild salt marshes are a favourite haunt of duck, geese and other birds. Up to
the present very little attempt has been made to manage such marshes for bird
life. Recently (8) experiments have been carried out on the management of saltings for wigeon (*Anas penelope*) at Bridgewater Nature Reserve in Somerset.
It was found that both wigeon (and sheep) feed best on mown saltings and that
a good sward of *Puccinellia/Agrostis* could be obtained by mowing.

The use of salt marshes for industry, housing and waste disposal, on all of
which monetary land values can be placed, has resulted in an attempt to put a
monetary value on wild marsh. Gosselink, Odum and Pope (37) have made a first
assessment and the figures they arrived at are set out in Table 4.5.

Using these values one can demonstrate that less economic damage is done to
salt marshes by putting roads over on pillars rather than as filled causeways.

On the Atlantic coast of the U.S.A. in the more populated states (Connecticut,
Massachusetts, New York, New Jersey, Delaware) it would seem that up to 25
percent of the total marsh area has been alienated in the last 25 years.
Prior to that marsh had certainly been reclaimed in the Bay of Fundy as well
as elsewhere. In Europe considerable areas have been reclaimed for farmland

TABLE 4.5

Value of U.S.A. Coastal Plain Marshes

Purpose	Ann. return/ acre	Capital value/ acre
1 Fish and food	$US 100	$US 2000
2 Oyster culture (maximum)	$ 900	$ 18 000
3 Sewage effluent treatment	$ 2500	$ 50 000
4 Life support value (based on Gross Primary Production)	$ 4150	$ 83 000

1 and 3 or 2 and 3 are compatible uses.

by dyking as well as reclamation (Thames estuary) for industry. One of the biggest reclamation projects is that of the Zuyder Zee in Holland where large areas have been reclaimed by one dyke put in at the mouth (20). So much reclamation has now taken place that the point has been reached where further alienation should only be permitted for very good purposes and where it can be shown that any remaining salt marsh will meet the needs of the local food chain. Gross productivity of salt marshes will be important in this connection and determination of values can be time consuming. Recently remote sensing by air photography (27) has been successfully used and this may enable determinations to be made more rapidly and also over large areas.

Recent years have witnessed major coastal oil spillages from accidents to tankers and some oil has got on to salt marshes. Provided it is not excessive there is little long term damage, especially to perennials, and the soil does in fact bring about a denaturing of the oil (20). There is, however, no cause for complacency.

THE VEGETATION

Sufficient should now have been said to indicate that as accretion takes place, the land gradually rises and the numbers of floodings become fewer and fewer. This decrease in floodings brings about other changes (see p. 123),

so that, as the environmental conditions alter, one vegetation type is
replaced by another. On the rocky sea-shore, the algal belts remain constant,
and represent the climax vegetation. On the salt marsh, the vegetation is
dynamic and the zonation to be observed in going from the seaward edge to the
upland behind is a developmental zonation or *succession* (see p. 2). The
succession is initiated on bare mud or sand that has not previously borne
vegetation, and the whole sequence therefore forms an excellent example of a
prisere. Because of the dynamic nature of the vegetation, normal seral terminology must be used in describing the different communities. One may therefore distinguish associes, consocies, socies, etc., among both the phanerogamic and cryptogamic vegetation.

Since the deposition of mud depends on tidal flooding, accretion ceases when
the land level is raised to extreme high tide mark. In fact it probably
ceases slightly below this level, where the submergences are so few that mud
deposition is negligible. At this level in Europe, there is generally a community dominated by the Sea rush, *Juncus maritimus* and in the U.S.A. by *Juncus
gerardi* or *J. roemerianus*. Provided the land is not sinking and there is no
influx of fresh water, further change will not take place. The *Juncus* represents the regional climatic climax, though it is potentially capable of
further development. For this reason, it is best termed the sere climax.
Should a fresh water stream or river enter the marsh area, it will be found
that the salt marsh passes imperceptibly into fresh water reed swamp (see p.
111).

SALT MARSH COMMUNITIES

The Arctic and subarctic salt marshes are characterised by the dominance of
the grass *Puccinellia phryganodes* which forms the primary marsh community.
In northern Canada down to the St. Lawrence and in Europe, though there may be
a lower Zosteretum, e.g. in the White Sea, *Carex subspathacea* dominates the
higher levels. These marshes exhibit very little vegetational variation and
the succession is simple. This is associated with the extreme temperature
conditions and probably also with the long twilight of the arctic summer. At
the higher levels a wide range of species may be found, especially in subarctic regions. *Stellaria humifusa, S. crassifolia, Cochlearia officinalis,
Triglochin maritima, Potentilla egedii* and *Montia lamprosperma* range from

northern Labrador, north Quebec through Greenland to northern Finmark (20,51, 57). The marshes of Iceland and northern Norway are to some extent transitional to the boreal European Atlantic salt marshes. *Puccinellia phryganodes* is less abundant and *P. maritima* or *P. retroflexa* (on sandy soils) enter in. Under brackish conditions *Agrostis stolonifera* and *Hippuris vulgaris* with, in places, *Eleocharis palustris*, are the primary colonists. In hollows with standing water *Carex mackenziei* and *C. salina* are the primary colonists together with *Agrostis* and *Triglochin palustris*. The highest salt marsh community at these high latitudes, ranging from Greenland to the White Sea, is a Festucetum rubrae-Caricetum glarecosae (20). Further study may show that this generalised community really exists in more than one facies. In Finland algal communities dominated by *Dichothrix gypsophila* have been recorded from the Caricetum subspathaceae and one dominated by *Phormidium corium* in the Juncetum gerardii (34).

It has already been indicated that the communities on any marsh are related to each other in space and time, and one of the problems of the ecologist is to try and work out these relationships. They can be expressed in terms of successional diagrams which are by no means as simple as earlier workers believed. It is possible to summarise such successional diagrams and indicate in a broad manner how communities on various types of marshes may be related to each other. For any given marsh area, only the major stages in the succession will be represented. A generalised schema for the successions in the arctic and subarctic is as follows:

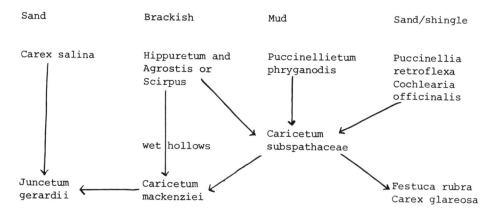

Sand	Brackish	Mud	Sand/shingle
Carex salina	Hippuretum and Agrostis or Scirpus	Puccinellietum phryganodis	Puccinellia retroflexa Cochlearia officinalis
	wet hollows	Caricetum subspathaceae	
Juncetum gerardii	Caricetum mackenziei		Festuca rubra Carex glareosa

The lowest phanerogam community (Zosteretum) in Europe is composed of the eelgrasses, *Zostera marina* and *Z. nana* (*Z. noltii*), which occur on mud flats that are exposed at low tide. These flats, and also those higher ones that are submerged daily by tides have been termed *"sloblands"*. Associated with the *Zostera* will be found a number of algae, and in some parts of Europe, where the water is rather more brackish, *Ruppia maritima* may also occur. Some years ago the eel grass beds were decimated by a disease (77), but since then there has been a recovery. There is generally a bare zone above the *Zostera* beds before the next phanerogam colonises the ground.

In eastern Europe south of the subarctic, i.e. Norway, Sweden, Denmark, the salt marsh vegetation can be regarded as falling into three seres depending on the salinity and nature of the soil (29). In the brackish water sere the Zosteretum, usually with *Ruppia* or a Ruppietum, is succeeded by *Eleocharis parvula* or *E. uniglumis* if the soil is sandy, and by a Scirpetum maritimi if the soil is muddy. The *Eleocharis* generally gives way to a Phragmitetum which is transitional to fresh water, whilst the Scirpetum passes into a Puccinelli-etum maritimae community. The final salt marsh community for both lines is generally dominated by *Juncus gerardi*.

In the normal saline sere the pioneer community, which is ephemeral owing to dominance of annual species, is dominated by *Salicornia strictissima* or *S. stricta* and is then succeeded by a Puccinellietum maritimae in which there is much Sea aster (*Aster tripolium*) unless there is heavy grazing. In depressed areas where water stands *P. maritima* is generally replaced by *Puccinellia distans*. The *Puccinellia* is commonly succeeded by the sere-climax of *Juncus gerardi* but in places (e.g. Sweden) an extensive community of *Festuca rubra/ Agrostis stolonifera* can be interposed.

In the hypersaline sere the primary colonist is *Salicornia ramosissima,* but *S. strictissima* and *S. leiosperma* are intermingled. The Salicornietum is succeeded by the inevitable *Puccinellia maritima* and then by *Juncus gerardi,* where, if the soil is sandy, *Plantago maritima* (Sea plantain) and *Halimione pedunculata* (Pedunculate purslane) can be subdominants. Where the ground is drier and rarely flooded *Glaux maritima* forms a distinct community. Around Göteborg in south west Sweden some species, e.g. *Archangelica officinalis, Carex recta, Ligusticum scoticum* reach their southern limit. A generalised schema for these eastern shores of the European north sea coast is as follows:

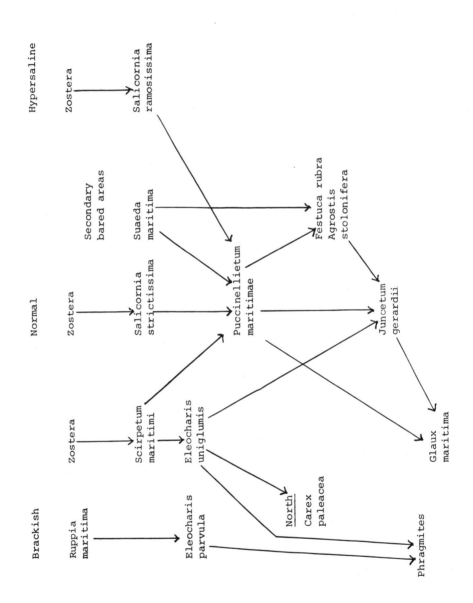

In the brackish Baltic (20) the Scirpetum matimi or Scirpetum tabernaemontani
is the principal pioneer followed by a community with *Triglochin maritimum*,
Aster trigolium and *Scirpus palustris* which in turn is succeeded by a Juncetum
gerardii, or Juncetum baltici.

Farther south in Denmark (Skälling, Fanø) the main sequence is essentially the
same but a number of other communities occur which are found westwards to
France and Great Britain. One significant community is the *Aster tripolium/
Puccinellia maritima* community on sandy soils which becomes the Asteretum
tripolii on muddy soils, and the other is a mixed community, the General Salt
Marsh community, comprising *Puccinellia maritima*, *Limonium vulgare*, *Plantago
maritima* and *Festuca rubra* as co-dominants. These same communities are to be
found on the north sea coast of Schleswig-Holstein and of Germany, though up
rivers such as the Elbe the Scirpetum maritimi is the primary colonist,
instead of *Zostera*, followed by *Salicornia*. In the Scheldt estuary (4) the
main sequence is *Zostera* - *Salicornia* - *Puccinellia* - General Salt Marsh -
Halimione portulacoides, though in the presence of grazing *Puccinellia maritima* remains as the dominant. On creek banks the primary colonist is *Suaeda
maritima* that gives way first to *Halimione* and then to a belt of *Artemisia
maritima*. The nature of the communities changes because of the major part
played, increasingly so, by the two hybrid cord grasses, *Spartina townsendii*
and *S. anglica*, and also by salt marsh fucoids. The relationship of the western and southern halophytic communities to those of the North Sea has been
discussed in some detail by Beeftink (3). If *Zostera* beds are present, there
will usually be a bare zone above them before the next phanerogam is able to
colonise the ground although *Spartina townsendii* can invade at the *Zostera*
level. On more sandy soils the primary community is likely to be either a
Salicornietum or a Puccinellio-Salicornietum. On the British east coast
these low communities may be intimately associated with two algal communities,
one a pure sward of the embedded *Fucus vesiculosus* ecad *caespitosus*, the
other a dense community of *Pelvetia canaliculata* ecad *libera* with which may
be associated the red alga *Bostrychia scorpioides*.

The Salicornietum is a primary community, not only on sandy marshes but also
on muddy flats as well. On the south and south-east coasts of Great Britain
and of Northern France it is commonly replaced by the hybrid Cord grass (78),
Spartina townsendii and *S. anglica*, which form a Spartinetum (18,36). These
are now spreading up the east coast of Great Britain and changing the success-

ion there. Small areas dominated by the original parents, *S. maritima* and *S. alterniflora* still persist in a few places.

On the sandy marshes of the west coast, much of the marshland is covered by two grass-dominated communities, the Puccinellietum and Festucetum rubrae. Workers on these marshes have sometimes divided both into upper and lower communities. Thus the lower Puccinellietum can be characterised by the presence of *Aster*, Sea arrow-grass (*Triglochin maritima*) and Sea lavender (*Limonium vulgare*), whilst the upper Puccinellietum possess Sea pink (*Armeria maritima*), *Limonium*, Creeping fescue (*Festuca rubra*), Sea milkwort (*Glaux maritima*), Sea plantain (*Plantago maritima*) and Long-leaved scurvy-grass (*Cochlearia anglica*). The lower Festucetum often contains abundant *Armeria*, and at higher levels Fiorin (*Agrostis stolonifera*), Mud rush (*Juncus gerardi*), Buck's-horn plantain (*Plantago coronopus*) are very common. On the rising (see p. 93) marshes, glycophytes such as White clover (*Trifolium repens*), Tormentil ((*Potentilla erecta*), and Autumnal hawkbit (*Leontodon autumnalis*) indicate the very rare flooding undergone by the Festucetum.

On the south coast, this zone is still occupied by *Spartina townsendii*, but, in places this is being replaced by *Phragmites communis*. This is probably due to opening of the *Spartina* sward by litter (see p. 100), further increase in soil level reducing salinity and light competition from the taller *Phragmites* The generalised succession here is shown on p. 109.

A community that is particularly abundant on the east coast but restricted elsewhere though extending eastwards to Denmark, is the one known as the General Salt Marsh community (G.S.M.). The co-dominants of the community in Great Britain are Sea pink (*Armeria*), Sea lavender (*Limonium*), *Spergularia marginata*, Sea plantain (*Plantago maritima*), *Triglochin* and at high levels Sea hard-grass (*Parapholis strigosa*). *Glaux maritima* (Sea milkwort) may also occur, especially with *Triglochin* (Arrowgrass) in the wetter depressions.

From the Asteretum stage to higher levels on the east coast, from the Spartinetum stage in the English Channel, and from the Puccinellietum stage on the west coast, the Sea purslane (*Halimione portulacoides*) forms a fringe along the banks of creeks, a fringe that becomes generally wider with age, unless the marshes are grazed. Changes in such marshes in the estuary of the Authie have been recorded since 1835 (46). There is reason to believe that *Halimone*

GENERALISED SUCCESSION - SOUTH COAST

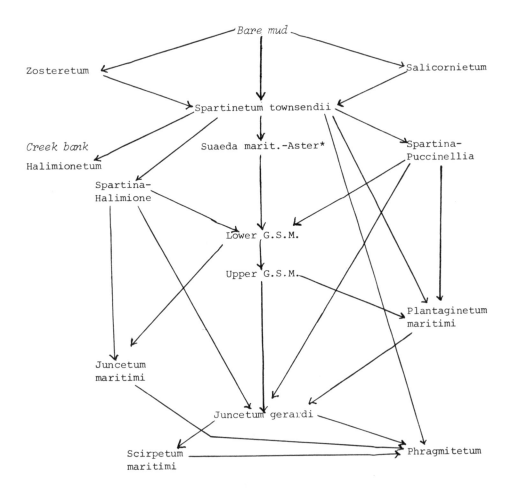

Note. in regions of reduced salinity one can have a direct transition from the Spartinetum to either a Phragmitetum or Scirpetum
maritimi, e.g. Poole Harbour, Lytchett Bay.

*North coast of France.

is restricted to places where drainage is good, hence it occurs along creek
banks and along the edges of shingle laterals (p. 236). At high levels it
may spread over the marshes and be associated with the Sea poa, *Puccinellia
maritima* which may even form a pure community (29). On the Norfolk coast at
Scolt Head, a peculiar variant of this community is found near the sand dunes:

this has been termed the Sandy Halimionetum and in such places *Halimione port-ulacoides* var. *parvifolia* tends to replace the common var. *latifolia*.

A high-level community common on some European marshes but not so frequent on British marshes in the Agrostidetum dominated by Fiorin (*Agrostis stolonifera*). A more frequent high-level community, especially on the muddy east coast marshes, is the Plantaginetum maritimi dominated by the Sea plantain, *Plant-ago maritima*, with *Agrostis, Festuca, Glaux* and *Armeria* commonly associated with it.

The uppermost levels of the marshes, where there is no influx of fresh water, are usually occupied by either a Juncetum gerardii, or a Juncetum maritimi or the two together: where both occur, local conditions seem to determine whether or not the *Juncus gerardi* occupies a higher or lower level than *J. maritimus*. Both species have certain salt marsh plants associated with them, essentially species that must be able to tolerate considerable reduction of light, e.g. *Armeria, Glaux*.   In the Solway area, where these upper levels only become flooded by extreme or storm tides, other plants such as Lesser spearwort (*Ranunculus flammula*), Brookweed (*Samolus valerandi*), Parsley water dropwort (*Oenanthe lachenalii*), Bird's foot trefoil (*Lotus corniculatus*) and Yorkshire fog (*Holcus lanatus*) enter the community and can clearly tolerate the brack-ish conditions.

It is in the Sea rush (*Juncus maritimus*) zone that the debris of the drift-line is generally to be found, and this can often be characterised by a zone of *Atriplex patula* var. *hastata*, *A. littoralis* or a belt of Sea wormwood (*Artemisia maritima*) or of *Suaeda fruticosa* and occasional plants of the beet, *Beta vulgaris* ssp. *maritima*.   These are probably nitrophiles and occur there for that reason and the fact that their seed is distributed by the tide along the drift-line (see also p. 152).

In the storm flood zone, open communities, including several annuals are not uncommon. Characteristic species are *Sagina maritima* and *Cochlearia danica*. The communities are generally fragmentary and of very local occurrence. From southern England to Portugal *Frankenia laevis* and *Limonium bellidifolium* are common and *Cochlearia* becomes scarcer. Another group of species can also be found colonising bare areas caused by cattle or human tracks or construction of sea walls. *Spergularia marina* and *Puccinellia distans* are distinct feat-

ures here. They are ephemeral and give way to a pure *P. maritima* or a G.S.M
community.

The common transitional community to fresh water is dominated by the tall
reed *Phragmites communis*, and there seems little doubt that the Phragmitetum
of the East Anglian fen country was the normal successor to a salt marsh community. It can also be seen occupying the same position on the south coast.

No single marsh area will provide an example of every one of the communities
that have been briefly described. The student must study each marsh area and
try and determine which major communities are present and whether there are
any variants.

The succession on lower marshes can take place relatively rapidly and vegetation maps prepared over quite a short period of years can indicate the rapidity of the changes. Such vegetation maps are therefore well worth making (15).

Apart from the algae (5,9,13) (and p. 46), very little work has been done on
the thallophyte flora of salt marshes. Recently, however, studies have been
made of the fungal and bacterial flora including the rhizosphere populations,
of a Lincolnshire salt marsh (60-62,81,82). As might be expected, the greatest
number of fungi and bacteria were recorded from mature marsh. An interesting
feature was a decrease in number of both organisms in the *Spartina* zone as
compared with the lower mud flats on the one hand and the higher marsh on the
other. At present, the significance of this is not known. It is evident,
however, that this rather difficult field of study, as the organisms are not
well known, presents considerable opportunities for future investigation.

On the temperate Canadian and American salt marshes the primary colonist is a
tall form of *Spartina alterniflora* (sometimes referred to as var. *glabra*).
This community extends up to the St. Lawrence estuary and probably even northwards. Behind the tall *S. alterniflora* there is generally a sward of low-
growing *S. alterniflora* (sometimes referred to as var. *pilosa*). The tall
Cord grass excludes light and as a result there are very few associated
species, *Salicornia* spp. being the most frequent. Behind the *Spartina alterniflora* zone there is a *Spartina patens* or *Puccinellia americana* (*P. paupercula?*) zone, the *Puccinellia* being predominant in Canada and northern U.S.A.
and *S. patens* southwards. The sward is generally so dense that there are few

other associated species, though it is at this level that the Sea lavender,
Limonium nashii is to be found. The final salt marsh community or sere climax is a Juncetum gerardii. In Canada the *Spartina* of wet depressions is
followed by a low forb community of annual *Salicornia* species (*S. europaea*
agg.), *Glaux maritima*, *Plantago oliganthos* and *Triglochin gaspense* which represents the European *T. maritima* complex in the west Atlantic. In the St.
Lawrence Gauthier (28) has described the transition to brackish communities
characterised by *Spartina pectinata*, *Scirpus acutus*, *Juncus balticus* and *Calamagrostis canadensis*.

Many of the Bay of Fundy marshes have been reclaimed, but there is still extensive wild marsh growing on a firm soil. They occupy a considerable vertical range because of the large range of the tide (40 ft) in the Bay of Fundy.
The communities are essentially the same as those found north and south except
that the *Spartina patens* zone has a rather greater abundance of associated
species (*Triglochin*, *Plantago*, *Glaux*, *Limonium*, *Festuca ovina*). On secondary
bare areas *Salicornia stricta* (part of *S. europaea* agg.) and *Suaeda maritima*
are the pioneer colonists.

The New England salt marshes, which develop in front of a hard rock upland,
are essentially built of a marine peat. The same sequence of communities
exist on these marshes as elsewhere. However, replacing the *Puccinellia* of
the northern marshes one finds the grass *Distichlis spicata* either co-dominant
with *Spartina patens* or forming local consocies. *Zostera* is frequently the
primary colonist, as in Europe, with *Ruppia maritima* in brackish places
(including salt pans). Similarly a mixed forb (General Salt Marsh) community
is often associated with pans and comprises much the same species as reported
above for Canada. *Gerardia maritima* and the Sea aster (*A. subulatus*) occur in
such places. Many of these marshes have been ditched in order to control
mosquitoes. The ditch turf line forms a good area for colonisation by annual
Salicornia, *Suaeda* and *Atriplex patula* var. *hastata* followed by *Iva oraria*.
As a result of his studies of Barnstaple marsh Redfield (63) has shown that *S.
alterniflora* only spreads at the rate of 1.33 ft/yr which is not as fast as in
other places. At higher levels *Iva oraria* (*I. frutescens* var. *oraria*) and
Baccharis halimifolia are significant features of the vegetation. The Juncetum gerardii represents the sere climax or where there is fresh water it
passes into a *Spartina pectinata* or *S. cynosuroides* community that in turn is
replaced by *Scirpus* spp. (including *S. americanus*) and ultimately by a reed

swamp of *Typha* and *Phragmites*.

The schema below summarises the general successions to be found on these
marshes.

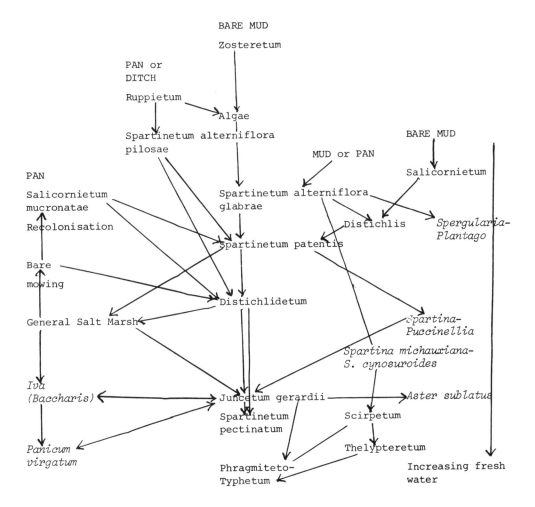

The salt marshes of New Jersey and Delaware form an ecotone between the peaty
New England marshes and the muddy coastal plain marshes from Virginia to
Florida (20,65,66). The pioneer and native marsh communities of the coastal
plain marshes remain the same but *Juncus gerardi* is replaced by *J. roemerianus* and *Limonium nashii* by *L. carolinianum*. In places the pioneer *Spartina*
may be replaced by *Salicornia ambigua* or *S. mucronata* as pioneers. In the
J. roemerianus, Iva oraria, Lythrum lineare and *Aster subulatus* are common,

whilst the marsh landward border is characterised by *Baccharis halimifolia*
and *Iva oraria* associated with a variety of other species, e.g. *Kosteletzyka
virginica, Panicum virgatum, Borrichia frutescens, Pluchea camphorata*, etc.
The transition to fresh water is again via *Spartina cynosuroides, Scirpus
maritimus* to *Typha* and *Phragmites*. On the North Carolina marshes, the
vegetation has been divided into high and low marsh (1). The low marsh communities include those with *Spartina alterniflora, Limonium carolinianum* and
Juncus roemerianus. The high marsh communities comprise those with *Spartina
patens, Aster tenuifolius, Distichlis spicata, Fimbristylis castanea* and
Borrichia frutescens. Farther south mangrove species become associated with
the salt marsh vegetation (see p. 217). The following schema illustrates the
general successional relationships on these coastal plain marshes. On the
whole they are simpler than those for New England (20).

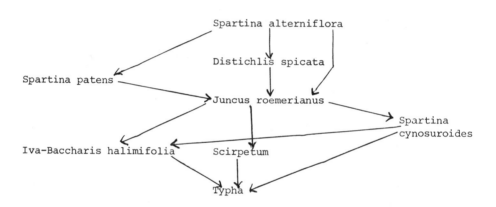

Apart from describing the various communities, it is possible on any salt
marsh area to make use of life-form spectra as a means of comparison. In
comparing the spectra, the values should be determined preferably on a frequency basis in order to allow for the significance of dominance (see p. 9).
Whilst no figures are immediately available for Great Britain, the kind of
results that can be obtained are indicated (p. 115) for the salt marshes of
the Oresund in Sweden (18).

It is evident from these figures that the hemicryptophyte element is the dominant, with the therophytes forming the next most important group. This
appears to be general over salt marshes from widely different parts of the
globe.

For those who wish to compare communities objectively from different areas,
there are various mathematical methods by which this can be done (see p. 7).
If any of these are used, their limitations should be borne in mind, and also
the fact that different methods may yield different results. It may, however,
well prove instructive to carry out such exercises; salt marsh communities,
because of their definiteness of character and the relatively few species
involved, form very suitable communities for analytical studies and consideration of the value of quadrats and other means of sampling vegetation (see
Chapter 1).

TABLE 4.6

Percentage of Life-forms

Community	Chamae- phyte	Hemicrypt- ophyte	Geophyte	Hydro helophyte	Thero- phyte
Salicornietum	-	57.5	11.5	-	31
Scirpetum maritimi	-	33	22.5	11.5	33
G.S.M.	5	52	10	-	32
Plantaginetum	6	57.5	12.5	-	24
Juncetum gerardii	4	58	8	-	30
Artemisietum maritimae	3.5	49	11	-	36.5
Suaedetum maritimae	-	50	17	-	43

REFERENCES

1   ADAMS D.A., Factors influencing vascular plant zonation in North Carolina
     salt marshes. *Ecol.*, 44, 445-456 (1963).

2   BARNES F.A. and KING C.A.M., A preliminary survey at Gibraltar Point,
     Lincolnshire. *Bird Obs. & Field Res. St. Gib. Pt. Lincs. Rept.*, 41-59
     (1951).

3   BEEFTINK W.G., Die zontvegetatie van zw-Nederland beschouwd in Europees
     verband. *Mededel. Land bouwhogesch wagen.*, 65(1), 1-167 (1965).

4   BEEFTINK W.G., Vegetation and habitat of the salt marshes and beach

plains in the south-western part of the Netherlands. *Wentia.*, 15, 83-108
(1966).

5   BLACKLER H., An algal survey of Loch Foyle, N. Ireland. *Proc. Roy. Ir.
Acad.*, 54B(6), 97-139 (1951).

6   BORER O., Recent coastal changes in south-eastern England. IV. Changes
in the Wash. *Geog. J.*, 93(6), 491-496 (1939).

7   BRACHER R., The ecology of the Avon banks at Bristol. *J. Ecol.*, 17, 35-
80 (1929).

8   CADWALLADER D.A. and MORLEY J.V., Further experiments on the management
of saltings pasture for wigeon (*Anas penelope*) conservation at Bridgewater Bay National Nature Reserve, Somerset. *J. Appl. Ecol.*, 11(2), 461-
6 (1974).

9   CARTER N., A comparative study of the algal flora of two salt marshes.
J. Ecol., 20, 341-370 (1932); 21, 128-208, 385-403 (1933).

10 CHAPMAN V.J., A note upon *Obione portulacoides* (L.) Gaert. *Ann. Bot. N.S.*,
1(2), 305-310 (1937).

11 CHAPMAN V.J., Marsh development in Norfolk. *Trans. Norf. Norw. Nat. Soc.*,
14(4), 394-397 (1938).

12 CHAPMAN V.J., Studies in salt marsh ecology. Sect. I-III. *J. Ecol.*, 26(1),
144-179 (1938).

13 CHAPMAN V.J., Studies in salt marsh ecology. Sect IV, V. *J. Ecol.*, 27(1),
160-201 (1939).

14 CHAPMAN V.J., Studies in salt marsh ecology. Sect VIII. *J. Ecol.*, 29(1),
69-82 (1941).

15 CHAPMAN V.J., Some vegetational changes on a shingle off-shore bar at
Thornham. *Trans. Norf. Norw. Nat. Soc.*, 24, 273-278 (1948).

16 CHAPMAN V.J., *Halimione portulacoides* (L.) Aell., *in* Biological Flora of
the British Isles. *J. Ecol.*, 38(1), 214-222 (1950).

17 CHAPMAN V.J., Studies in salt marsh ecology. Sect. IX. *J. Ecol.*, 47(2),
619-639 (1959).

18 CHAPMAN V.J., *Salt Marshes and Salt Deserts of the World.* Leon. Hill,
London. (1960).

19 CHAPMAN V.J., The Ecology in *Scolt Head Island.* Ed. J.A. Steers. Heffer,
Camb. (1960).

20 CHAPMAN V.J., *Salt Marshes and Salt Deserts of the World.* 2nd Ed. Cramer,
Lehre. (1974).

21 CHATER E.H., Recent changes in the halophytic vegetation of the Rye
coastline. *Hastings Nat.*, 5(1), 3-20 (1934).

22   CHATER E.H. and JONES H., Some observations on *Spartina townsendii*. H
      and J. Groves in the Dovey estuary. *J. Ecol.*, 45(1), 157-167 (1957).

23   CONWAY V., Further observations on the salt marsh at Holme-next-the-Sea.
      J. Ecol., 21, 263-267 (1933).

24   COTTON A.D., Clare Island survey. Part 15: Marine algae. *Proc. Roy. Ir.
      Acad.*, 31, 1-178 (1912).

25   DAVIES M.R. and LAMBERT J.M., A sandy area in the Dovey estuary. *J. Ecol.*,
      28, 453-464 (1940).

26   DIXON E.E. *et al.*, The geology of the Carlisle, Longtown and Silloth
      districts. *Mem. Geol. Surv. U.K.* (1926).

27   GALLAGHER J.L., REIMOLD R.J. and THOMPSON D.E., Remote sensing and salt
      marsh productivity. Proc. 38th Ann. Meet. Amer. Soc. Photogram., pp. 338-
      48 (1970).

28   GAUTHIER B., Récherches floristiques sur l'hydrolittoral de l'Archipel
      de Montmagny. M.Sc. Thesis, Univ. Laval, Quebec.

29   GEHU J.M. and GHESTEM A., Zonation végétale en baie de Cauche. *Bull. Soc.
      Bot. Nord. Fr.*, 16(1), 27-33 (1963).

30   GILLHAM M.E., Vegetation of the Exe estuary in relation to water salin-
      ity. *J. Ecol.*, 45(3), 735-756 (1957).

31   GILLHAM M.E., Coastal vegetation of Mull and Iona in relation to salin-
      ity and soil reaction. *J. Ecol.*, 45(3), 757-778 (1957).

32   GILLNER V., Vegetations - und standorts - Untersuchungen in den Strand-
      wiesen der Schwedischen westküste. *Act. Phyt. Suec.*, 43, 1-198 (1960).

33   GIMINGHAM C.H., Contributions to the maritime ecology of St. Cyrus, Kin-
      cardineshire. III. The salt marsh. *Trans. Bot. Soc. Edin.*, 36, 137-164
      (1953).

34   GODWIN H., Studies in the post-glacial history of British vegetation.
      III-IV. *Phil. Trans. B.*, 230 (570), 239-343 (1940).

35   GOOD R.D'O., Contributions towards a survey of the plants and animals of
      South Haven Peninsula, Studland Heath, Dorset. II. General ecology of
      the flowering plants and ferns. *J. Ecol.*, 23, 361-405 (1935).

36   GOODMAN F.J., BRAYBROOKS E.M. and LAMBERT J.M., Investigations into "die-
      back" in *Spartina townsendii* agg. I. *J. Ecol.*, 47, 651-677 (1959).

37   GOSSELINK J.G., ODUM E.P. and POPE R.M., The value of the tidal marsh.
      Center for Wetland Res., Louisiana State Univ. (1973).

38   GRAY A.J., The ecology of Morecambe Bay. V. The salt marshes of More-
      cambe Bay. *J. Appl. Ecol.*, 9(1), 207-220 (1972).

39   HÄYREN E., Über die algenvegetation des sandigen geolitorals am Meere

in Schweden und in Finland. *Svensk. Bot. Tid.*, 50(2), 257-69 (1956).

40 HESLOP-HARRISON J.W., A survey of the lower Tees marshes and of the reclaimed areas adjoining them. *Trans. Nat. Hist. Scot. Northumb.*, N.S. 5(1) (1918).

41 KING C.A.M., *Beaches and Coasts*. Arnold (1959).

42 LINDER E., Red hill mounds of Canvey Island in relation to subsidence in the Thames estuary. *Proc. Geol. Ass.*, 51(3), 283-290 (1940).

43 LYON C.J and HARRISON W., Rates of submergence of coastal New England and Arcadia. *Science*, 132, 295 (1960).

44 MARSH A.S., The maritime ecology of Holme-next-the-Sea. *J. Ecol.*, 3, 65-93 (1915).

45 MARSHALL D.R., The morphology of the upper Solway salt marshes. *Scott. Geog. Mag.*, 78, 81-99 (1962).

46 MOCQUETTE M., GEHU J.M. and FAUQUET M., Contribution a l'étude phytosociologique de l'éstuaire de L'Authie. *Bull. Soc. Bot. Nord. Fr.*, 18(2), 114-143 (1965).

47 MORSS W.L., The plant colonisation of merselands in the estuary of the River Nith. *J. Ecol.*, 15, 310-343 (1927).

48 MOSS C.E., Geographical distribution of vegetation in Somerset. *Roy. Geog. Soc. Spec. Publ.* (1957).

49 NEWMAN L.F. and WALWORTH G., A preliminary note on the ecology of part of the S. lincolnshire coast. *J. Ecol.*, 7, 204-210 (1919).

50 NIELSEN N., Eine methode zur exakten sedimentationsmessung. *Kgl. Dansk. Videns. Selsk. Biol. Meddel.*, 12(4), 1-97 (1935).

51 NORDHAGEN R., Studies on the vegetation of salt and brackish marshes in Finmark (Norway). *Vegetatio*, 5/6, 381-94 (1954).

52 OLIVER F.W., Some remarks on Blakeney Point, Norfolk. *J. Ecol.*, 1, 4-15 (1913).

53 OLIVER F.W., Blakeney Point reports. *Trans. Norf. Norw. Nat. Soc.*, 9-12 (1925-29).

54 O'REILLY H. and PANTIN G., Some observations on the salt marsh formation in Co. Dub lin. *Proc. Roy. Ir. Acad.*, 58B(5), 89-128 (1957).

55 PERRATON C., Salt marshes of the Hampshire-Sussex border. *J. Ecol.*, 4(2), 240-247 (1953).

56 PETHICK J., The distribution of salt pans on tidal salt marshes. *Journ. Biogeog.*, 1, 57-62 (1974).

57 POLUNIN N., Botany of the Canadian Eastern Arctic. III. Vegetation and ecology. *Bull. Nat. Mus. Can.*, 104, 1-304 (1948).

58 PRAEGER R.L., Phanerogamia and Pteridophyta *in* Clare Island survey. Part X. *Proc. Roy. Ir. Acad.*, 31 (1911).

59 PRIESTLEY J.H., The Pelophilous formation on the left bank of the Severn estuary. *Proc. Bristol. Nat. Soc.*, 4th ser. 3 (1911).

60 PUGH G.J.F., The fungal flora of tidal mud flats, in *The Ecology of Soil Fungi*. Liverpool Univ. Press (1960).

61 PUGH G.J.F., Fungal colonisation of a developing salt marsh. *Nature*, 190, 1032-1033 (1961).

62 PUGH G.J.F., Studies in fungi in coastal soils. I. *Trans. Brit. Mycol. Soc.*, 45(2), 255-260 (1962).

63 REDFIELD A.C., Development of a New England salt marsh. *Ecol. Mono.* 42(2), 201-37 (1972).

64 RICHARDS F.J., The salt marshes of the Dovey estuary. IV. The rates of vertical accretion, horizontal extension, and scarp erosion. *Ann. Bot.*, 48, 225-259 (1934).

65 SILBERHORN G.M., Lancaster County Tidal Marsh Inventory. Virg. Inst. Mar. Sci. pp. 1-92 (1973).

66 SILBERHORN G.M., Mathews County Tidal Marsh Inventory. Ibid. pp. 1-10 (1974).

67 SLATER L., Sedimentation on the salt marsh on Scolt Head Island. *Trans. Norf. Norw. Nat. Soc.*, 13(2), 133-140 (1931).

68 SMITH W.G., Botanical survey of Scotland. III-IV. Forfar and Fife. *Scot. Geog. Mag.*, 73 (1905).

69 STEERS J.A., The East Anglian Coast. *Geog. J.*, 69, 24-48 (1927).

70 STEERS J.A., Scolt Head Island. *Geog. J.* 83(6), 479-502 (1934).

71 STEERS J.A., Some notes on the north Norfolk coast from Hunstanton to Brancaster. *Geog. J.* 87(1), 35-46 (1936).

72 STEERS J.A., The rate of sedimentation on salt marshes on Scolt Head Island, Norfolk. *Geol. Mag.*, 75(883), 26-39 (1938).

73 STEERS J.A., *The Coastline of England and Wales*. C.U. Press (1946).

74 STEERS J.A., Accretion on Scolt Head Island marshes. *Trans. Norf. Norw. Nat. Soc.*, 24, 279 (1948).

75 STEERS J.A., Twelve years measurement of accretion on Norfolk salt marshes. *Geol. Mag.*, 85(3), 163-166 (1948).

76 STEERS J.A., The Physiography in *Scolt Head Island*. Ed. J.A. Steers. Heffer, Camb. (1960).

77 STEERS J.A., Physiography in *Wet Coastal Formations*. Ed. V.J. Chapman. (in press).

78   SWANN E.L., *Spartina* (Gramineae) in W. Norfolk. *Proc. Bot. Soc. Brit.*
      Isles, 6(1), 46-7 (1965).

79   TANSLEY A.G., *The British Islands and their Vegetation*. C.U. Press
      (1939).

80   THOMPSON H.S., Changes in the coast vegetation near Berrow, Somerset.
      J. Ecol., 10, 53-61 (1922).

81   TURNER M. and GRAY T.R.G., Bacteria of a developing salt marsh. *Nature,*
      London, 194, 559-560 (1962).

82   TURNER M. and PUGH G.J.F., Species of *Mortierella* from a salt marsh.
      Trans. Brit. Mycol. Soc., 44(2), 243-252 (1961).

83   TUTIN T.G., The autecology of *Zostera marina* in relation to its wasting
      disease. *N. Phyt.*, 37(1), 50-70 (1938).

84   WIEHE P.O., A quantitative study of the influence of the tide upon popu-
      lations of *Salicornia europaea*. *J. Ecol.*, 23, 323-333 (1935).

85   YAPP R.H. *et al.*, The salt marshes of the Dovey estuary. II. The salt
      marshes. *J. Ecol.*, 5, 65-103 (1917).

CHAPTER 5

THE SALT MARSH ENVIRONMENT

THE TIDES

Just as the tides and tidal phenomena form the principal environmental feature
in marine algal and mangrove ecology, so the tides represent the major phenomenon of the salt marsh habitat. The vegetation of salt marshes is subject to
periodic inundation by sea water, the lower the marsh the more frequent the
inundation. During the periods of flooding in daylight, photosynthesis of
phanerogamic plants will be reduced because the supply of carbon dioxide is
diminished and silt in the water reduces the light supply. Irrespective of
when the flooding occurs, the environment of the root may also be altered and
the oxygen supply reduced so that respiration is affected. In the case of
the seaweeds, the reverse phenomena are likely to occur, photosynthesis and
respiration being reduced during the periods of exposure. There is also the
effect of saline water on the metabolic plant processes, especially those of
the phanerogams.

At low tide the vegetation will be subject to the normal regional and local
climate. Thus a flooding tide may leave the marsh and be followed by a heavy
downpour, resulting in a rapid change of salinity in the soil water. In
summer, when the tide leaves the marsh the vegetation may become exposed suddenly to high temperatures. On the other hand, the vegetation does not suffer
from drought conditions even in the driest summer. It must be evident, therefore, that the periods of submergence and exposure are of profound significance to the plants, both phanerogams and algae. In addition to all these
effects, there is also a purely mechanical effect exerted by the tide.

The tide is generally responsible for the conveyance of seeds over the salt
marsh. At middle and high levels, these seeds become trapped in the vegetation, and are left when the tide recedes. Success in germination and growth
depends here, as in any other phanerogamic community, on the environment,
availability of space and competition. At the lower levels where there may be
much open ground, the problem is essentially one of successful establishment
before the seedling can be washed away by the tide. We know very little
about establishment on low marshes though it is a problem that does not present any great difficulties in investigation. Wiehe 41 used the density of

Salicornia seedlings on low marsh in relation to frequency of flooding tides, and his data suggest that the lower limit of the plant is set by the mechanical removal of seedlings. In Fig. 5.1 it will be seen that there is a sharp rise in disappearance (mortality rate) at the level where there is daily flooding (neap-tide zone). Field observations such as the above, however, need to be coupled with germination and growth studies under controlled conditions in order to determine rate of root and shoot growth. Studies of this nature have been carried out with *Spartina alterniflora* in the U.S.A. (33). It

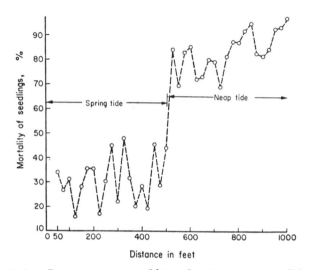

FIG. 5.1. *Percentage mortality of* Salicornia *seedlings along a transect (after Wiehe).*

would seem that with the annual species of Glasswort (*Salicornia*), seedlings need to be left uncovered for 2 to 3 days, and this will only happen during neap-tide periods above the level of mean high water mark of neap tides (see p. 124); in that period, the root can penetrate the soil to a sufficient depth to anchor it when the marsh is next flooded and so prevent it being swept away. It would therefore be most desirable to have information on root growth and soil penetration for primary colonists such as the various species of Glasswort (*Salicornia*), Seablite (*Suaeda maritima*), Sea poa (*Puccinellia maritima*) and indeed all salt marsh species.

It is not, however, sufficient to determine the minimum period of continuous exposure required for successful anchorage. It is essential that the period must occur at the normal time for germination, which will be some time in the spring. For this reason, the lower limit of an annual *Salicornia* may fluctuate from year to year depending on the period when neap tides coincide with germination. The present writer has shown that Sea aster (*Aster tripolium*) seedlings normally need 5 days before they are properly anchored. This, therefore, represents the minimum exposure time required. On the Norfolk marshes, the lower limit of abundant *Aster* is at +7.5 ft O.D.*, whilst the lowest is at +6.4 ft O.D. The maximum period of continuous exposure is 7 days at the former level and it occurs in February. At the lower level, the period is 5 days and it occurs in March. It is true there is still a 5-day exposure at +6.1 ft O.D., but it occurs in April and May, after the normal germination time. It seems, therefore, that the lower limit of *Aster* on the Norfolk marshes may be determined by the establishment period and the time of its occurrence at the lower levels.

From the above, it is evident that much valuable information can be secured by carrying out levelling surveys on the marshes and finding the vertical ranges of major species and the principal communities. If the levels are related to the nearest tide levels, it is then possible to determine not only the maximum periods of continuous exposure at each level, but also the expected number of submergences each day during daylight.

On this basis (13 the marshes fall into upper and lower marshes, the principal feature separating the two being the period of continuous exposure, which increases greatly in passing from the top of the lower marshes to the bottom of the upper marshes. It appears that the boundary between these two groups lies near mean high water. At present the only set of data refer to the Scolt marshes in Norfolk (13) and the Lynn marshes in U.S.A. (15), and it would be highly desirable to obtain more information for other salt marsh areas. Using Scolt data, the lower marshes there commonly undergo more than 360 submergences per annum, though this value for other places may well depend upon tidal range and the character of the tides (see p. 57). The maximum period of continuous exposure never *exceeds* 9 days and the mean daily submergence in daylight is more than 1.2 hours. So far as the period of continuous exposure is concerned, it may change from a maximum of 8 days on lower marshes to one of 16 days on higher marshes, with change of level of only 0.2 ft. It is easy to see that such a change could be of profound importance to many plants, not only in respect of germination and establishment

* Ordnance Datum.

but also in the effect it could have during a hot, dry summer.

Phanerogams and algae appear about equally affected by this division into upper and lower marshes. Thus, twelve phanerogamic species occur wholly on one type or the other, whilst six are common to both: among the algae, twenty-seven species are restricted, and nine are common to both. This result only applied to East Anglia and will differ in other regions. On Romney marsh (U.S.A.) ten phanerogams occurred wholly on one type or the other and seven on both: among the algae the situation was reversed as compared to Scolt, seven species being restricted and twenty-nine covering both (15). The algae restricted to the upper marshes are mostly members of the Myxophyceae which, as a group, are well adapted to withstand long periods of desiccation. It seems that very few phanerogams are able to tolerate more than 3 hours' submergence in daylight. This, however, is an aspect that requires further study with detailed measurements of photosynthesis and respiration under conditions of submergence and exposure.

After a levelling survey has been carried out, it is possible to plot the continuous exposure periods for individual species at the upper and lower limits (Fig. 5.2). For a given species one would expect the diagrams to be comparable for different salt marsh areas, particularly if the tidal phenomena represent the principal causal factors. This aspect needs much further study, since at present comparable data are only available for Scolt and Massachusetts. One species, *Salicornia stricta*, though listed by some as taxonomically identical, has such different responses (Fig. 5.3) that the plants may belong to different physiological races or even to different species. It can, however, be noted that Sea purslane (*Halimione portulacoides*) appears to be a species limited by tidal phenomena since the number of submergences per annum at its upper level on both Scolt and Dublin marshes is between 100 and 104. It has been suggested that a tidal range of more than 8 m enables the Halimionetum to develop at a lower level than usual.

Adult plants or seedlings can be transplanted from one marsh level to another in order to determine the impact of submergence-exposure upon them. Thus in the U.S.A. marshes can be divided into low low (tall *Spartina alterniflora*), high low (dwarf *S. alterniflora*), low high (*Salicornia, Limonium, S. alterniflora*) and high high (*S. patens*). Of the species studied *Salicornia virginica* of low high grew satisfactorily in high low and low and *Limonium carolin-*

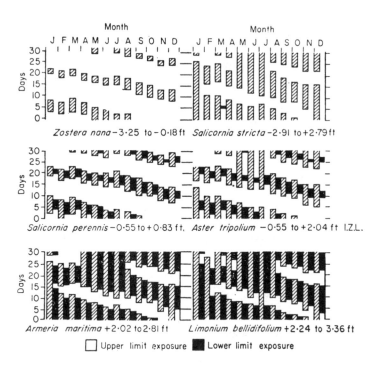

FIG. 5.2. *Charts indicating features of continuous exposure for salt marsh plants at the upper and lower limits of their vertical range at Scolt (after Chapman). I.Z.L. = Island Zero Level.*

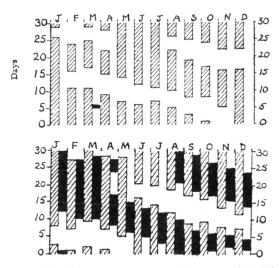

FIG. 5.3. *Continuous exposures at upper (hatching) and lower limits (solid black) of* Salicornia stricta *at Scolt in Norfolk (above) and at Saugus in U.S.A. (below) (after Chapman).*

ianum also grew satisfactorily in high low (34).

Certain algal species have representatives common to both salt marsh and
rocky coast. No detailed work has as yet been undertaken to ascertain if
such plants occupy comparable levels on the two types of shore in relation to
the tides. Thus *Pelvetia canaliculata* and its ecad *libera* would be ideal to
study in this respect, as also *Fucus vesiculosus* and its salt marsh ecads
volubilis, caespitosus and *muscoides*.

WATER TABLE

Apart from the major effect of periodic floodings and the intervening periods
of exposure and the indirect effect of these phenomena upon water loss and
basic metabolic processes of the plants, there is the influence of the tides
upon the soil water table, an influence which can be counteracted or complemented by the incidence of rainfall. The movement of the water table can be
of profound significance should it result in water-logging of the roots for
any appreciable period, and furthermore, variation in water movements with
distance from major creeks may result in a vegetation zonation correlated with
it. Indeed there seems little doubt that the zone of Sea purslane (*Halimione
portulacoides*) found along creeks is related to the better drainage conditions
(11,17). According to Brereton (8) the distribution of *Puccinellia maritima* is
partly controlled by water table and partly by salinity.

Water table conditions on a marsh are related not only to the proximity of
creeks, but also to soil structure. For this reason a study of the soil is
an essential feature of any salt marsh investigation. In so far as the soil
water table is usually not far below the surface, the soil study can generally
be prosecuted effectively by digging pits.

SOIL STRUCTURE

The broad features of salt marsh soils have already been indicated. It is
apparent that they are formed generally on a sand base, more rarely on a rocky
one, and that the deposited material is either windblown sand, water-borne
clay and silt, plant remains or a combination of any of these.

In the U.S.A. marshes in Canada and New England have been studied in some detail. In the Bay of Fundy the marine silt overlies remains of beech and pine forests indicating a relatively recent subsidence. The silt is mostly reddish but in places a blue soil can be found which is associated with badly drained areas (18). The New England marshes consist essentially of a fibrous peat, mainly consisting of remains of *Spartina alterniflora*. The kind of sequence in building up the soils of these marshes is illustrated in Fig. 5.4.

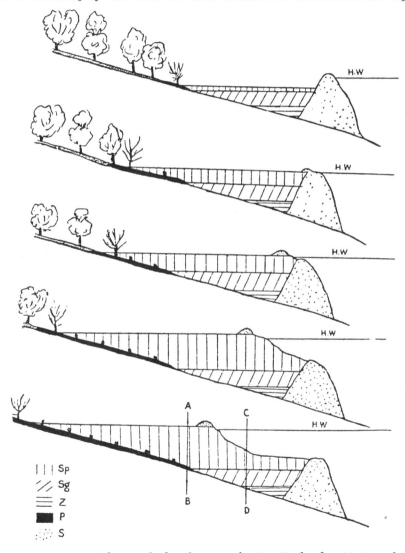

FIG. 5.4. *Salt marsh development in New England. At* AB *only*
Spartina patens *peat would be found.* Sp = Spartina patens *peat;*
Sg = S. alterniflora *(tall form) peat;* Z = Zostera *mud;* P =
freshwater peat; S = *sand (after Chapman).*

A study of the geological structure of salt marshes requires amplification by the carrying out of simple mechanical analyses using a standard sedimentation technique that will be found in any book on soil analysis. The result of such an analysis reveals essentially the proportions of coarse sand, fine sand, clay and silt that are present. Marshes with a high proportion of the first two will possess good drainage and will generally carry a grass-dominated vegetation. Marshes with a high proportion of clay and silt will tend to be poorly drained, except near creeks, but such marshes have a much higher agricultural potential when they have been reclaimed by the building of sea walls.

The relative proportions of the sand fractions to those of clay and silt largely determine the pore space of the soil, and this affects the drainage conditions. This can affect plant distribution. · Thus *Suaeda maritima* var. *macrocarpa* is found on muddy soils subject to flooding, whilst var. *flexilis* occurs on more sandy soils with better drainage. The pore space of a peat soil may vary between 75 and 90 percent, whereas that of a clay soil will range between 50 and 65 percent and that of a sandy soil will be rather less. Although the sandy soil may have the lowest pore space, water movement will be rapid because there is a low proportion of soil colloids to which water can become tenaciously bound. The actual spaces, though fewer than the numerous minute capillaries of a clay soil, are probably larger, and hence offer less resistance to water movement.

In addition to the above features, the height of the marsh itself plays a part in determining the depth of the water table, because the higher the marsh, the less frequent the submersions and the lower will be the water table, though the marsh is potentially more influenced by heavy rainfall than is a lower marsh. The higher marshes also have a greater depth of surface mud which will impede water movement and for this reason is of great importance (see p. 130). On marshes of all levels there is generally a raised zone along creeks, where coarser material is deposited at flooding tides (18), another raised zone around the landward edges and a flat zone in between.

WATER MOVEMENT

The access of water to a marsh and its subsequent removal after high tide have been summarised in Fig. 5.5. As the tide begins to rise, water commences to

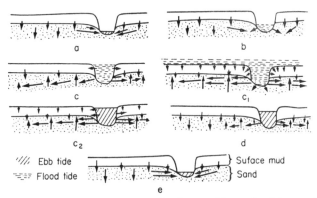

FIG. 5.5. *Water movements during a diurnal tide cycle.* a,b,c,d,e, *non-flooding tide,* c-c$_1$-c$_2$-d, *flooding tide. Surface mud remains as an aerated layer (after Chapman).*

seep laterally into the creek, the rate of such lateral seepage depending on the nature of the soil strata. Where there is a deposit of mud on the banks, as in older creeks, the rate of seepage may be reduced. Seepage will not, of course, commence until the level of water in the creek exceeds that of the soil water table in the adjacent marsh. As the tide rises, the amount of seepage increases, though when the surface mud layer is reached, a back pressure is set up due to air trapped in the soil (see later). So far as the soil water table is concerned, the extent of the tidal influence upon it will depend on the distance apart of the creeks, the size of the creek and the height of the marsh. As water movement is greatest nearest the creek, close proximity of creeks will increase the movement of the water table. The larger and deeper the creek, the greater the water pressure and again the greater will be the lateral soil water table movement. Eventually flooding of the marsh will occur, this happening more frequently with the lower marshes, and seepage then takes place vertically into the surface soil layers.

When the tide turns the flooding surface water is removed first of all and as it pours over the creek edges erosion slowly but surely takes place. Shallow pools of water persist in the slight irregularities of the marsh surface, and slowly disappear by seepage and evaporation. These shallow pools do, however, make it difficult to determine exactly when a marsh is re-exposed. Such pools disappear more rapidly in summer than winter and also more rapidly at the commencement of a spring tidal cycle rather than at the end when the soil may be approaching saturation. The entry of water by gravitational and lateral seep-

age results in the gradual elevation of the soil water table over a spring
tidal cycle, whilst during the neap-tide cycle the water table slowly falls.
Superimposed upon this cyclic movement will be the effect of each single tide,
though the effect here is likely to be restricted to a zone adjacent to each
creek. Water will not effectively start to drain out of the soil into the
creeks until the water level in the creeks is below that of the soil water
table in the adjacent marsh. Because of the occlusion of air in the surface
mud layer, it is not really possible to follow water table movements by digging pits in the soil. The movement can be followed by using tubes perforated
in the lower portion, the bottom opening being closed by a wooden plug, and
employing a graduated stick to determine the water level in the tubes. Between measurements the upper opening is kept closed by a cork. An electrical
circuit recording technique has also been used (14) with success on marshes,
though it cannot be used where there is a peat soil, which tends to remain
saturated.

AERATED LAYER

Use of tubes and recorders has shown quite clearly that the soil water table
never rises completely to the surface, even during a flooding tide(13). Therefore there is always an aerated layer just below the surface. How the recorders and tubes demonstrate the existence of this layer is illustrated in Fig.
5.6. Further evidence of the aerated layer can be obtained by plunging a
stick into the soil when the tide is covering it, and then on withdrawing the
stick bubbles of gas emerge. This gas can be collected over a glycerine-sea
water mixture and analysed. As may be expected, the composition is quite
different from that of the atmosphere, the oxygen content being greatly reduced and the CO_2 content greatly increased (Table 5.1).

This gas must have an influence upon root respiration and the low oxygen may
account for the development of aerenchyma* that seems to have occurred with
many salt marsh species.

The composition of this gas varies considerably over a single marsh and from
marsh to marsh, and probably seasonally as well. Manometers which can be

* Tissue with numerous large air spaces: usually cortex and pith.

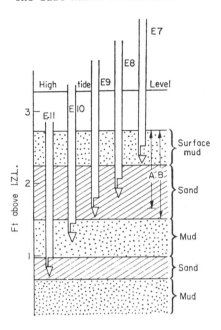

FIG. 5.6. *Plover marsh, Scolt Head Island, away from a creek.*
Morning tide, 28 June 1934. E 10, E 11 *flooded;* E 11 *recorded;*
E 7 *to* E 9 *no record.* A, *definite aerated layer;* B, *probable*
extent of aerated layer.

TABLE 5.1

Percent composition of Salt Marsh Gas

	Asteretum				Limonium bellidifolium	
	a	b	c	d	a	b
$CO_2 + H_2S$*	2.99	2.55	3.26	4.22	1.46	0.93
O_2	1.61	0.82	0.71	1.42	10.5	17.5

* This is present in small amounts.

carefully inserted into the soil at different depths also demonstrate the
existence of the aerated layer, and confirm that during a flood tide the
rising water table exerts a pressure upon the occluded gas (Fig. 5.7). When
the distribution of roots in the various soil strata is studied, the great

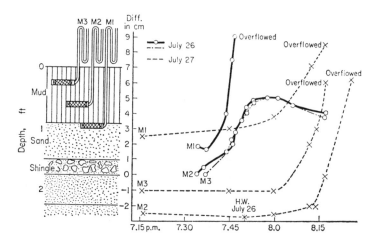

FIG. 5.7. *Effect of rising tide on aerated layer in a Juncetum. Manometers during evening tides, 26 and 27 July 1934 (after Chapman).*

majority are found to be in the surface mud layer, which is mostly occupied by the aerated zone. The great importance of this aerated layer to the plants cannot be over-estimated, and it is likely that many species would not be able to grow at low levels on the marshes without it.

SOIL SALINITY

Of the chemical constituents in the soil, the chloride and sodium ions are by far the most important.* They determine the salinity of the environment, and the amount present is dependent upon a number of factors first enunciated by Morss (26). Some of these factors have already been mentioned in connection with other aspects of the habitat: such factors are height of the preceding tide, i.e. whether flooding or restricted to creeks; rainfall, which can bring about downward leaching of salts; proximity to creeks (drainage); mechanical composition of the soil, the soil colloids of a clay soil binding sodium ions more strongly than in a sandy soil; height of marsh in relation to frequency of flooding; proximity of any fresh water inflow; depth of water table, as

     * In the following pages, salinity studies have been expressed in terms of osmotic pressure, percentage of NaCl, or percentage of soluble chloride.

the nearer this is to the surface the more constant will be the soil salinity; presence of vegetation and the type of vegetation. The plants reduce evaporation from the soil surface and their transpiration is responsible for a continual rise of soil water from the lower layers.

It is very difficult to distinguish between the effect of the tides (through submergence and emergence) and of salinity in determining the zonation that can be observed on salt marshes (8,26). One answer to this problem rests with experimental work on the salinity tolerance of the dominant species, associated with extensive field sampling of soils over extended periods of time (23,29, 38). Any experimental work on salinity tolerance must take into consideration the age of the plant, because it seems likely that adult plants are very much more tolerant than seedlings. Seedling establishment is the first essential, and it is therefore of greatest importance to study the effect of salinity on germination and early stages of growth. Experimental studies have shown (38) that some species do not grow under optimal conditions in nature, presumably as a result of plant competition.

Salinity and Germination

The results obtained to date indicate that the great majority of salt marsh plants show maximum germination under fresh water conditions. It will be indicated later (p. 137) that germination time for many species on salt marshes is correlated with a period of minimum surface soil salinity, and it is this that enables some species, at least, to occur where they do. So far as germination is concerned, the effect of high salinity is essentially to inhibit the process, because if ungerminated seeds are transferred to fresh water they will then germinate. There is evidence that the prehistory of the parent plants may play some part in growth of the seedlings of some species.

Recent work (18) has extended our knowledge considerably about the effect of salinity upon germination and it has suggested that species can be placed into one of three categories:

1   Glycophyte group, e.g. *Juncus maritimus, Beta maritima* where a low
            salinity is essential. These species are found on high marsh where
            winter rains lower the salinity.

2   Eury-halophytes with a wide range of tolerance, e.g. *Aster tripol-ium*, *Spergularia marginata*.

3   Species with a narrow salinity tolerance, e.g. *Salicornia stricta*, *Triglochin maritima*.

Despite the new work it would seem that further study is still needed before any final conclusions can be drawn. Some typical germination results that have been obtained are set out in Table 5.2.

TABLE 5.2

Percentage Germination after 28 Days

	Spartina townsendii *	*Phragmites communis*	*Aster tripolium*	*Spergularia marginata*	*Salicornia stricta*	*Suaeda maritima*	*Juncus maritimus*	*Artemisia maritima*	*Halimione portulacoides ecovar latifolia*	*H. portulacoides ecovar parvifolia*
Tap water	80	4	45	66	93	4	50	86	83.3	25
1 percent NaCl	21	32	25	4	45	0	18	8	50	8.3
2 percent NaCl	15	16	10	0	36	4	5	0	8.3	0
Sea water	3	0	0	0	38	0	0	0	0	0
5 percent NaCl	0	0	0	0	36	0	0	0	0	0
10 percent NaCl	0	0	0	0	12	0	0	0	0	0

* Jacquet 1949.

It is evident that very few species will tolerate more than 2 percent sodium chloride, and that of the species tested the annual *Salicornia stricta* is the only one with any real tolerance and this explains why it is such a success-ful colonist, not only at low levels but also on salt pans at high levels where soil salinity can rise to very high values. There is also some evidence (16) that lowering the temperature enables germination of certain species to take place at increased salinities. This is certainly the case with *Spergu-*

laria marginata, but it is an aspect which requires much more experimental work in relation to concurrent field studies. It has also been reported that light intensity affects the germination of seeds of Sea arrow-grass (*Triglochin maritima*), *Spergularia marginata* and Sea milkwort (*Glaux maritima*). Since plants from inland salt regions of Europe were used for this work, its repetition and extension, using maritime plants, is essential. Suitable simple experiments would not be difficult, using lattice screens to provide different degrees of light intensity.

Salinity and Growth

Once the seeds have germinated, subsequent growth is also affected by soil salinity. Thus with Annual glasswort (*Salicornia stricta = S. europaea*) optimum growth occurs between 1.5 and 2.5 percent NaCl (5,18,24), whereas with Sea aster (*Aster tripolium*) it lies between 0.5 and 1.0 percent. This, however, is a field in which much more experimental information is required, correlated with salinity determinations from the marshes. Ultimately it will be necessary to try and relate growth phenomena to either the sodium or chloride ions, since there is no doubt that the effect of these two ions is quite different on the development of morphological features such as succulence. In the meantime, the operation of NaCl upon growth needs much more investigation. The general effect appears to be one of dwarfing of plants, such reduction being commonly ascribed to the high osmotic pressures engendered in the cells. There are, however, other possibilities, such as the water-logging of very clayey soils through the effect of sodium on soil colloid dispersion, with the result that reducing conditions inimical to plants are produced. Other possibilities involve ion antagonism and the effect of sodium on the calcium metabolism. Salinity as such cannot be the only factor affecting growth and it must need be studied in relation to other factors of the environment, such as light intensity and drainage. In the case of *Salicornia* and *Puccinellia maritima*, which are often "clumped", the distribution is probably controlled by a combination of salinity and drainage (1,8, both related to number of inundations. In the case of adult plants, there is evidence that *Salicornia* spp., *Spergularia marginata*, Sea aster (*Aster tripolium*), *Glaux*, Sea plantain (*Plantago maritima*), Sea poa (*Puccinellia maritima*), Sea lavender (*Limonium vulgare*) and *Spartina* spp., are all tolerant of high salinities, so that their occurrence in an area may well depend upon the tolerance of the seedlings. On the other hand, Mud rush (*Juncus gerardi*), Fiorin (*Agrostis stolonifera*) and *Scirpus* spp. are intolerant of high salinity. More work has been done in the United States (15,23,29,38) on this aspect than in Europe and further work on European (28) species is much to be desired.

In some of the work in this field, the salinity of both soil solution and of the plants growing in the soil has been expressed in terms of osmotic pressures, the argument being that because of the high excess of sodium chloride the osmotic pressures will be proportional to the amount of NaCl present. This, however, is not always true, because in the Shrubby seablite (*Suaeda fruticosa*) only 42 percent of the osmotic pressure is due to the chloride ion, whereas in *Salicornia stricta* it is 91 percent. Further examples of such variations are given in Table 5.3.

TABLE 5.3

Osmotic Pressures of Cell-sap of Various Halophytes and Proportion Due to Chloride Ion (after Arnold)

Species	No. of determinations	O.P. sap (atm)	Proportion O.P. sap due to Cl⁻ (atm)	Cl⁻ as percent O.P. sap
Atriplex patula var. *hastata*	6	31.6	13.3	42
Suaeda fruticosa	15	35.2	15.3	43
Glaux maritima	2	14.6	7.4	51
Juncus gerardi	3	27.8	15.5	56
Triglochin maritima	10	24.6	16.1	66
Scirpus maritimus	2	14.7	10.4	71
Salicornia rubra	11	44.3	31.5	71
Spartina patens	4	20.9	15.7	75
Salicornia ambigua	6	42.5	34.1	80
S. stricta (herbacea)	10	39.7	35.9	91
S. mucronata	3	34.0	31.5	93
		Av. 32.6		

A further complication is that the osmotic pressures of different parts of the plant can vary, that of leaf cells commonly being much higher than those of roots or stem. This means that a great deal of the earlier work will need to be repeated.

Salinity Variations

A detailed study by the present writer (14) of the Scolt marshes indicated that a fairly regular horizontal gradient in the soluble chloride could be observed in the 3 in. and 9 in. soil layers of the principal prisere communities. The same gradient existed in the surface layer during the winter, but evaporation during the hot summer months exerts a profound effect upon bare soil and upon high marshes with low vegetation, such as the General Salt Marsh and Plantaginetum maritimi (p. 110). In the Juncetum the tall character of the vegetation lowers evaporation and hence surface salinity does not rise in the summer. In the Phragmitetum the habit of the dominant species (*Phragmites communis*) and also the influence of fresh water modify the salinity.

While some workers (32,36) have recorded salinity gradients with increasing soil depth, irregularities have been recorded elsewhere. During parts of the year there may be a gradient with depth but on English marshes studied (14) there is a lack of regularity. In a New England marsh the vertical gradient increased with depth from October to April, whilst from May to September it decreased with depth. Rainfall can have a marked temporary effect upon the salinity gradient, particularly at the higher levels on a marsh. The lower communities show the least effect of rainfall (Fig. 5.8) whilst the higher communities exhibit the greatest influence of rainfall and tidal inundation. One may expect to find some form of salinity gradient with depth, but it is likely to be more pronounced in summer on high marshes with low vegetation, and it also can be subject to modification by excessive rainfall and abnormal tides.

The seasonal changes in salinity on salt marshes are perhaps of most importance because they affect germination and seedling establishment (p. 133). On the Norfolk marshes, the principal feature is an early spring fall in the soluble chloride of the surface soil (Fig. 5.9). This spring fall has been recorded for salt marshes in the U.S.A. (Fig. 5.10) and New Zealand, and it is this lowering of the surface salinity that permits the germination of salt

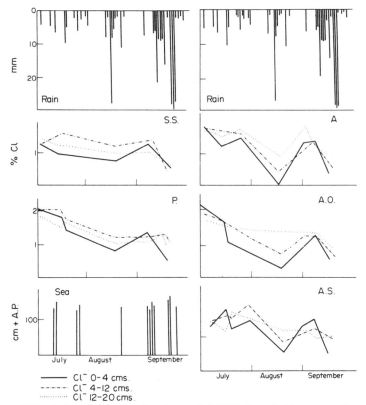

FIG. 5.8. *Effect of rain and tidal inundations on the salinity of a Dutch salt marsh.* S.S. = *Salicornieto-Spartinetum townsendii;* P = *Puccinellietum;* A = *Artemisietum;* A.O. = Artemisia-Halimione; A.S. = Artemisia-Limonium; *Bottom left, sea = abnormal high waters expressed as cm. above normal (A.P.).*

marsh species. The extent to which the salinity is lowered must vary from year to year and hence the occurrence of annuals for any year will vary somewhat from marsh to marsh.

Sodium Ion

A similar study has been made of the exchangeable sodium present in these soils. Since the sodium ion is adsorbed to the clay particles, it will not always be present in the exchangeable form in a molecular ratio to the soluble chloride. In fact, the exchangeable sodium at Scolt only accounted for a fraction of the total soluble chloride in the surface and 3 in. layers. In

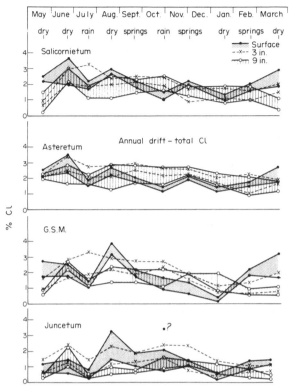

FIG. 5.9. *Annual drift at surface, 3 in. and 9 in. levels of the total chloride in four Norfolk salt marsh communities. The widths of the bands indicate the degree of variation found on each soil level (after Chapman).*

the more sandy subsoil at 9 in. there is less adsorption of the sodium and the values obtained frequently equalled those expected on a molecular ratio basis. There is, however, no comparable seasonal drift with a January-February minimum as is found with the soluble chloride, nor was there any real correlation between the behaviour of the soluble chloride and exchangeable sodium. This, however, is by no means universally true and the Norfolk phenomena may be associated with the considerable variation exhibited by the different salt marsh soils. It is possible that on the sandy marshes of the west coast, where the soil is more uniform, that a correlation between the behaviour of the two ions would be found.

It is interesting to compare the variations that occur in the chloride and sodium of plants growing on salt marsh soils with the corresponding values for

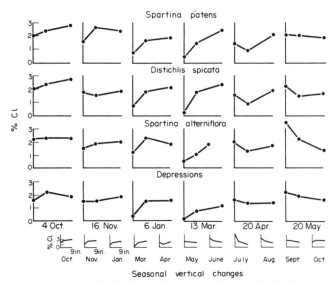

FIG. 5.10. *Annual drift and seasonal vertical changes (mean values) in the chloride in the soil of New England salt marsh communities (after Chapman).*

the soils. This has been done for the annual *Salicornia stricta* (Fig. 5.11), and it will be seen that for this species, at least, there is no correlation between the amounts absorbed by the plants and those present in the soil. This, however, is only an isolated investigation and other species may behave quite differently, but at present we have no data.

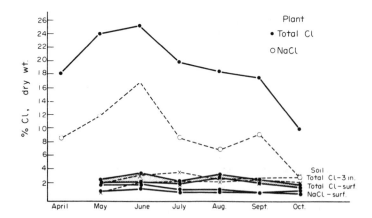

FIG. 5.11. *Relation of total chloride and chloride equivalent of the exchangeable sodium in plants of* Salicornia stricta *compared with the amounts in the surrounding soil (lower bands) (after Chapman).*

There is still plenty of scope for further studies on all aspects of salinity
and salinity tolerance of salt marsh species, as also on the control of high
osmotic pressures arising from habitats rich in sodium chloride and also on
the effect of high salinities upon transpiration, though this last probably
plays little or no part in controlling zonation on marshes. So far as osmotic pressure control is concerned, salt marsh plants can be grouped into three
classes:

(a) Succulents, in which salt uptake is compensated for by water intake,
though at the end of the season the succulent portion may dry up and be
sloughed off, e.g. *Salicornia* species.
(b) Salt excreting forms, e.g. *Limonium, Spartina, Glaux, Halimione,* where
special glands remove salt to the exterior, though the extent to which the
amount of salt removed prevents the osmotic pressure from rising is not known.
In the case of *Halimione* there is clear evidence of secretion against a gradient (5).
(c) No special mechanism other than leaf death at the end of the season. If
the leaves contain much accumulated salt, their death and decay removes the
salt from the plant.

Salinity and Transpiration

Studies on the effect of salinity upon transpiration are difficult to inter-
pret because of the various criteria used to express the transpiration rate,
e.g. dry weight, surface area, fresh weight. There seems little doubt that
halophytes have a lower number of stomata per unit area than do non-halophytes,
but if transpiration rate is expressed on a leaf area basis, the rate can be
higher than that of non-halophytes. The fact that a halophyte can transpire
1-2½ times its weight of water daily would seem to indicate that salt marsh
plants have no undue difficulty in absorbing water from their apparently unfavourable medium, and that transpiration proceeds at a rate not far different
from that of non-halophytes. There is also some evidence (11) which indicates
it is the effect of specific ions upon the transpiration rate that is more
important than molecular substances such as excess sodium chloride.

OTHER IONS

Apart from sodium and chloride ions, relatively little work has been carried
out upon other ions present in salt marsh soils(31). Some data are available
for areas in Holland (2,6), Denmark, the U.S.A. and the Southern Hemisphere
and some for Great Britain(22). This is perhaps surprising when one considers
a little the potential agricultural value of the marshes once they have been
reclaimed. Indeed, it would be of the utmost value to follow the changes that
occur, not only in the vegetation (31), but also in the soil chemistry and
physics when a salt marsh is enclosed. Whilst salt marsh soils are potentially rich in nutrients their reclamation is not easy because of the extreme
dispersion of the soil based on the excess exchangeable sodium, which has
first to be removed (16).

In Morecambe Bay phosphorus, potash, nitrogen all decrease seawards whereas
calcium increases landwards. On the European coast carbonate content decreases from 35 percent or more in Brittany salt marshes to 0.5-5 percent on
the Jutland marshes (39). There is also a decrease as one proceeds up estuaries. On the other hand an earlier worker could not find any significant horizontal changes on a Dutch salt marsh. Potassium content is closely related
to the percentage of clay particles in the soil so that input takes place as
silt is deposited(42). Phosphorus on the other hand, appears to be more closely correlated with humus content. Another major nutrient, nitrogen, is derived either from flooding tides, fixed from the air by blue-green algae (37,43)
and bacteria or is liberated from plant debris. This latter is highly significant at the drift-line. There is also some evidence that the presence of
soluble iron may be important for some species. Thus it has been suggested
this could be a reason for the restriction of *Spartina alterniflora* to low
marshes.

On the Norfolk marshes, changes in exchangeable calcium have been followed,
but it was not possible to correlate them with either rainfall or tidal inundations. The data did indicate the existence of a horizontal gradient between
communities in most of the soil layers but until further work has been carried
out on other marshes it would be premature to make any generalisation.

SOIL MOISTURE

The moisture content of salt marsh soils has been studied in some detail (18),
but in view of its great variability it cannot be regarded as a factor that
plays a part in determining zonation of the vegetation. In some cases a gradient may exist (1) whereas in other cases (15) it is absent or barely detectable.
It is therefore apparent that further work on the soil moisture content would
be very desirable. The nature of any vertical gradient would appear to depend on the geological structure of the marsh, and in particular on the nature and depth of the surface mud. Where there is a transition from clay to
sand, there will be a marked gradient, particularly on high marshes where the
soil water table is likely to be at some depth.

TEMPERATURE

This factor mainly affects the geographical distribution of species. This is
a field where more work is required. The present writer (17) has suggested that
the northern limit of *Halimione portulacoides* may be correlated with the 60°F
July isotherm (see p. 146) and the northern limit of *Suaeda fruticosa* with
the 61°F isotherm for August. On the Atlantic U.S.A. marshes there is a northern limit for *Juncus roemerianus* and other southern species which are likely
to be temperature determined. The effect of temperature upon growth has been
much neglected. In the case of *Puccinellia maritima* optimum growth (19) occurs
between 17-23°C with two ten minute inundations per day.

BIOTA

Natural animals, though present on salt marshes, do not form such an integral
part of the ecosystem as they do on a rocky sea coast (p. 79). Molluscs and
crabs can be abundant, especially on bare mud flats and pans that dry out
fairly regularly. High marshes adjacent to dunes that carry a rabbit population are subject to grazing, the plants mainly browsed being the grasses, *Aster*
and *Plantago*. As may be expected more animals, crustacea, fish etc. are found
in the creeks and pools and the few species found on the marshes themselves
have little or no direct effect upon the vegetation. Numerous birds visit the
marshes and there is no doubt that the vegetation is very important to them,

especially the ducks. Other birds, e.g. Clapper Rail, make their nests on
the higher marshes. Pfleger (30) has contributed greatly to our understanding
of Foraminifera on marshes, each environment having its distinctive assemblage.
Mosquitoes and their larvae are very evident on all marshes, especially those
of the western Atlantic, where ditching was resorted to as a means of control.

LIGHT

Whilst light obviously affects photosynthesis, and the light can be reduced
considerably at low levels during tidal inundation, especially if much sediment is carried in the water, this aspect has not been subject to much study.
In the case of *Puccinellia maritima* day length has a significant effect upon
the habit of the plant: with a 16 hr day and 10 000 lux it produces long
creeping stolons whilst under a 12 hr day and 10 000 lux it becomes tufted 40.

PANS

The pans that form such a characteristic feature of salt marshes are worthy
of study because they can well be compared with rock pools. Apart from their
existence in upper or lower marshes (p. 123), they have been subdivided into
hard and soft-floored pans (18) or into saline and less saline pans (27). The
salinity of the water depends on height and hence frequency of flooding, rainfall, whether there is layering or not, and the nature of the mud bottom.
Layering will only occur if the pan is deep, but it may be quite significant
(Fig. 5.12). After a dry period, if the pan becomes filled with rain water,
there will be diffusion of salt outward from the mud so that the lower water
layers are more saline than the upper. The oxygen content of the pan water
depends upon the type and abundance of animal and plant life as well as upon
the height of the pool in relation to tidal flooding. As one may expect,
there is generally a rise in the oxygen concentration around midday (Fig. 5.
12) as a result of photosynthesis. Remarkably little study has been undertaken of salt pans, both in regards to their flora and the conditions under
which it exists. In view of the circumscribed nature of the habitat, salt
pans are as excellent for field study as are rock pools.

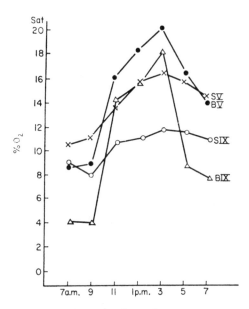

FIG. 5.12. *Diurnal variations in oxygen concentration in a diatom pool (pool* IX*), and in pool* V (Enteromorpha-Ulva). B, *bottom layers;* S, *surface layers (after Nichol).*

AUTECOLOGY

In so far as many of the species found on salt marshes are restricted to the salt marsh habitat, there is plenty of scope for autecological studies. This is an aspect of salt marsh ecology that has not received much attention, though valuable work has been done on the hybrid Cord grass, *Spartina townsendii* and increasingly on *Spartina alterniflora*. Thus its germination and growth requirements, soil preferences and climatic limits are quite well known. We also know that there is much dissemination by means of rhizome fragments being carried around by the sea, that under certain conditions individual plants develop into clumps, the centres of which subsequently die and become invaded by secondary growth(9), that under certain soil toxic conditions "die back" occurs (20,21), that its great success may be correlated among other things with the presence of two kinds of root, fine absorbing rootlets and deep, stout anchoring roots and quick-growing runners.

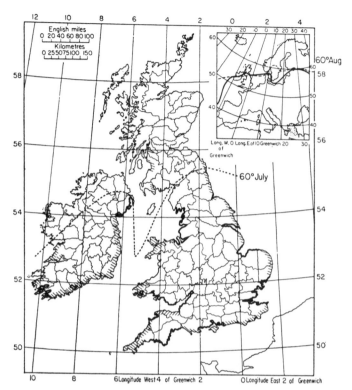

FIG. 5.13. Halimione portulacoides *(L.) Aell. Distribution in British Isles and (inset) northern limits in Europe.* ■■ *= extant.* /////= *probably extinct.* \\\\\\ *= recorded in these vice-countries but not seen by author or other persons other than where full black (after Chapman).*

A study (11,17) of Sea purslane (*Halimione portulacoides*) has shown that there are two main varieties, *latifolia* and *parvifolia*, which differ in their eco-logical requirements, the former being characteristic of creek banks and shingle borders and the latter of high sandy marshes. Both require good drain-age conditions and var. *latifolia* seems to be susceptible to stock grazing. There is a close correlation between the 60° July isotherm and the northern limit of the species in Great Britain (Fig. 5.13) so that the northern limit could well be determined by temperature. In Great Britain the tetraploid *Salicornia dolichostachya* is characteristic of open habitats and the diploid *S. europaea* agg. in places associated with *Suaeda* or grasses. The habit of some of the *Salicornia* species is controlled by soil water content, soil text-ure and light intensity (18). A major study of *Limonium vulgare* and *L. humile* has revealed the fact that the distribution of these two species is based on intrinsic, environmental, historic or interspecific factors (6). Autecological studies are important because they help us to understand the limiting factors and behaviour within the habitat of a particular species. Only by combining field investigations with experiments under controlled conditions near the laboratory, can the autecology of any species be understood.

REFERENCES

1   ADAMS D.A., Factors influencing vascular plant zonation in North Carolina salt marshes. *Ecol.*, 44, 445-456 (1963).

2   ADRIANI E.D., Sur la phytosociologie, la synécologie et le bilan d'eau de halophytes de la region néerlandaise méridionale, ainsi que de la Mediterranée francaise. *S.I.G.M.A.*, 88, 1-217, Groningen (1945).

3   ARNOLD A., Die Bedeutung der Chlorionen fur die Pflanzen. *Bot. Stud.*, Vol. 2. Jena (1955).

4   BAUMEISTER W. and KLOOS G., Uber die Salzsekretion bei *Halimione portulacoides* (L.) Aell. *Flora*, 163, 310-326 (1974).

5   BAUMEISTER W. and SCHMIDT L., Uber die Rolle des Natriums in Pflanzlichen Stoffwechsel. *Flora*, 152(1), 24-56 (1962).

6   BOORMAN L.A., Studies in salt marsh ecology with special reference to the genus *Limonium*. *J. Ecol.*, 59(1), 103-120 (1971).

7   BOUCAUD J., Nutrition azotée sur les sols littoraux. Cas de *Suaeda macrocarpa* Moq. Sur vases littorales, comparaison avec les glycophytes. *Oecol. Plant.*, 5(1), 87-98 (1970).

8   BRERETON A.J., The structure of the species populations in the initial stages of salt marsh succession. *J. Ecol.*, 59(2), 321-338 (1971).

9   CALDWELL P.A., The spatial development of *Spartina* colonies growing without competition. *Ann. Bot.*, N.S. 21(82), 203-214 (1957).

10 CAREY A.E. and OLIVER F.W., *Tidal Lands: a Study of Shore Problems.* Blackie, London (1918).

11 CHAPMAN V.J., A note upon *Obione portulacoides* (L.) Gaert. *Ann. Bot.*, N. S. 1(2), 305-310 (1937).

12 CHAPMAN V.J., Marsh development in Norfolk. *Trans. Norf. Norw. Nat. Soc.*, 14(4), 394-310 (1938).

13 CHAPMAN V.J., Studies in salt marsh ecology, I-III. *J. Ecol.*, 26(1), 144-179 (1938).

14 CHAPMAN V.J., Studies in salt marsh ecology, IV-V. *J. Ecol.*, 27(1), 160-

201 (1939).

15   CHAPMAN V.J., Studies in salt marsh ecology, VI-VII. *J. Ecol.*, 28, 119-
      152 (1940).

16   CHAPMAN V.J., The new perspective in the halophytes. *Quart. Rev. Biol.*,
      17(4), 291-311 (1942).

17   CHAPMAN V.J., *Halimione portulacoides* (L.) Aell. in *Biological Flora of
      the British Isles. J. Ecol.*, 38(1), 214-222 (1950).

18   CHAPMAN V.J., *Salt Marshes and Salt Deserts of the World.* 2nd Ed. Cramer,
      Lehre (1974).

19   DAIBER F.C., Salt marsh plants and future coastal salt marshes in relat-
      ion to animals in *Ecology of Halophytes* ed. Reimold and Queen. Acad.
      Press, N.Y. p. 475-510 (1974).

20   GOODMAN P.J., Investigations into "die-back" in *Spartina townsendii* agg.
      II. *J. Ecol.*, 48, 711-724 (1960).

21   GOODMAN P.J. and WILLIAMS W.J., Investigations into "die-back" in *Spart-
      ina townsendii* agg. III. *J. Ecol.*, 49(2), 391-398 (1961).

22   GRAY A.J. and BUNCE R.G.H., The ecology of Morecambe Bay. V. Soils and
      vegetation of the salt marshes: a multivariate approach. *J. Appl. Ecol.*,
      9(1), 221-34 (1972).

23   HARSHBERGER J.W., The vegetation of the salt marshes and of the salt and
      freshwater ponds of northern coastal New Jersey. *Proc. Acad. Nat. Sci.
      Philad.*, 1909, 373-409 (1909).

24   MONTFORT C. and BRANDRUP W., Physiologische und pflanzengeographische
      Seesalzwirkungen. II: Ökologische Studien über Keimung und erste Ent-
      wicklung bei Halophyten. *Jb. Wiss. Bot.*, 66(5), 902-946 (1927).

25   MONTFORT C. and BRANDRUP W., Physiologische und Pflanzengeographische
      Seesalzwirkungen. III. *Jb. Wiss. Bot.*, 67(1), 105 (1928).

26   MORSS W.L., The plant colonisation of merselands in the estuary of the
      River Nith. *J. Ecol.*, 15, 310-343 (1927).

27   NICHOL E.A.T., The ecology of a salt marsh. *J. Mar. Biol. Ass. U.K.*, 20,
      203-261 (1935).

28   NIENBURG W. and KOLUMBE E., Zur Ökologie der flora des Wattenmeeres, II.
      Wiss. Meer. Kiel. N.F. 21-22, 77 (1931).

29   PENFOUND W.T. and HATHAWAY E.S., Plant communities in the marshlands of
      south-eastern Louisiana. *Ecol. Monog.*, 8, 1-56 (1938).

30   PHLEGER F.B., Foraminifera populations and marine marsh processes. *Limnol.
      Oceanog.*, 15, 522-34 (1970).

31   PIGOTT C.D., Influence of mineral nutrition on the zonation of flowering

plants in coastal salt marshes, in *Ecological Aspects of the Mineral Nutrition of Plants*. Ed. I.H. Rorison. pp. 25-35. Blackwell.

32   PURER E.A., Plant ecology of the coastal salt marshlands of San Diego County, California. *Ecol. Monog.*, 12, 81-111 (1942).

33   SENECA E.D., Germination and seedling response of Atlantic and Gulf Coast populations of *Spartina alterniflora*. *Amer. J. Bot.*, 61(9), 947-56 (1974).

34   STALTER R. and BATSON W.T., Transplantation of salt marsh vegetation, Georgetown, South Carolina. *Ecol.*, 50, 1087-89 (1969).

35   STEERS J.A., *Scolt Head Island*. The physiography and evolution. Heffer, Cambridge (1960).

36   STEINER M., Zur Ökologie der salzmarschen der Nordöstlichen vereinigten Staaten von Nordamerika. *Jb. Wiss. Bot.*, 81, 94-202 (1934).

37   STEWART W.D.P, Nitrogen turnover in marine and brackish habitats. II. *Ann. Bot.*, 31, 385-40 (1967).

38   TAYLOR N., Salt tolerance of Long Island salt marsh plants. *Circ. N.Y. State Mus.*, 23, 1-42 (1939).

39   VERHOEVEN B., On the calcium carbonate content of young marine sediments. *Inter. Inst. Land Reclam. Improv. Bull.*, 4, 27pp. (1963).

40   WEIHE K VON and DREYLING G., Kulturverfahren zur Bestimmung der Salz- und Überflutungsverträglichkeit von *Puccinellia* spp. (Gramineae). *Helogland. wiss. Meeresunter.*, 20, 157-171 (1970).

41   WIEHE P.O., A quantitative study of the influence of the tide upon populations of *Salicornia europaea*. *J. Ecol.*, 23, 323-333 (1935).

42   ZONNEVELD I.S., *in* BEEFTINK W.G., The coastal salt marshes of Europe (*Wet Coastal Formations*, Elsevier (in press)).

CHAPTER 6

SAND DUNE VEGETATION

OCCURRENCE

The accumulations of sand that go to form sand dunes are almost entirely confined to coastal regions in Europe, though elsewhere far greater areas are
occupied by dunes in the interior arid and semi-arid continental regions.
Like the marshes maritime dunes are essentially confined to coastal plains,
and are not to be found where there are steep cliffs just behind the beach.
The habitat, particularly in its early stages, is characterised by special
features, and in consequence the plants that occupy the early phases of sand
dunes are restricted to certain species that can tolerate these conditions.
The flora of the dunes as a whole contains a proportion of characteristic
species, but is not so specialised as that of salt marshes. For this reason
the flora is much richer than that of salt marshes. Salisbury (53) recorded
over 400 species but if exotics are added the list is probably around 1000 (47).
Dune systems such as the Culbins carry 400-500 species. Westhoff (1952)
recorded as many as 31 exotics in the Dutch shrub-dune phase. On the dunes
of the Dutch Voorne area 29 groups of plants and animals, 700 species of vascular plants (= 52 percent of Dutch flora) and 111 species of breeding birds
(= 66 percent of Dutch birds) have been recorded (1). Some interesting species
are, however, recorded in the dune flora, such as *Primula scotica* from Caithness and the Mediterranean ball rush (*Holoschoenus vulgaris*) from Somerset (53).
Some species in recent years, because of climatic changes, have altered their
distribution. Thus *Glaucium flavum* is no longer found in Scotland and *Parnassia palustris* has disappeared from dune slacks in southern England (46).

The names applied locally to sand dunes vary in different parts of Great Britain. Thus in East Anglia they are known as "meols" or "meals", whilst in
Cornwall and Devon they are called "towans" or "burrows"; in Wales they are
known as "warrens" and in Scotland as "links". The maximum height reached by
dunes in England and Wales is about 20 m, but in the Culbin Sands they may
reach an elevation of 30 m. There appears to be no reason why these heights
should not be exceeded, as they certainly are in other parts of the world.
Thus in the Coto Donano in Spain they reach a height of 100 m (46).

FORMATION

There are two major phenomena that enable maritime dune formation to proceed.
The first and most important is a supply of sand together with wind to move
it, and the second is plant colonisation. The supply of sand comes from the
sand flats that are exposed at low tide, and on a windy day the movement of
sand can not only be seen but felt. Blown sand is deposited wherever the
wind drops, as in passing over a hillock or if it meets an obstacle, and the
sand accumulates on the protected lee side (Fig. 6.1). Plant colonisation in
the early stages assists in the further growth of dunes because plants represent obstacles, whilst the roots at the same time help to "fix" the sand already there although this function is not important. As the cover becomes
more and more complete and other dunes form in front and cut off the sand
supply, so the dune first gradually ceases to grow higher and is finally stabilised. Apart from this substrate mobility there is also a lack of water and
nutrients.

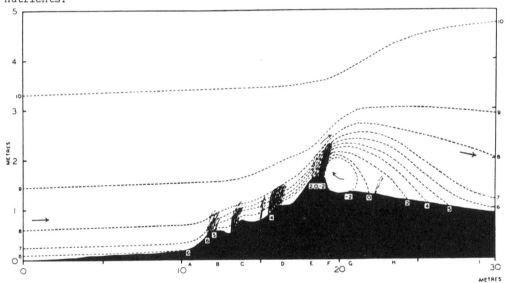

FIG. 6.1. *Effect of wind over sand dune grass clump (after Ranwell)*

After dunes have been colonised and covered by plants, erosion may take place
(see p. 210) should the vegetation cover become broken. When this happens,
the wind can act on the exposed bare sand and secondary movement of sand then
takes place. In the early stages the excavated area is known as a "blow-out",
and, if not stopped, erosion proceeds until the whole dune has been removed,
very often with the formation of a mobile dune.

DRIFT-LINE

Dune formation often begins on the drift-line where, amidst the mass of sod-
den flotsam and jetsam, plants can and do make their appearance (6) The litter present on the drift-line ameliorates the general lack of nutrients and
instability. Around these plants, small mounds develop, though whether any
further growth occurs depends on how high the sand rises, which may be as
much as 2 m. We may therefore commence our study of sand dunes by a brief
look at the drift-line vegetation.

Over a year more than one drift-line can be observed on a beach, but plants
are generally restricted to the uppermost line, where there is the greatest
stability. The drift-line occurs not only on the foreshore, but, in the case
of off-shore barrier islands and spits, it is also represented on the protected shoreward side where it rests at the base of the dunes or shingle ridges
or else is evident on the highest marshes. The foreshore drift-line, which
can be subject to storm tides, is poor in species, though these can be, and
often are, the fore-runners of dunes. The plants are generally scattered,
and there is no development into any form of closed vegetation.

Most of the drift-line species are annuals and belong to about three families
(Cruciferae, Chenopodiaceae and Polygonaceae). The principal foreshore representatives are *Cakile maritima* (Sea rocket), *Salsola kali* (Saltwort) and
Atriplex littoralis (Shore orache) which are widespread on all north Atlantic
coasts from the far north of Norway, Labrador and New Foundland to Portugal
and south-east U.S.A. (12,13,14,24,41). In the far northern areas a further
characteristic plant is *Mertensia maritima* (Northern shore wort).

Nordhagen (34) in his study of the Norwegian drift-line recognised four communities: (a) *Cakile maritima* with *Salsola kali*, (b) *Atriplex littoralis* community with *A. latifolium* and *Agropyron repens*; (c) *Atriplex latifolium* community with *Matricaria maritima* and *Agropyron*, (d) *Atriplex sabulosum* community
with *A. latifolium* and *Agropyron junceiforme*. All these could be succeeded
at higher levels by an *Agropyron repens* maritime community. The *Atriplex*
littoralis community, which is the only *Atriplex* north of the Arctic circle,
could be succeeded by an *Agropyron repens-Rumex crispus* community with *Mert-*
ensia , *Crambe maritima* (Seakale), *Glaucium flavum* (Sea poppy) and *Beta*
maritima (Sea beetroot).

On temperate European shores additional species associated with the three ubiquitous species (see above) include *Honkenya peploides* (Sea sandwort), *Elymus arenarius* (Lyme grass), *Atriplex hastata* (Hastate orache) and *Atriplex
arenaria* (Sand orache). The last named species occurs from the Breton dunes
(11) south to the Gironde (14). South of La Rochelle *Salsola soda* occurs as a
further species together with *Euphorbia peplis* and *Polygonum maritimum*.

On western Atlantic shores additional species found in the drift-line of Labrador and New Foundland are *Lathyrus maritimus* (Sea pea), *Potentilla anserina*
and *Archangelica atropurpururea* (24). Additional warm temperate species are
also found in the south-eastern States, including *Euphorbia polygonifolia*
(Polygonate-leaved spurge), *Spartina patens* and *Fimbristylis castanea*.

In the protected localities behind dunes and on marshes, the same species may
occur, but others also enter into the community and very often are more abundant. Thus the landward drift-line of the south-eastern States possesses
Criton punctatus and *Cenchrus tribuloides*. Similarly at Scolt Head in Norfolk,
the drift-line between dune and salt marsh may possess the Shrubby sea-blite
(*Suaeda fruticosa*), *Artemisia maritima* (Sea wormwood), *Beta vulgaris* ssp. *maritima* (Sea beet), Danish scurvy-grass (*Cochlearia danica*) and Buck's horn plantain (*Plantago coronopus*). Elsewhere in other parts of Great Britain Seakale
(*Crambe maritima*), Woody nightshade (*Solanum dulcamara*), Sea radish (*Raphanus
maritimus*), Shore knotgrass (*Polygonum littorale*), Ray's knotgrass (*P. raii*),
Sea knotgrass (*P. maritimum*), and Babington's orache (*Atriplex glabriuscula*)
belong to this community. In Sweden *Juncus bufonius, Potentilla anserina* and
Rorippa islandica may be found (41). In all localities one can find casuals
that clearly come from some other habitat - dune or shingle, e.g. Sea heath
(*Frankenia laevis*), Sea spurge (*Euphorbia paralias*), Curled dock (*Rumex crispus*), Matted sea lavender (*Limonium bellidifolium*) and Sea campion (*Silene
maritima*).

The species of Orache (*Atriplex*) are often the most abundant, though on salt
marsh *Artemisia maritima* can form extensive areas. Whether the latter is a
characteristic drift-line species, or is rather a denizen of the salt marsh,
has yet to be settled. It is regarded as a nitrophile, and there is no doubt
that the drift-line is very rich in nitrogen from the decaying organic matter.

Not only is the drift-line habitat extremely unstable, since there is the ever-present prospect of smothering from sand or a fresh supply of debris, but the soil water, particularly on the foreshore, does not depart very greatly from the composition of sea water. Up to the present, the drift-line community has not been subjected to serious study and, apart from *Suaeda fruticosa*, very little is known about the requirements of the individual species, or even about the nature of the environment. One interesting feature about it is that the working depth for the roots of different species is about the same (19) (Table 6.1).

TABLE 6.1

(After Gimingham)

	Depth of longest root in inches		Length of longest lateral in inches		Position of longest lateral below surface in inches		
	Mean	Max.	Mean	Max.	Mean	Min.	Max.
Salsola kali	8.8	14.5	8.0	13.0	2.8	1.5	4.5
Atriplex glabriuscula	9.5	13.5	8.7	16.0	2.7	2.0	3.5
A. sabulosa (laciniata)	6.7	8.5	3.3	4.0	2.4	2.0	3.0
Agropyron junceiforme	8.2	10.0	6.3	12.5	1.5	1.5	2.0

Sometimes these plants do not appear to be located in relation to the current drift-line, but if they are excavated it will be found that their roots are associated with a buried former drift-line (17). Although the species grow at the upper tidal limit, they cannot endure prolonged immersion in sea water. Characteristically they have fleshy leaves and provision for water storage, either in the leaves (*Cakile*, *Honkenya*) or in special hairs (species of *Atriplex*), such water storage being regarded as one means of meeting the considerable osmotic pressures of tissues that result from the roots being in highly saline water. Thus Salisbury (53) records the following osmotic pressures in these plants:

Honkenya peploides	15.5-18.5 atm
Atriplex littoralis	37+ atm

| *Euphorbia peplis* | 9-20 atm |
| *Salsola kali* | 11-30.6 atm |

In the non-halophytes the osmotic pressure of the sap is around 5-7 atm.

The common Sea rocket (*Cakile maritima*) appears capable of tolerating some degree of sand covering, but it succumbs if the process is too frequent or the covering too great (7): Sand couch grass (*Agropyron junceiforme*), on the other hand, is capable of thriving under such conditions.

The Mediterranean *Suaeda fruticosa* (Shrubby seablite) reaches its northern limit in Norfolk and South Wales. Experiments have shown (6) that it is not tolerant to water-logging, but apart from this factor two requirements are essential for its successful establishment. The first is the tide which brings the seed and the seed-bed material (debris). The second is a period of quiescence, when the drift-line is not disturbed, so that young plants do not become buried by sand or shingle before they are established. Once they are established, further burying stimulates them to send up new shoots (see p. 243). The conditions under which plants such as *Salsola*, *Mertensia* and *Cakile* will exist need to be determined and then experimental work undertaken to confirm them. The drift-line is a fertile field of investigation that quite clearly merits much further work.

DUNE CLASSIFICATION

Before describing the various stages of dune building and the plants associated with them, some brief mention must be made of dune classification. Various authors have attempted to classify dunes - mainly from a physiographic viewpoint. One simple classification (57) is as follows:

(a) *Accumulation forms*. In these dunes the vegetation becomes predominant and a successive series of new dunes arise in front of each other.

(b) *Fixation forms*. These refer to the older dunes in a series of ridges, which have been gradually deprived of their sand supply. The valleys or hollows that exist between such dune ridges are known as "slacks" or "lows" (see p. 172 et seq).

(c) *Remanié forms*. These result from erosion of the fixation forms as a

result of wind attack if the vegetation cover is broken by some agency. If a
dune undergoing erosion is stabilised, it represents a moderate remanie form,
but in other cases practically the entire dune may be removed and in its
place a mobile dune appears.

(d) *Parabolic dunes*. These can arise as above, or they may develop where the
sand supply is particularly plentiful and the vegetation covering is inadequate, particularly in the centre of the dune as compared with the sides. In
such cases the higher central part continues to grow and move forward. The
continual moving of the sand over the top forms a sharp lee side, and gradually a parabolic dune is formed, i.e. a dune concave to the direction of the
prevailing wind, the sides of which are held back by the vegetation covering.
These dunes are the exact opposite of the crescentic dunes or barchans so
typical of deserts, where there is no vegetation to control the two ends,
which then move faster than the centre. Such dunes may later be broken
through by a wind channel in the centre leaving two flanks on either side (28).
The orientation of the two flanks could lead one to think that wind was not
involved in their formation. It has been pointed out (4) that records of wand-
ering parabolic dunes in Europe are all of relatively recent date, and the
question has been asked whether such dunes are the result of man's negligence
or over-exploitation. There is no doubt that elsewhere desert conditions
have been induced by man (Egyptian desert and central Otago desert in New Zealand), and mobile coastal dunes may therefore be symptomatic of the same
cause.

There is, however, another possible explanation. Mobile dunes may be associated with sinking shore-lines, when the sea increasingly brings about erosion of the fore-dunes. It is therefore worth noting that the present land
sinking (south-east England and the Low Countries) commenced relatively recently (geologically speaking) (see p. 94 and Fig. 4.8).

Several authors (32,55,60) have proposed more elaborate systems of dune classification but these go beyond the scope of this book.

One classification that should perhaps be mentioned is that where six types
are recognised (46,47):

(a) Dunes on off-shore islands, e.g. Georgia coast, Scolt Head.
(b) Dunes on spits, e.g. Blakeney.

(c)   Dunes on nesses such as Dungeness, Cape Hatteras.

(d)   Bay dunes at the back of bays.

(e)   Hindshore dunes comprising successive dune ridges and slacks, e.g. Lancashire dunes, Newborough Warren (Anglesey) and elsewhere.

(f)   Sand plains, which in Scotland are termed machairs.   Some authors suggest
Frontshore dunes for (a)-(c) and Hindshore for (d)-(f) but these seem to be
misnomers.

In the case of hindshore dunes one either finds a succession of prograding
dune ridges with slacks in between or else a ridge forms and before it is
stabilised by vegetation it moves landwards and then another ridge forms in
the same place. At Newborough Warren it takes 50 years for a dune to build
(28) to maximum height, and with a landward movement of 6-7 m per year it takes
a further 20 years before the space is available for a new dune to form (see
p. 187). If a dune becomes too high a wind break can occur and a U-shaped
dune appears.

WIND AND VEGETATION

Emphasis has been laid throughout upon the importance of wind 28. On the
western coasts of Europe, westerly winds blow steadily for most of the year.
In the presence of drift-line vegetation these winds produce a succession of
dune ridges which pass through the stages of vegetation development described
in the next section. Elsewhere parabolic dunes are produced and the result-
ant dune mass must be interpreted in the light of the various stages of mobility and erosion, as well as whether they occur singly, overlapping each other
or in laterally connected bands. Such dune complexes are well exemplified at
Braunton Burrows (66) and Newborough Warren (42,43,44). On other coasts, especially those of the Atlantic U.S.A., the westerly winds are not important, and
dune growth is dependent almost wholly upon local on-shore winds, especially
those of storm periods. On the European west coast, the prevailing westerly
winds encourage the formation of parabolic dunes which move landward and in
so doing generally break down and leave the flanks behind (see p. 188). Stabilisation of such dunes, apart from the flanks, may take a long time to
effect, and, because of the movement over a bare, damp sand substrate important relations exist between the slacks and dune vegetation (see p. 176). The
flanks of eroded parabolic dunes will pass through vegetation phases compar-

able to those found on parallel dune ridges, though the embryo dune phase
will be missing. Because of the different stages of formation and decay the
parabolic dunes have reached, it is much more difficult to trace the vegetation succession in such areas.

The prevailing mobility of dune systems on the west coast has meant that old
concepts (5) based upon relatively stable dunes have had to be extensively revised in such ever-changing areas. For some years now, dune areas have been
favourite locations for military exercises, and whilst these activities undoubtedly have done much to keep such dunes in a mobile condition, there is
little doubt that on the west coast the dynamic nature of the dunes is of
very long standing (see also p. 187).

DUNE VEGETATION

We may now turn to a study of dune formation in relation to the vegetation
cover. Here it is evident that the dune vegetation is ultimately related to
the two main types of dune, i.e. calcareous and non-calcareous. In the former, the high proportion of calcium carbonate results in a flora that contains
a calcicole or "chalk-favouring" element, whereas in the latter, conditions
become acidic and lead to plants typical of heath formations.

Embryo or Fore Dune

The early stage of dune formation is known as the *embryo* dune phase and is
very often an Agropyretum junceiformi. Here small mounds of sand accumulate
on the foreshore around plants of the drift-line, especially Sea rocket (*Cakile*), Saltwort (*Salsola*), Sea sandwort (*Honkenya*) and Sand couch grass (*Agropyron junceiforme*). As the mounds rise, the couch grass becomes more prominent and Marram grass (*Ammophila arenaria*) is able to invade as the possibility
of tidal inundation decreases. This species is very successful because of its
capacity to produce vertical and prostrate rhizomes. In the eastern U.S.A.
it is replaced by *A. breviligulata* in the north and by *Uniola paniculatum* in
the south (24). The mounds gradually spread and eventually fuse to give a small
fore-dune. The dominant plant on the European fore-dune is commonly *Agropyron*
because it is able to withstand occasional wetting with sea water. It readily

thrives with 1.5 percent salt in the soil and can temporarily tolerate up to
6 percent. Apart from its tolerance towards sea water, it is a valuable
plant in dune formation because it possesses extensive underground rhizomes
which send up new aerial shoots. The aerial shoots assist in the accumulation of more sand, whilst the roots help to bind the sand that is deposited.

It has been found that the earliest tillers of *Agropyron* are markedly prostrate, and give rise to a rosette of shoots adpressed to the sand. When several such young plants are adjacent, a network of shoots is formed and these
gather sand to form a low hummock. With increasing age and density, the prostrate habit of the shoots is replaced by an erect habit. Horizontal rhizomes
then grow out to a distance of 2-3 ft from these patches, and in the succeeding year they produce a new rosette of tillers. In this manner a whole series
of embryo dunes is gradually built up.

In the absence of sand couch grass, the fore-dunes are generally colonised by
the Lyme grass (*Elymus arenarius*) or by *Ammophila* spp., either of which invades hummocks that have developed around the drift-line plants. The success
of *Ammophila* invasion is, however, dependent upon there not being any frequent tidal flooding. In Sweden *Lactuca tatarica* has recently become abundant on the Marram-Lyme grass community(41).

The Lyme grass reaches its western and southern limit at Mont St. Michel(14),
on the Atlantic coast dunes of France *Euphorbia paralias, Eryngium maritimum*
and *Calystegia soldanella* become more prominent whilst *Honkenya* becomes less
common. Warm temperate southern elements, such as *Matthiola sinuata* and
Diotis candidissima enter the community as newcomers (12).

Yellow Dune

The embryo dune phase is succeeded by the *yellow dune* phase, so called because
there is still much bare sand to be colonised. Studies of maps of rapidly
growing areas, such as Scolt and Blakeney, can give a fair indication of the
rate of growth of dunes to the yellow dune stage.

The increase in height through sand trapped by the *Agropyron* and other drift-
line plants enables *Ammophila* spp. to enter the community and form an Ammo-

ophiletum characteristic of this phase. Earlier entry by Marram grass is
prevented by its reaction to salt, since it cannot tolerate more than 2 percent in the soil. The erect shoots trap more sand, and indeed the more the
sand covering, the more vigorous are the *Ammophila* plants (see p. 189). At
the same time the horizontal rhizomes and the deep-going roots act as most
effective sand stabilising agents. Despite the deep roots the open *Ammophila*
habitat is one in which drought conditions may prevail, especially in summer
months. Structurally, the leaf possesses xeromorphic features, and in dry
weather it also curls over so that water loss is still further reduced.

It appears that the advent of the *Ammophila* can be by seed or by fragments of
regenerating rhizome, rather like Cord grass (*Spartina townsendii*) (see p.
145). Generally it is likely that seedling establishment is sporadic but more
observations are required. From the seedling or the rhizome fragment, a new
horizontal rhizome appears (Fig. 6.2A-D). In the early stages the leafy
shoots are generally unbranched and are not sufficiently dense to cause differential sand accumulation. When a shoot is overwhelmed by sand, one or more
buds develop to produce a vertical shoot which develops leaves on reaching the
surface (Fig. 6.2F). If sand accumulation continues, more shoots develop and
the tussock habit, so characteristic of old dunes, is produced; the old rhizome then disintegrates (Fig. 6.2G), and is replaced by new adventitious roots
nearer the soil surface (15,21). Indeed, a characteristic feature of many dune
plants is their capacity to renew growth in response to sand covering. This
can often be seen if a rooting system is carefully excavated.

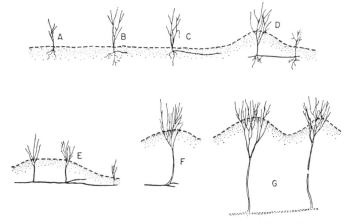

FIG. 6.2. *Diagrammatic representation of the mode of origin of a
sand dune system caused by the growth of* Ammophila arenaria *(for
explanation, see text) (after Greig-Smith et al.).*

In the south-eastern states of the Atlantic seaboard of the U.S.A. *Uniola paniculata* plays the same role as *Ammophila* and its response to the environment is very similar.

It has been pointed out (7) that *Agropyron* and *Ammophila* or *Uniola* on the embryo and yellow dunes respectively demonstrate how dominance can be achieved through unfavourable environmental conditions depressing or inhibiting potential competitors. The capacity of *Agropyron* to tolerate sea water enables it to dominate fore-dunes; the power of *Ammophila* or *Uniola* to react vigorously to sand covering enables those species to dominate the yellow dune phase. Indeed, once the remaining bare sand has become covered by plants and there is no further supply of sand, *Ammophila* tussocks commence to disintegrate. Short horizontal rhizomes are produced and these give rise to small, scattered leafy shoots that remain in the new vegetation. Whether the *Ammophila* actually becomes senescent or the response is to less favourable conditions has still to be established (see p. 189). It is a problem that should be capable of solution through experimental work. It has been suggested (58) that increased competition for water, lack of oxygen, or increased carbon dioxide in the soil atmosphere may be responsible. Alternatively, rate of growth may, normally, in the absence of sand covering, be so slow that it can no longer compete with other plants with a greater rate of growth.

Gehu and Petit (14) consider that the principal European community from Holland northwards is dominated by *Ammophila* and *Elymus*. South and westwards they regard the community as an *Ammophila-Euphorbia paralias* one which becomes replaced in Portugal by an *Ammophila arundinacea-Pancratium maritimum* community. Around Charante and Vendee there is an ecotonal variant with several local endemics (*Silene thorei, Linaria thymifolia, Artemisia lloydii*). On the islands of Honat and Hoedic (12) *Diotis candidissima, Matthiola sinuata, Galium arenarium* are associated with the *Ammophila-Pancratium* community. On these two islands an alternate yellow dune community is a Festucetum (*F. dumetorum* or *F. rubra* var. *arenaria*) with *Galium arenarium, Medicago marina* and *Ononis repens*. Associated species of the yellow dune in the U.S.A. include *Vicia cracca, Euphorbia polygonifolia, Cenchrus tribuloides, Oenothera humifusa* (Evening primrose) and *Panicum amarum*. As many of these associated species have not been subjected to detailed study, they offer a fruitful field for investigation.

Some of the dune species spread into the community through vegetative growth, e.g. Sand sedge (*Carex arenaria*): others come from seed and produce a vertical root very rapidly and hence are soon anchored. This rapidity can be compared with much slower rooting establishment on low salt marsh (see p. 123). In the case of the Sea spurge (*Euphorbia paralias*), during the first 3-4 days after germination the root grows to a depth of 5-6 cm before the cotyledons have emerged, and within a fortnight the roots are down 10-15 cm into permanently moist sand.

The species (totalling about 26) (26) found in the early yellow dune phase or Ammophiletum of Europe can be regarded in the main as characteristic dune plants which are rarely found elsewhere. The principal species are as follows:

Agropyron junceiforme	*Ammophila arenaria*
Carex arenaria	*Honkenya peploides*
Eryngium maritimum	*Calystegia soldanella*
Euphorbia paralias	*Elymus arenarius*
E. portlandica[+]	*Festuca rubra* var. *arenaria*
Rhynchosinapis monensis[*]	*Thalictrum minus* ssp. *arenarium*
Viola tricolor ssp. *curtsii*	*Corynephorus canescens*

With increasing age, other species arrive, becoming ever more and more abundant, until eventually the vegetation cover closes. Hepburn[26] noted over 250 species in dune localities with eight or more species widely dispersed on dune systems, though also occurring in other habitats.

It is very evident from published lists of species from dunes in different parts of the British Isles, (4,7,10,19-21,23,26,36-38,44,53,54,65,66) that there is a great diversity in the Ammophiletum. Apart from those already mentioned, other species, which are generally present in such a community, include Wall-pepper (*Sedum acre*), *Erodium cicutarium* ssp. *dunense*, Ragwort (*Senecio jacobaea*), and species of Chickweed (*Cerastium*). Many additional species are only sporadic and occur locally or are not present every year. This fact, coupled with the great variability of the associated flora of older dunes, is almost certainly due to accidental seeding, either by wind transport or by human

* West coast and Isle of Man.
+ South and west coasts and Ireland.

agency. An example of the latter can be observed in places such as the tern-
ery on Scolt Head Island, where the numerous visitors are probably responsible
for many of the casuals that have been recorded. The erection of holiday huts
on dunes often results in a localised, associated flora introduced over the
years consciously or unwittingly by the hut occupants.

In the dunes of the Atlantic coast of the U.S.A. the vegetation of the yellow
dune phase changes from north to south. From the Gulf of St. Lawrence south
to North Carolina *Ammophila breviligulata* is the dominant (in New Jersey it
forms 82 percent of the vegetation (31). In the Gulf and New Brunswick associated species include *Rumex acetosella*, *Botrychium ternatum*, *Rosa lucida* and
Vicia cracca. In the New England states and down to New Jersey *Solidago sempervirens*, *Xanthium canadense*, and *Euphorbia polygonifolia* are associates. On
the Maryland, Virginia and Carolina yellow dunes species such as *Panicum amarum*, *Solidago sempervirens*, *Cenchrus tribuloides*, *Oenothera humifusa* and *Xanthium strumarium* enter the community (27). In the far south on the Florida dunes
the *Uniola* is associated with *Spartina*, *Panicum*, *Ipomvea pes-caprae*, *Yucca*,
Croton and *Euphorbia polygonifolia* (37).

Moss Colonisation

In the later stages of the Ammophiletum, particularly in depressions where the
sand is fairly stable, mosses make their appearance and help in a minor manner
to stabilise the sand. The principal species are *Tortula ruraliformis*, *Barbula fallax*, *Bryum pendulum* and *Brachythecium albicans*, though others may occur
locally. Pioneer mosses, such as *Tortula*, are acrocarpous whereas mosses of
later stages, e.g. *Hypnum*, are pleurocarpous. In the case of *Barbula fallax*
(11) there are regular growth increments with a heavy production of rhizoids at
all subsurface levels. The net result is a cushion of some depth and sand-
binding capacity. *Bryum pendulum* produces new shoots after burial, so that
unless the sand is excessively mobile it readily becomes established (Fig.
6.3). Experimental work carried out by transplanting mosses to various dune
sites or by burying them under known depths of sand (3) showed that no species
appeared capable of tolerating a sand cover of 4 cm depth, but that species
typical of the yellow dune phase were capable of emerging from under 3 cm.
In the sand-covering experiments, marked powers of regeneration and recovery
were also shown by *Pohlia annotina*, *Polytrichum piliferum* and *P. juniperinum*

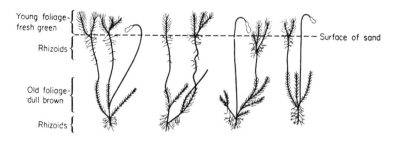

FIG. 6.3. *Diagram of excavated shoots of* Bryum pendulum *Schp. (after Gimingham).*

(Fig. 6.4). Despite this capacity to tolerate sand coverage, these last three species are generally restricted to the older stable dunes, and it may be that moisture requirement or some other factor prevents them from establishing themselves in the early dune states.

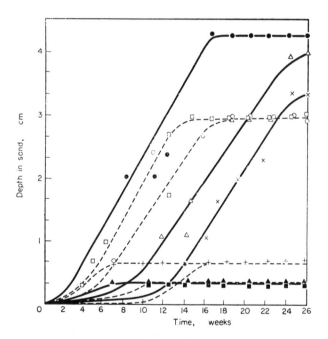

FIG. 6.4. *Time in weeks taken to recolonise half the area after burial under various depths of sand.* ●, Pohlia annotina; Δ, Polytrichum piliferum; X, P. juniperinum; □, Tortula ruraliformis; O, Brachythecium albicans; +, Rhytidiadelphus squarrosus; -, Bryum argentetum; ▲, Rhacomitrium canescens; ■, Pleurozium schreberi *(after Brise* et al.*).*

It has been pointed out (2) that dune mosses fall into three growth types, short turfs, mats and wefts (Fig. 6.5). Short turf mosses are essentially characteristic of the yellow dune phase whilst mats, represented by species such as *Brachythecium albicans*, *Eurhynchium praelongum*, are more abundant in the next stage - the grey dune phase, whilst on dune pasture or machair one finds the wefts, such as *Hylocomium splendens* and *Hypnum cupressiforme*. Where there is abundant lime in the dune soil, *Camptothecium lutescens* will be present in quantity.

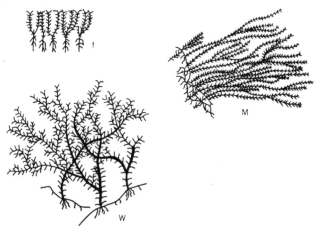

FIG. 6.5. *Diagrams of the three chief growth-form types repres-*
ented. t, short turf (viewed from side); M, mat (viewed from
above); W, weft (viewed from side) (after Brise and Gimingham).

Grey Dune

The yellow dune phase is succeeded by the fixed or *grey* dune phase, in which there is a complete vegetation cover. The species involved are extremely varied and it is not easy to provide any very generalised account. Some are strictly dune plants (see p. 162), but the great majority occur in other habitats. The name grey dune (an alternative is fixed dune) has been given to this stage because of the lichen invasion that occurs and gives a grey covering to the sand, the principal lichens being species of the genus *Cladonia*. The name could, however, well be applied to the greyish colour of such dunes when viewed from a distance, which is produced primarily by the glaucous green colour of the leaves of Marram. In the U.S.A. the term used for this group of dunes is "scrub dune" because the principal vegetation cover is a thicket of low shrubs.

Because there is such a great variation in the floras, dunes in different areas must be studied and lists of the species prepared. As Harshberger (34) and Tansley (58) have indicated, the plants are extremely varied and form, according to geographical situation, climatic region, and various physiographic, edaphic and particularly biotic factors, a considerable series of different communities. The final stage is either (a) grassland (machair), especially on calcareous dunes (where grazing by rabbits or domestic animals takes place or the dunes are converted to golf courses, e.g. St. Cyrus, Southport, St. Andrews); (b) *Calluna* heath on non-calcareous dunes; (c) forest, especially on the Atlantic coast of the U.S.A. The most successful trees on sand are species of pine, juniper or birch (acid dunes) and plantations are not uncommon in many parts of the British Isles. Such plantations provide an extremely effective means of stabilising sand dunes and are planted for this purpose in many parts of the world. The great bulk of the British dunes terminate as grasslands, but Calluneta are recorded from Dorset (20), Walney Island (39), and in eastern Scotland (56), whilst at Newborough in Anglessey (44) *Calluna* is associated with *Salix repens* in the slacks (see p. 174).

Before the final stages are reached in western Europe the *Ammophila* is gradually superseded by Creeping fescue (*Festuca rubra* var. *arenaria*) and Sand sedge (*Carex arenaria*, with or without *Corynephorus canescens*, together with a host of associated plants including weft mosses and lichens. A feature of many of the phanerogams is their shallow rooting system, rather surprising in a habitat of this nature. The continual addition of plant remains brings about marked darkening changes in soil colour. Originally this is white, if the sand has a high proportion of calcareous shell fragments, or yellow if it is largely composed of silica.

The grey dunes of Europe exhibit distinct seasonal aspects though these have not been widely studied. In the spring one can find a mass of ephemerals such as *Stellaria* spp., *Cerastium* spp., *Aira* spp. Later in the year taller plants, many of them perennials, take their place and give a splash of colour to the otherwise dull grey foliage of the grasses. The colour-providers include Lady's bedstraw (*Galium verum*), Restharrow (*Ononis repens*), *Thalictrum minus* ssp. *arenarium*, *Lactuca virosa*, Bird's foot trefoil (*Lotus corniculatus*), *Cirsium* spp. and Ragwort (*Senecio jacobaea*). Many of the species that occur

are, as in the yellow dune phase, casuals, or else they are species with potential seed parents not too far away from the dunes. For full lists of species, reference should be made to the various accounts of dune systems that
have appeared (see end of chapter). Among the lichens, which are essentially
restricted to the grey dune phase, especially where there has been rabbit dis-
turbance, the most important genera are *Cladonia* and *Peltigera*, the former
being particularly abundant and represented by about ten species. The entry
of lichens into dune vegetation is dependent upon earlier moss colonisation.
Liverworts are generally rare, except in dune hollows where fresh water may
be very near the surface or even form a pond.

In the Wadden area of Holland and eastwards the sand is chalk deficient (0.2-
1%) and the grey dune phase is dominated by *Ammophila* and *Festuca*. At the
estuaries of the Rhine, Meuse and Scheldt the sand is richer in chalk (3-20%)
and the yellow dunes are invaded first by *Sambucus nigra*, then by *Rosa* spp.,
Cratagus monogyna and *Ligustrum vulgare* that ultimately give way to a dune
scrub of *Hippophäe* (59,62,63,64). On the Atlantic coast dunes of France the
yellow dune phase is first invaded by mosses, then by *Helichrysum staechas*.
This is followed by *Ephedra distachya* and lichens and ultimately a grey dune
shrub phase develops that has been termed a Rosa-Ephedretum. In this community can be found the endemic *Dianthus gallicus* (12,14).

On the Atlantic coast of the U.S.A. the grey dune phase is essentially represented by a shrub community. From the Gulf of St. Lawrence south to the Carolinas the dominant is the beach heather, *Hudsonia tomentosa*, which in the south
eastern States is replaced by *Myrica cerifera* (this reaches its northern limit
in Maryland). In the northern States species associated with *Hudsonia* include
Juniperus sabina, *Vaccinium pennsylvanicum*, *Prunus maritimus* and *Rosa lucida*.
In New Jersey *Hudsonia* forms up to 70 percent of the vegetation cover with
Panicum amarum, *Cyperus grayii* and *Lechea maritima* forming the other 30 percent (31). On the central Atlantic coast *Myrica cerifera* with its associated
species forms an ecotone between the foredune and *Hudsonia* grey dune communities. On the Assateague shores two shrub zones have been recognised, one
about 1 m high with numerous climbers and characterised by *Amelanchia canadensis* and *Pyrus angustifolia* var. *spinosa*, the other more than 1 m high with
fewer climbers and dominated by the beach heather (27). In the south eastern
States *Quercus virginiana*, *Prunus serotina* and *Rhus copallina* can all be associated with the *Myrica* (37).

It is perhaps appropriate to make reference here to a recent study on dune annuals in relation to density and nutrition (40). In pure populations of the following annuals, *Aira praecox, A. caryophyllea, Cerastium atrovirens* and *Vulpia membranacea* 90 percent of their seedlings will survive irrespective of density or of nutrient regime. Increasing the density does, however, result in a remarkable plastic response. In mixed populations of all four annuals *Vulpia* eventually suppresses the other three and *Cerastium* suppresses both species of *Aira* irrespective of nutrient regime. In the presence of abundant *Festuca rubra* all four annuals are suppressed or eliminated, thus suggesting that perennials on dunes probably have an ecological advantage over annuals.

Final Stages

With increasing age a greater proportion of non-maritime species enter the dune community, the exact nature of these species being determined to some extent by the acidity or alkalinity of the dune soil. Many of them can be regarded as "grass-heath" species which combine to give a dune pasture. In a comparison (46) of species lists for grey dunes at Blakeney (anon-calcareous dune region in eastern England) and in Co. Galway in western Ireland (a highly calcareous dune system), only seven were common to the two areas though each supported about forty species. If grazing is at all persistent or severe most of the maritime species disappear. The bracken will invade non-calcareous dune pasture if given an opportunity, and if not checked a closed bracken community can result. Such a community contains a few species not found on adjacent grass dune. The bracken will not, however, descend into damp hollows where there may be winter flooding. Once bracken is established on a dune system its further spread is almost wholly by vegetative means. On Braunton Burrows the mean rate of extension was found to be about 49 cm per year (56) so that its advance is slow but sure.

The flat grassland machair of Scotland is essentially a vegetation-land form complex forming shallow sand pasture overlying other substrata. The sand is highly calcareous so that some species such as *Carex arenaria* and *Tortula ruraliformis* (moss) are reduced or lacking. There are some distinctive species including *Achillea millefolium, Galium verum, Euphrasia* spp., *Trifolium repens* etc., but Gimingham (18) points out that machair is best distinguished by less constant species that fall into several groups:

(1) Species associated with a wet soil or high water table, e.g. *Salix*
     repens, *Carex flacca*.

(2) Orchids.

(3) Annuals and species of open communities.

(4) A few arctic-alpines, e.g. *Dryas octopetala*, *Oxytropis halleri*.

On acid soils heath vegetation develops, usually following on after the grassland stage (Walney) or direct from the Ammophiletum (Studland, Dorset). In
such a heath both *Calluna vulgaris* and *Erica cinerea* are conspicuous elements.
On the continent *Calluna* may be associated with *Genista littoralis* or *Ulex*
europeus. In Sweden the sand heath is characterised by the presence of *Fest-*
uca polesica and *Corynephorus canescens* (41.) Associated species in the heath
stage are *Agrostis* sp., Sand sedge (*Carex arenaria*), Wavy hairgrass (*Deschamp-*
sia flexuosa), Dwarf furze (*Ulex gallii*), and Gorse (*U. europeaus*). It is,
however, impossible to provide a "typical" list because of the great local
variations.

Dune scrub can be regarded as the fore-runner to indigenous forest, though in
Great Britain even the scrub phase is not common. It consists of any of the
spinous shrubs which can grow on light sandy soils. The Burnet rose (*Rosa*
spinosissina) is a common species on calcareous dunes, whilst Bramble (*Rubus*
sp.), *Ulex* (Gorse), Blackthorn (*Prunus spinosa*), other species of wild rose,
and Elder (*Sambucus*) are also common components. There is only one shrub
characteristically confined to the maritime dune habitat. This is the Sea
buckthorn, *Hippophäe rhamnoides*, which is only indigenous on British east
coast dunes. It is very much more abundant on continental maritime dunes,
where it is often associated with Privet (*Ligustrum vulgare*) and the two build
up a form of macchia. With the reduction in rabbits from myxomatosis, *Hippo-*
phae is invading more and more dune systems and is almost proving a nuisance
(54).

On the Dutch dunes the final stage is a low birch wood with *Hippophäe*, *Euony-*
mus, *Ligustrum*, *Cratageus* and *Berberis* into which the oak, *Quercus robur*, may
eventually enter if the soil is poor in lime (6). On the French Atlantic coast
dunes the final stage is a *Quercus ilex* woodland or a conifer woodland of
Pinus pinaster (14). In the Studland dunes, birch is to be found now and these
trees may be the fore-runners of a birchwood. The final stage in northern
Europe (and this would presumably apply also to Great Britain if the opportun-

ity were available) is conifer forest or deciduous woodland which can be regarded as belonging to the Quercetum atlanticum in one or more of its forms.

On the Atlantic coast of the U.S.A. dune scrub is the major fore-runner to
dune forest, but neither scrub nor forest has received the amount of study
they merit. On the northern dunes of New Brunswick the final stage is a conifer forest. On the New Jersey dunes red cedar and the pine *P. rigida* represent the final stage, the former species continuing further south where it is
associated with *Ilex opaca, Quercus lyrata, Acer rubrum* and *Prunus serotina*
with the vines *Ampelopsis, Vitis* and *Tecoma radicans*. The forest on Assateague Island (27) is dominated by *Pinus taeda* with *Quercus falcata, Ilex opaca*
and *Vaccinium atrococcum*. Going farther south *Q. virginiana* replaces *Q. falcata* and *Ilex vomitoria* replaces *I. opaca*. Here in these south eastern dunes
one also finds *Quercus laurifolia* and *Carpinus caroliniana*. The oaks are typ-
ically festooned with the lichen *Usnea* and the bromeliad *Tillandsia usneoides*.

CRYPTOGAMIC VEGETATION

Sand dunes would not normally be regarded as a habitat in which many fungi
could be found. Perhaps because of this relatively little work has been carried out upon them. When a list was made for the dunes of Scolt Head Island,
it was found that there were no less than 15 Pyrenomycetes, 3 Discomycetes, 12
Fungi Imperfecti, 20 rust fungi, 5 smut fungi, 20 Agarics, 4 puff ball species,
and the Stinkhorn, *Phallus impudicus*. Seven species of slime fungi (Myceto-
zoa) were also recorded. Whether this is typical of dune areas as a whole it
is not possible to say, but it could be expected that the tall grasses, especially of the grey dune phase, would stop evaporation and keep the soil remains
sufficiently moist for even agarics to grow satisfactorily. A number of the
species found are of course parasites upon members of the phanerogamic vegetation (see also p. 208 for soil fungi). There is, however, also some evidence that open sand may be moister than that of grey dune, probably associated with no transpiration loss and a higher surface dew formation.

An interesting problem is presented by the development of the diatom flora of
sand dunes. This has been studied by Round (50,51) for Braunton Burrows and
Harlech (we are only concerned here with the actual dunes, not the "slacks",
for which see p. 174). On the dunes the diatom flora is restricted to the

mosses, and it was shown that this epiphytic flora had been derived from the existing damp sand flora of the dune hollows or slacks.

SUCCESSION

The dune succession as described above is quite clearly a prisere, and since it develops on sand it is often known as a Psammosere. The principal communities of the European succession are shown schematically on p. 172, though this "ideal" sequence is rarely found. On the west coast mobility of the dunes and the resulting interaction of dune and slack vegetation make for great complexity (see p. 176).

When grey dune or older dune pasture suffer a blow-out, provided the entire dune is not eroded away the blow-out may recolonise naturally and new dune builds up if there is still a source of sand. Under such circumstances one has an example of a cyclic process (see schema, next page).

The use of biological spectra has been referred to previously (see pp. 9, 10 and 15), and when such spectra are calculated for dunes and slacks, it is seen that the vegetation of European dunes, like that of salt marshes, is essentially a hemicryptophyte flora. On the U.S.A. Atlantic dunes the flora has a high proportion of phanerophytes.

Spectra for Newborough Warren (after Ranwell)

	Ph.	Ch.	H.	G.	H.	Th.
Dunes	4	11	40	5	0	40
Slacks	0	9	57	9	9	16

There is commonly a high proportion of annuals (Therophytes) upon the dunes. These are primarily spring and early summer plants completing their growth and setting seed after the damp winter and before the onset of the dry summer.

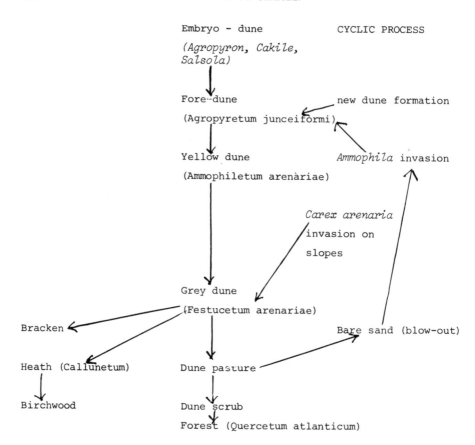

DUNE SLACKS

One of the characteristic features of dunes are the damp or wet hollows, commonly called slacks, left between successive dune ridges (Fig. 7.6), or which
have been formed as a result of complete blow-outs. In such places the ground
water may reach the surface throughout the year or only in the winter months,
and this undoubtedly greatly influences the vegetation, not only as regards
composition and distribution, but the plants themselves are often depauperate
as compared with the same species elsewhere.

When water is present throughout the year, a pond of varying size is present
with its attendant aquatic plants. In the water one finds species of Pondweed
(Potamogeton), Shore-weed (Littorella uniflora) and, in some localities, Horned pondweed (Zannichellia palustris), whilst round the edges the vegetation

does not vary greatly from that found around any inland pond. Where there is
only standing water in the winter or where the soil is marshy, four or five
species of rush (*Juncus*) can be found together with a variety of other marsh
plants, including orchids (59). Such places usually have but a minor proportion
of strictly maritime plants such as Sea milkwort (*Glaux maritima*), *Juncus balticus*, Sharp rush (*J. acutus*), Sea rush (*J. maritimus*), Sea club-rush (*Scirpus
maritimus*) and Brookweed (*Samolus valerandi*), unless open to occasional
flooding by the sea. A number of species of the moss genus *Hypnum* occur in
such localities and it is here also that some hepatics, particularly *Riccia*
has tended to disappear.

On Braunton Burrows three separate rush communities have been listed (66), the
Juncetum maritimi, Juncetum acuti and Holoschoenetum vulgaris. There is also
a damp pasture - *Carex nigra-Hydrocotyle* community and another community co-
dominated by Buck's-horn plantain (*Plantago coronopus*) and Hairy hawkbit
(*Leontodon leysseri*). The latter community forms a sparse soil cover and many
of the associated plants possess a rosette habit or are creeping. The damp
pasture is to be found in the most landward of the slacks or even landward of
the last dune ridge. The composition varies greatly and, in some cases at
least, differences are brought about by variations of level and flooding.
Thus where there is prolonged flooding, *Hydrocotyle* is often the dominant
plant.

Whilst most of the species to be found in dune slacks are common or reasonably
common, there are a number of interesting varieties that have been recorded
from various parts of Europe. These include Coral-root (*Corallorhiza trifida*),
Lesser twayblade (*Listera cordata*), *Cicendia filiformis* and Yellow bartsia
(*Parentucellia viscosa*), whilst in the Caithness dunes there is *Primula
scotica* and *Polygonum minus*. The actual vegetation of a slack is primarily
determined by chance in which man and cattle can play a major part.

In many dune systems one can recognise three levels of plant growth in relation to the water table as well as the dunes

(a) Semi-aquatic. Water table never more than 0.5 m below surface and often
     flooded so that aquatics and semi-aquatics occur.
(b) Wet slacks with the water table not more than 1 m down. Bryophytes and
     rushes are typical of this type.

(c) Dry slacks with grasses and the water table 1-2 m down.

Algae are to be found in this habitat, though very little work has been carried out on the algae of dune ponds. Myxophyceae, *Vaucheria*, *Chara*, *Mougeotia*
and *Tribonema* have all been recorded, and Round (50,51) has listed the diatom
flora of such slacks. Because the water level fluctuates and the ponds may
dry up, there is an absence of members of the Chlorococcales and Volvocales.
In a Lancashire slack, the benthic (bottom-living) diatomaceous flora was well
developed, and although the number of species was small, the actual number of
individuals was very large. The samples from slacks at Harlech contained
fewer species than either of those in Lancashire or Devon.

It appears that the damp sand flora is essentially a remnant of the pond
flora, which is not surprising in view of the fluctuating water level, with
the addition of a single variety of a species of *Nitzschia*. On the newly
exposed floor of slacks, algae and mosses are commonly the first colonists.

On the west coasts of Great Britain, the damp soil of the slacks is colonised
by a carpet of the Creeping willow, *Salix repens*, which forms a Salicetum
repentis (Fig. 6.6). *S. atrocinerea* is rather less common in this type of
habitat. With the disappearance of rabbits *Alnus* also invades such areas. In
the Dutch dune area (Terschelling Is.) the Salicetum is preceded by dwarf
shrub valleys with *Oxycoccus marcocarpus*. The Salicetum slacks reach a climax
at the rear of the dunes with *S. cinerea*, *S. aurita* and *Betula pubescens* (63).
If the surrounding dunes are stable, no sand is blown on to the *Salix* plants,
and the surface soil remains wet, supporting a variety of marsh species together with mosses and liverworts. Peripheral growth of *S. repens* is very slow,
so that its capacity to spread from damp slacks to the adjacent dunes is extremely limited. If sand is blown onto the *Salix*, hummocks are formed through
which the shoots of the willow grow up. Since seedling establishment of *Salix*
only occurs on moist ground, it is clear that the optimum habitat for entry
into a dune system is quite different to the conditions required for optimum
growth. With the production of hummocks, the soil becomes drier and the nature of the community changes.

It appears that *S. repens* cannot thrive in permanently water-logged habitats,
and its lower limit in slacks is therefore set by the degree of water-logging.
This is in contrast to a suggestion (53) that water deficiency determines plant

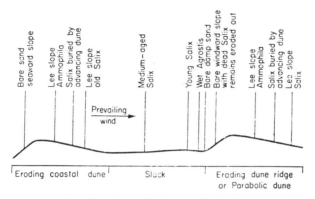

FIG. 6.6. *Distribution of dune and slack vegetation in a typical coastal region of Newborough Warren (after Ranwell).*

limits in slacks, though this may be true for species other than *S. repens*. With the creeping willow, so long as the surface soil is not water-logged in the main growing season, the plants grow rather higher, whereas in the lower, temporarily wet areas, the plants remain dwarfed. Salinity may be a factor, especially in slacks nearest the sea, since the seeds germinate in 30 percent sea water but rarely if the salinity is much higher.

In acidic dunes, the slacks eventually carry a vegetation dominated by *S. atrocinerea* and *Betula pubescens* (e.g. Studland in Dorset) into which other species may enter. Thus Gresswell (23) reports the presence of the Larger wintergreen (*Pyrola rotundifolia* ssp. *maritima*) and Yellow bird's-nest (*Monotropa hypopithys*) living on the Lancashire dunes on the humus formed from decay of the willow leaves. Ranwell (44) also records the entry of *Pyrola* into the Anglesey dunes, where it is possible that a *Pyrola-Salix* community will develop. With the advent of still more sand, larger *Salix* dunes are formed and the associated flora becomes very similar to that of the Ammophiletum, the only essential difference being in the dominant.

Particular attention has been paid (44) to the *Salicetum repentis* of the dune slacks at Newborough Warren (Anglesey). The pattern of the vegetation suggested that cyclic changes occurred, and that the sequence depends on whether there is a mobile *Ammophila* dune associated with a wet slack (Fig. 6.7), or turf associated with a dry slack. In the former case it was estimated that the full cycle takes about 80 years to complete.

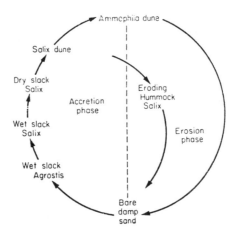

FIG. 6.7. *Cyclic sub-seral succession in the mobile dune-slack complex at Newborough Warren (after Ranwell).*

A more recent study (29) of changes in dune slack vegetation has been carried out using a combination of permanent plots and successive mapping. Between the years 1956 and 1968 it became evident that both progressive succession and retrogression had taken place. Some of the changes may have been cyclic but there was a general trend towards either *Salix repens (± Hippophäe)* or *Phragmites* as the following schema shows.

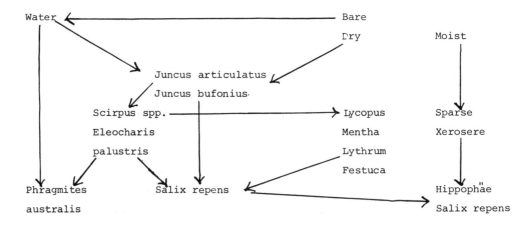

The final sequence in this area is extremely complex and although the main dune succession may appear simple, when one comes to analyse the slacks, and probably also the lows (see following), the story may be exceedingly complex. The mobility of the dunes on the European west coast makes for this complexity,

which is less evident on British east coast dune systems where the spatial
succession is in close approximation to the temporal succession.

In the U.S.A. the comparable physiographic features are termed swales. In
New Brunswick dunes *Festuca rubra* and *Fragaria virginiana* are characteristic
plants. In New Jersey damp swales are occupied by *Carex* sp., *Cyperus*, *Juncus*,
Oenothera perennis, *Osmunda* sp. etc. In older swales *Rhus toxicodendron*,
Myrica pennsylvanica and *Juniperus virginiana* are to be found whilst in the
oldest *Vaccinium corymbosum*, *Acer rubra*, *Rosa rugosa* and *Dryopteris thely-*
pteris are typical species (31). On Assateague the swales contain *Juncus marg-*
inatus biflorus, *J. gerardi*, *Pteridium aquilinum*, *Osmunda regalis* and *Panicum*
sphaerocarpum. It is quite evident from this brief account that the inter-
dune depressions on both sides of the Atlantic have very different floras,
and on the Atlantic U.S.A. coast there is a significant floristic change from
north to south.

LOWS

On the Norfolk coast, other depressions called "lows" have been described by
the present writer (17). These differ physiographically from dune slacks in
that they are depressions enclosed by two laterals, usually with a break in
the shingle laterals so that at high spring tides the sea has access. If the
laterals are dune-covered such lows look very much like slacks. Because of
the access of salt water, their flora is rather different from that of true
slacks and it differs somewhat from the flora of adjacent dunes and salt marshes. The soil varies from bare sand to mud, the more sandy lows being adjacent to dunes. After flooding by the tide, water may remain in the low for
some time and in the summer it is not uncommon to find salt efflorescence on
the soil surface. Where there is a proportion of shingle in the soil, the
typical species of the habitat are *Limonium bellidifolium*, Sea heath (*Frank-*
enia levis), and Shrubby seablite (*Suaeda fruticosa*), though this last-named
is a relic from the drift-line. Where the soil is more sandy, dwarf and
prostrate forms of Seablite (*Suaeda maritima* var. *macrocarpa*) and Glasswort
(*Salicornia prostrata*, *S. appressa*) are predominant, though the erect species
may also be present. Other plants of this habitat are Sea poa (*Puccinellia*
maritima) and var. *parvifolia* of *Halimione portulaccoides* (Sea purslane).

BIOTA

In conclusion, a few words may be said about the biota of the dunes. Birds
play a part in that they are almost certainly responsible for the entry of
scrub species, since most of them possess succulent fruits. An excessive gull
population can change an *Ammophila* dune to an area of annuals such as *Stellaria media*. Enrichment may be so great that slack species such as *Dactylorchis* can grow. Reference has already been made to the effect of grazing (52) and
the subsequent perpetuation of a grass heath stage on old dunes. In the past
browsing by rabbits produced a tussocky appearance to bushes of *Suaeda fruticosa* (7) near the dunes. When no grazing takes place (7,45,66,66) dune grasses,
especially *Festuca rubra*, and Sand sedge (*Carex arenaria*) become more luxuriant and many of the herbs drop out, presumably because of light competition.
The changes essentially affect secondary species and there is no reversal of
the ordinary dune succession. Ranwell (45) reports that at Newborough Warren
(Anglesey), decrease in rabbit browsing brought about an increase in *Festuca
rubra* and a decrease in *Agrostis tenuis*. The sharp reaction of the last-
named species to grazing, together with evidence from other areas, suggests
that at Anglesey the species is near the limit of its ecological range (see
also effect of grazing on cliff vegetation, p. 256). Worms may be common in
wet slacks and in the *Salix repens* zone at Newborough the biomass of worms per
acre approximated to that of woodland. Worms and arthropods undoubtedly contribute to the aeration and fertility of these soils that suffer temporary
water-logging. The invertebrate population may be very considerable, e.g. up
to 2000 species may occur. On the Terschelling dunes 368 arthropods were recorded (Fig. 6.8).

One other example of plant-animal relationships is that of the cinnabar moth
and the Ragwort, *Senecio jacobaea* (7). When the caterpillars are abundant the
Senecio plants are so decimated that very little seed is set. Fewer plants
are available the subsequent year and they become completely destroyed. In
the following years, the caterpillars have no food, and so the moth population
decreases to the point when the *Senecio* can re-establish and so the cycle
continues.

Finally, man with his increasing pressures on the coast is responsible for considerable dune damage especially in areas dominated by *Agropyron junceiforme*
and *Ammophila arenaria*.

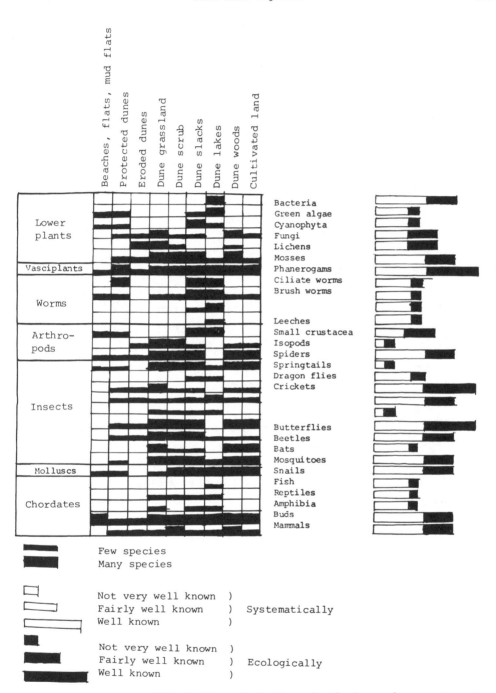

FIG. 6.8. *Distribution of plants and animals on dune systems at Voorne (Netherlands) illustrating densities, ecological knowledge and taxonomy (after Adriani and van der Maarel).*

REFERENCES

1   ADRIANI M.J. and VAN DER MAAREL, Voorne in de Branding. Sticht. Wetensch-
     app. Duinonder. Oostvoorne. 104pp. (1968).

2   BRISE E.L. and GIMINGHAM C.H., Changes in the structure of bryophytic
     communities with the progess of succession on sand dunes. *Trans. Brit.
     Bryol. Soc.*, 2(4), 523 (1955).

3   BRISE E.L., LANDSBERG S.Y. and GIMINGHAM C.H., The effects of burial by
     sand on dune mosses. *Trans. Brit. Bryol. Soc.*, 3(2), 285 (1957).

4   BRUCE E.M., The vegetation of the sand dunes between Embleton and Newton.
     The Vasculum, 17, 94 (1931).

5   CAREY A.E. and OLIVER F.W., *Tidal Lands: a Study of Shore Problems.*
     London. Blackie (1918).

6   CHAPMAN V.J., *Suaeda fruticosa* Forsk. in *Biological Flora of the British
     Isles. J. Ecol.*, 35, 293-302 (1947).

7   CHAPMAN V.J., The plant ecology of Scolt Head Island in *Scolt Head
     Island*. Ed. J.A. Steers. Heffer. Camb. (1962).

8   DOING-KRAFT H., Zonerung in landschap en plantengroei van de Duinen bij
     Bloemendaal en Velsen. *Levende Natuur*, 61(10), 219-227 (1958).

9   ELLISTON-WRIGHT F.R., Ecological studies, Braunton Burrows, in MARTIN W.
     K., and FRASER G.T., *Flora of Devon*. Arbroath (1939).

10   FOTHERGILL P.G., The Blyth-Seaton sluice sand-dunes. *The Vasculum*, 20, 23
     (1934).

11   GÉHU J.M., Un site célèbre de la côte Nord Bretonne: Le Sillon de Talbert
     (C-du-N). Observations phytosociologiques et écologiques. *Lab. Mar.
     Dinard*, Fasc. 46, 193-113 (1960).

12   GÉHU J.M., La végétation psammophile des îles de Honat et de Hoedic.
     Bull. Soc. Bot. Nord Fr., 17, 238-266 (1964).

13   GÉHU J.M. and GHESTEM A., La mineralisation expérimentale de l'azote
     organique de deux systèmes pédobioligiques littoraux naturels (Dunes et
     Prés Salès). *Ann. Inst. Pasteur.* 109 (suppl.). 136-152 (1965).

14   GÉHU J.M. and PETIT M., Notes sur la végétation des dunes littorales de
     Charante et de Vendée. *Bull. Soc. Bot. Nord Fr.*, 18, 69-88 (1965).

15   GEMMELL A.R., GREIG-SMITH P. and GIMINGHAM C.H., A note on the behaviour
     of *Ammophila arenaria* (L.) Link, in relation to sand-dune formation.
     Trans. Proc. Bot. Soc. Edin., 36(2), 132 (1953).

16   GIMINGHAM C.H., The role of *Barbula fallax* Hedw. and *Bryum pendulum* Schp.
     in sand-dune fixation. *Trans. Brit. Bryol. Soc.*, 1(2), 70 (1948).

17   GIMINGHAM C.H., Contributions to the maritime ecology of St. Cyrus, Kin-
      cardineshire. II. The sand dunes. *Trans. Proc. Bot. Soc. Edin.*, 35(4),
      387-414 (1951).

18   GIMINGHAM C.H., Plant communities of the Machair and floristic relation-
      ships with non-dune vegetation in *Sand Dune Machair*. Nature Environ. Res.
      Counc. Inst. of Terrest. Ecol. Norwich (1974).

19   GIMINGHAM C.H., GEMMELL A.R. and GREIG-SMITH P., The vegetation of a
      sand-dune system in the outer Hebrides. *Trans. Proc. Soc. Edin.*, 35(1),
      82 (1948).

20   GOOD R.D.'O., Contributions towards a survey of the plants and animals
      of the South Haven peninsula, Studland Heath, Dorset. *J. Ecol.*, 23, 361-
      405 (1935).

21   GREIG-SMITH P., GEMMELL A.R. and GIMINGHAM C.H., Tussock formation in
      Ammophila arenaria (L.) Link. *New Phyt.*, 46(2), 262-268 (1947).

22   GRESSWELL R.K., The geomorphology of the south-west Lancashire coast
      line. *Geog. J.*, 90, 335-348 (1937).

23   GRESSWELL R.K., *Sandy shores in south Lancashire.* Liverpool (1953).

24   HARSHBERGER J.W., Phytogeographical survey of North America. 2nd Ed. repr.
      Weimar (1958).

25   HEERDT P.F. VAN and MORZER BRUYNS M.F., A biocenological investigation in
      the yellow dune region of Terschelling. *Tijdschr. Ent.*, 103, 225-75
      (1960).

26   HEPBURN I., The vegetation of the sand dunes of the Camel Estuary, north
      Cornwall. *J. Ecol.*, 32, 180-192 (1945).

27   HIGGINS E.A.T., RAPPLEYE R.D. and BROWN R.G., The flora and ecology of
      Assateague Island. Bull. A-172, Univ. Maryl. Agric. Expt. Stat. 70pp.

28   LANDSBERG S.Y., The orientation of dunes in Britain and Denmark in
      relation to wind. *Geog. J.*, 122(2), 176-189 (1956).

29   LONDO G., Successive mapping of dune slack vegetation. *Vegetatio*, 29, 51-
      61 (1974).

30   McLEAN R.C., The ecology of the maritime lichens at Blakeney Point, Nor-
      folk. *J. Ecol.*, 3, 129-148 (1915).

31   MARTIN W.E., The vegetation of Island Beach State Park, New Jersey. *Ecol.
      Monog.*, 29(1), 1-46 (1959).

32   MELTON F.A., A tentative classification of sand dunes and its application
      to dune history in the southern high plains. *J. Geol.*, 48(2), 113-145
      (1940).

33   MOORE S.J., The ecology of the Ayreland of Bride, Isle of Man. *J. Ecol.*,

19, 115-136 (1931).

34   NORDHAGEN R., Studien über die Maritime vegetation Norwegens. Bergens
     Mus. Arbok 1939-40 Natur vitens. rekke, Nr 2. 123 pp. (1940).

35   OLIVER F.W., Blakeney Point Reports, 1913-1929. *Trans. Norf. Norw. Nat.*
     Soc., Vols. of same years.

36   OLIVER F.W. and SALISBURY E.J., *Topography and Vegetation of Blakeney*
     Point, Norfolk. Lond. Univ. Coll.

37   OOSTING H.J., Ecological processes and vegetation of the maritime strand
     in the south-eastern U.S.A. *Bot. Rev.*, 20, 226-62 (1954).

38   ORR M.Y., Kenfig Burrows: an ecological study. *Scot. Bot. Rev.*, 1, 209
     (1912).

39   PEARSALL W.H., North Lancashire sand dunes. *Naturalist*, p. 201 (1934).

40   PEMADASA M.A. and LOVELL P.H., Interference in populations of some dune
     annuals. *J. Ecol.*, 62(3) 855-868 (1974).

41   PETTERSSON B., Maritime Sands. Act. Phytogeog. Suec. 50, 105-110 (1965).

42   RANWELL D., Movement of vegetated sand dunes at Newborough Warren, Angle-
     sey. *J. Ecol.*, 46, 83-100 (1958).

43   RANWELL D., Newborough Warren, Anglesey. 1. The dune system and dune
     slack habitat. *J. Ecol.*, 47, 571-602 (1959).

44   RANWELL D., Newborough Warren, Anglesey. 2. Plant associes and succession
     cycles of the sand dune and dune slack vegetation. *J. Ecol.*, 48, 117-142
     (1960).

45   RANWELL D., Newborough Warren, Anglesey. 3. Changes in the vegetation on
     parts of the dune system after the loss of rabbits by myxomatosis.
     J. Ecol., 48, 385-396 (1960).

46   RANWELL D., *Ecology of Salt Marshes and Sand Dunes*. Chapm. & Hall (1972).

47   RANWELL D., Machair in relation to the British sand dune series in *Sand*
     Dune Machair. Nature Envir. Res. Council, Inst. of Terr. Ecol. (1974).

48   RICHARDS P.W., Notes on the ecology of the bryophytes and lichens at
     Blakeney Point, Norfolk. *J. Ecol.*, 17, 127-140 (1929).

49   ROUND F.E., The algal flora of Massom's slack, Freshfield, Lancashire.
     Arch. f. Hydrobiol., 54(4), 462 (1958).

50   ROUND F.E., Observations on the diatom flora of Braunton Burrows, N.
     Devon. *Hydrobiol.*, 11(2), 119-127 (1958).

51   ROUND F.E., A note on the diatom flora of Harlech sand dunes. *J. Roy.*
     Micr. Soc., 77 3/4, 130-135 (1959).

52   ROWAN W., Note on the food plants of rabbits on Blakeney Point, Norfolk.
     J. Ecol., 1, 273-274 (1913).

53 SALISBURY E.J., *Downs and Dunes*. Bell (1952).

54 SKINNER E.A., Survey of the dunes between Meggies Burn and Seaton Sluice. *The Vasculum*, 20, 122 (1934).

55 SMITH H.T.U., Coast Dunes. Coastal Geog. Conf. 1954. Off. Naval Res. 51-56 (1954).

56 STEERS J.A., The Culbin Sands. *Geog. J.*, 90, 498-528 (1937).

57 STEERS J.A., *The Coastline of England and Wales*. C.U. Press (1946).

58 TANSLEY A.G., *The British Islands and their Vegetation*. C.U. Press (1939).

59 VAN DER MAAREL E. and WESTHOFF V., The vegetation of the dunes near Oost-voorne (The Netherlands) with a vegetation map. *Wentia*, 12, 1-61 (1964).

60 VAN DIEREN J.A., *Organogene Dunenbildung*. (1934).

61 WATSON W., Cryptogamic vegetation of the sand dunes of the west coast of England. *J. Ecol.*, 6, 126-143 (1918).

62 WESTHOFF V., Gezelschappen met hontige gewassen in de duinen en langs de binnenduinrand. *Dendrol. Jaarbk.*, 1952, 9-49 (1952).

63 WESTHOFF V., Die Dunenbepflanzung in den Niederlanden. *Angew. Pflanzen-sociol.*, 17, 14-21 (1961).

64 WESTHOFF V., VAN LEEUWEN C.G. and ADRIANI M.J., Enkele Aspekten van vege-tatie en Bodem der Duinen van Goeree, in het bijonder de Contactgordels Tussen zont en Zoet milieu. *R.I.V.O.N. Mededel.*, 109, 47-91 (1961).

65 WHITE D.J.B., Some observations on the vegetation of Blakeney Point, Norfolk, following the disappearance of the rabbits in 1954. *J. Ecol.*, 49(1), 113-118 (1961).

66 WILLIS A.J., FOLKES B.F., HOPE-SIMPSON J.F. and YEMM E.W., Braunton Burrows: the dune system and its vegetation. *J. Ecol.*, 47(1), 1-24, 249-288 (1959).

CHAPTER 7

SAND DUNES-THE ENVIRONMENT

The principal feature of the dune environment is the sand that forms the
dunes, because from it stem nearly all the other characteristics that make up
the peculiarities of the habitat. The actual major physical and biological
processes concerned in dune formation have already been outlined in the previous chapter, but there are some aspects, such as sand movement and soil formation, that need to be considered in more detail.

WIND AND SAND MOVEMENT

The material of which the dunes are built is composed of grains of silica in
the case of siliceous dunes, and silica grains mixed with a varying proportion
of shell fragments in the case of calcareous dunes.

The material, whether it be silica grains or shell fragments, varies in size
and its distribution is therefore dependent upon wind velocity, the larger
the grain or fragment the greater the wind velocity necessary to move it.
Since size determines how far movement occurs, the actual proportion of the
different sized grains in any part of a dune system depends on the mean average wind velocity. An experiment to demonstrate this phenomenon can easily
be set up with the aid of a hair drier placed at varying distances from a
heap of sand, the resulting wind velocities being measured by means of a portable anemometer. Table 7.1, which gives the figures for the different sized
grains in the Southport and Blakeney dunes (26) provides and example of how the
proportion of grains moved is related to the mean average wind velocity.

Grains in categories 1 and 2 generally roll, whilst those in the other size
classes are often carried in the air. Grains of group 4 require a minimum
wind speed of 1 m.p.h. before they will start to move. With the greater velocity of the prevailing westerly winds at Southport, it can be seen why there
is a higher proportion of larger and heavier grains. Since movement will only
take place when the grains are dry, the time of exposure to both wind and sun
is of considerable importance. As the dunes increase in age and become more

TABLE 7.1

Proportion of Different Sized Grains in Dune System

	Grain Size	Southport	Blakeney
		percent	percent
1	Over 1 mm	1.2	0
2	0.3 - 1 mm	90.5	17.9
3	0.25 - 0.3 mm	3.0	68.9
4	0.2 - 0.25 mm	3.0	8.9
5	> 0.2 mm	2.0	4.1

closely clothed with vegetation, surface water loss is reduced, not only because of decreased surface evaporation, but also because the gradual and
steady increase of humus increases the water-holding capacity of the sand and
it therefore dries out less frequently as well as being less mobile.

It should be evident that in any dune area the annual incidence of gales and
their direction, as also the direction of the prevailing winds, is of the
greatest significance. Upon these rests the sifting process that is apparent,
upon inspection, in all dunes, the coarser and heavier particles comprising
the fore-dunes, the finer and lighter grains forming the bulk of the landward
dunes. The construction of a *wind rose** is therefore almost a necessity in
any ecological study of sand dunes.

On a very windy coast there will be a proportion of large grains in the dune
and therefore water loss will be great, not only through drainage but also
through evaporation. In addition there will be excessive sand movement so
that the net result is a sand dune environment which is the least favourable
for plants. As the dunes become older and more fore-dunes form, the size of
the deposited particles on the hind-dunes decreases as only the lighter ones
now reach them. A soil profile on an old dune should therefore yield an in-

* Term applied to a diagram that shows the percentage of winds
coming from different compass points over a year.

creasing proportion of larger particles with increasing depth. In calcareous
dunes, shell fragments are commonly lighter than siliceous grains and hence
are carried farther inland, but again the proportion of shell will be higher
near the surface as the strata below represent the younger stages of the dune.

A clear understanding of sand movement and the effect of vegetation in relation to dune formation cannot be achieved without making actual field observations with a portable anemometer. If this is done it will be found that results comparable to the following are likely to be obtained: the wind velocity
will increase with height above the dune surface but it will also vary depending on the location (windward face, crest, leeward or in a slack) (Fig. 7.1).

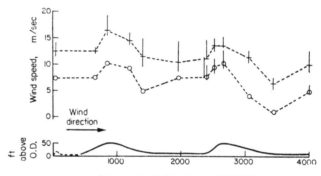

FIG. 7.1. *Wind speeds recorded at 5 cm (0————0) and 1 m*
(+————+) above the ground surface on profile T1-T4 during a
south-west gale of 40 knots (20 m/sec) at Newborough Warren.
The verticals on the curves show the range of speeds recorded at
individual sites. The point where the dotted lines cut the vert-
icals is the estimated average speed at the site (after Ranwell).

The effect of vegetation is to increase the difference between surface and
upper velocities. Thus over bare dunes the velocity at the surface may be
half that at 2 ft above, whilst with sparse Marram the surface velocity may be
one-quarter that at 2 ft above. The mere presence of the vegetation therefore
lowers the surface wind velocity considerably. For example, Salisbury (26)
records a wind velocity of 8.3 m.p.h. at 2 in. on bare dune whilst in adjacent
Marram it was 1.7 m.p.h. at the same height. In the case of marram grass the
individual tufts can have, as may be expected, a considerable effect upon wind
velocity. Thus a wind velocity of 4.4 m.p.h. in front of a tuft can drop to
2.3 m.p.h. behind the tuft. Figures such as these indicate the great importance of aerial shoots as obstacles leading to sand accumulation (Fig. 6.1).

Unless the root systems are extremely extensive they are not nearly so efficient a protection against sand removal as are the shoots.

DUNE MOVEMENT

The brief background of sand grain movement and the factors controlling such
movement given above enable us to progress to a consideration of the movement
of dunes as a whole.* So far as coastal dunes in Great Britain are concerned,
the rate of movement appears to vary considerably, obviously depending on
mean wind velocities, the degree of vegetation cover and degree of protection
by other windward dunes. Maximum dune movement at Morfa Harlech is around
3.7 m/annum, at Morfa Dyffryn 6.1 m/annum. Much lower values have been recorded for Great Crosby dunes (1.1 m/annum) and Norfolk dunes (1.5 m/annum),
whilst at Freshfield higher values 5.5-7.3 m/annum) represent the situation
(20).

One of the more detailed studies of dune movement has been carried out over a
period of 3 years by Ranwell (20) on sand dunes at Newborough Warren in Anglesey.
It has already been noted that wind velocity varies with topography (Fig. 7.1)
so one can anticipate that the movement of different parts of a dune system
will also vary. Using stakes placed firmly in the sand and making careful
measurements Ranwell was able to show that the rates varied from zero to 65 ft
per annum, the maximum rates being on the leeward side up to the crest, since
it is in this region that the sand is most mobile. There is no doubt that
movement takes place also on the windward side but as the sand is continually
being added here from the beach it is less obvious. In the slacks behind the
dunes there is little or no sand movement (Fig. 7.2). Where dune movement of
the nature described above is taking place the windward side of the dunes is
steeper than the landward. This contrasts with the kind of profile found on
shingle beaches, where, as a result of wave action and water percolation, the
lee side may be much steeper than the seaward side (see p. 239).

In any dune system the fluctuations in movement, and the effect of such fluctuations upon the dune profile, can be considerable, especially over a single

        * More detail will be found in KING C.A.M., *Coasts and Beaches*.
Arnold (1959).

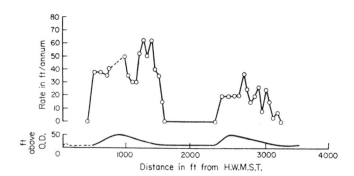

FIG. 7.2. *Rates of inland movement of different parts of a dune section in Newborough Warren (after Ranwell).*

gale period, and it is therefore the annual changes that are the more meaning-
ful. The amount of sand annually deposited on an accreting lee slope may
amount to 2-3 ft, whilst on very mobile dunes the windward slope may decrease
in height by a comparable amount as a result of erosion. During a gale great
changes can occur and variations in level of 1½ ft are not impossible. Some
indication of the extent of short period changes is provided in Fig. 7.3
showing the height of sand at certain pole sites over a period of years. The

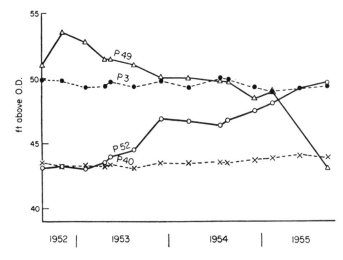

FIG. 7.3. *Short-period changes in sand level at a selection of
different pole sites on the dune transects at Newborough Warren.
P49, a vegetated crest site changing from accretion to erosion.
P3, a non-vegetated crest site. P52, a rapidly accreting vegetated lee slope site. P40, a slowly accreting vegetated lee slope
site (after Ranwell).*

very rapid changes of an eroding vegetated dune (p. 156) and of a vegetated
accretion lee site (p. 160) show how, on the one hand, a dune can be eroded
away to a remanié form, and on the other hand how the Marram (*Ammophila*) and
other plants must be able to respond to considerable smothering. Viable buds
have been recorded in *Agropyron junceiforme* at a depth of 60 cm, which appears
to be maximum covering it will tolerate. *Elymus arenarius* is more sensitive
and a cover of 7-8 cm seems to be the limit (21). In the case of *Ammophila*
seedlings it appears that an accretion rate of 15 cm per year is the maximum
they can tolerate with a further maximum of 2.5-5 cm at any one time (i.e.
any one gale). If accretion stops, the vigour of the *Ammophila* plants is
reduced because the old roots die and are not replaced by new ones as in the
case with continual accretion (16). In the case of *A.breviligulata* there is
abundant seed production, but few seedlings appear, due either to excessive
sand burial immediately after germination, or lack of water later (15).

When sand accumulates behind tufts of Marram, it is the leeward side of the
tuft that received the stimulus and the new shoots grow out (see p.160) on
this side so that the tuft gradually moves in the same direction as the dune.
In some respects this is similar to the movement of shrubby seablite up a
shingle beach (see p. 243). The data obtained from the Newborough dunes is of
the greatest importance in our understanding of the dynamics of dune systems.
However, dune systems vary substantially and for this reason data from other
dunes is greatly to be desired. Much of it can be obtained by simply driving
poles marked in feet and tenths of a foot into the dunes at strategic places.

TEMPERATURE

On the fore-dunes and in the yellow dune phase, where there is open soil, the
soil temperatures may reach values as high as $60^{\circ}C$ in summer. Sand is a poor
conductor of heat and therefore the soil temperature drops very rapidly with
depth, even in the first 5 cm. Dune temperatures also exhibit a daily rhythm
which is very much more pronounced on the sparsely vegetated yellow dunes,
where heat can be absorbed and lost more rapidly than on grey dunes (Fig. 7.4).
These particular temperature records also show that at night the surface temperature can fall below the dew point, so that dew then forms on the surface
and drains down into the sand. This is a different phenomenon to that of internal dew formation when the internal dune temperatures are below the dew

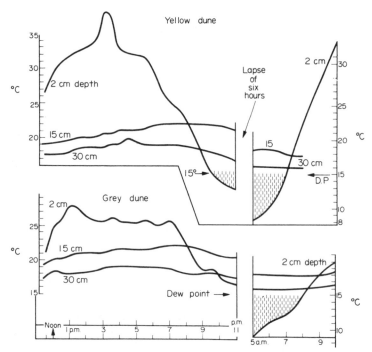

FIG. 7.4. *Dune temperatures showing daily rhythm. Note the fall below the dew point in the surface temperature at night and the more marked extremes in the yellow dune than in the maturer soil of the grey dune (after Salisbury).*

point (see pp. 201 and 249).

The surface sand temperature is affected not only by the degree of plant cover, litter and the amount of sunlight received but also by the rainfall and exposure to wind. Litter, for example, can reduce a summer temperature of the sand from 25°C to 7°C (17). In a *Tortula* matt the summer temperature can be 9°C higher on the south than on the north slope of a dune. In yellow dune with open *Ammophila* maximum temperatures occur at the sand surface whilst in closed *Ammophila* communities the maximum temperatures are some distance above the soil. Rather surprisingly, it seems that a moss mat results in a more extreme microclimate (1). All of these factors need to be taken into account when considering diurnal and seasonal temperature fluctuations.

SOIL FORMATION

Whilst development of the sand to form a soil must commence from the moment of establishment of the first plants, it is evident that, until the dune becomes stabilised, the rate of soil development is going to be very slow. A variety of processes are involved in soil formation. These include leaching, which removes chemicals from the surface layers to lower layers, removal of nutrients by the roots of plants and replenishment of these nutrients together with humus at the surface from dead and decaying plant material.

In the early stages of dune development, removal proceeds at a greater rate than replenishment. Pits dug in the sand generally show a uniform profile which may suggest that little redistribution of nutrients is taking place, whereas in fact the very reverse is the case. To some extent this must be associated with a high percentage pore space, e.g. 40 percent recorded at Braunton Burrows (25). With increasing stabilisation of the dunes the degree of leaching increases because there is no steady supply of new sand, but this leaching will depend to some extent on the vegetation cover, the less the cover the greater the leaching. If trees are either planted on dunes or arrive naturally, their roots will tap the lower soil layers and remove nutrients, and in the case of dune afforestation it is likely that in the first 15-20 years the drain on the soil can be very severe. Subsequently, downward leaching from the litter will tend to restore the balance (33,34).

Effective studies of dune soils can only be carried out if it is possible to give a date, even if only approximate, to the various dune ridges. One obvious way of doing this is by a study of old maps (25), which may show when a dune system was or was not present. It is now also possible to arrive at dune dating by making use of the ^{14}C technique in which the amount of ^{14}C present provides a measure of the age. This is based upon the half-life disintegration period of the ^{14}C atom, and the proportion that is generally present in living material as compared with the amount present in occluded soil organic matter.

WATER RELATIONS

Since sand dunes can be regarded as edaphically dry habitats, the moisture content of the dunes and also the behaviour of the water table is of paramount interest. Digging down into the sand of maritime dunes soon shows that the subsurface layers are moist, this moisture being derived mainly from the process of internal dew formation (see p. 201) as well as from rain. The dry character of the habitat is therefore more apparent than real, and provided plants can rapidly put out long roots (see p. 161) water should not be a major limiting factor. Indeed, it seems evident that on young dunes it is the mobility of the sand and possible damage from sea spray that are more restrictive.

In those systems where the nature of the water table has been studied it appears to be dome-shaped, a feature common to isolated granular deposits where drainage is maximal at the margins (Fig. 7.5). Since the water table

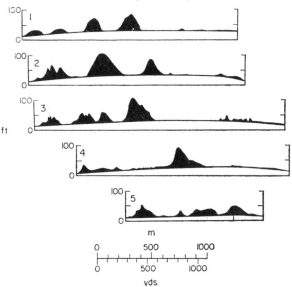

FIG. 7.5. *Profiles across the dune system with slacks, Braunton Burrows. Heights, obtained by survey, are given in feet O.D. The sand above the water table of June 1952 is shown in black (after Willis et al.).*

is close to the surface in the slacks the sand there remains moist and stable, though wind velocities in such places are also much less (p. 187), and would generally be insufficient to move the grains. Although the water table over the dune system as a whole tends to be dome-shaped, minor variations can occur. Thus at the transition from slacks to dunes the water table, especial-ly in winter, undergoes a distinct rise (Fig. 7.6). This is probably associ-ated with the greater accumulation of water in the dune under winter condit-ions together with the greater depth of soil in which water can accumulate.

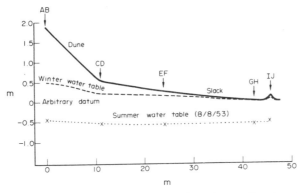

FIG. 7.6. *The free water table levels at the junction between dune and slack on Newborough Warren (after Ranwell).*

The importance of the water table in the slacks in relation to the type of vegetation has already been mentioned (see p. 172). The control of Creeping willow (*Salix repens*) by water-logging is one aspect of this, whilst another is the relationship of wet plant associes, e.g. *Juncus maritimus*, *Agrostis-Juncus articulatus*, and *Littorella-Samolus*, with slacks where the water table is never more than 1 m below the surface. Where the table descends to 1-2 m one finds dry slack associes dominated by *Salix repens* or *Festuca-Calluna*. If the water table descends still deeper true slack communities become replac-ed by dune communities. There is some evidence that plants of dunes and slacks behave differently in respect of transpiration and development of water deficits. Dune plants may be able to regulate transpiration rate more efficiently than slack plants (30). However we still have insufficient inform-ation about this issue. Fig. 7.7 illustrates the distribution of vegetation on dunes in relation to water level.

Experimental work has shown that *Agrostis stolonifera* and *Festuca rubra* grow better under dune than under slack conditions, the former species being less affected by water table level than the latter (13). In the case of *Carex serotina*, *Leonotodon taraxacoides* and *Plantago coronopus* the slack water table is the most significant factor with exchangeable Na^+ and Ca^{++} as the sole

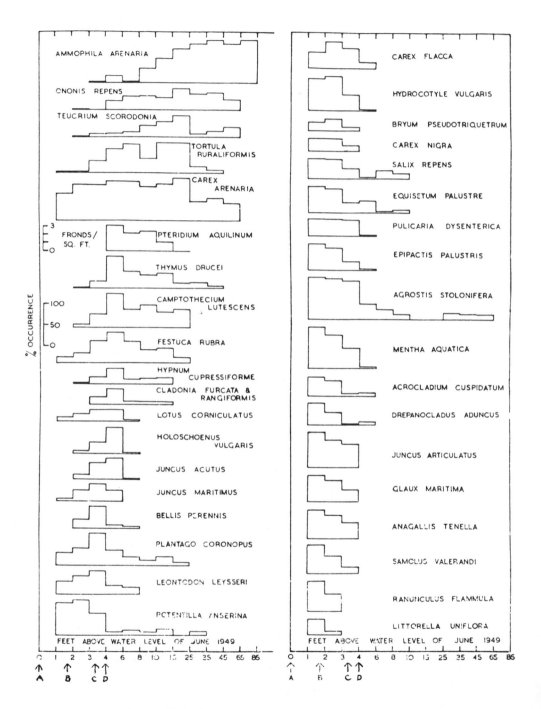

FIG. 7.7. *Distribution of vegetation on dunes in relation to water level (after Willis et al.).*

second group (19).

Whether one is investigating fore-, mid- or rear-dunes, it will be found that the water is fresh so that the roots of the plants are always in fresh water, and the only problem associated with excess salt is related to the amount deposited by wind-borne spray (see p. 205). The dune water table can be regarded as potentially subject to four major types of change: (a) seasonal, (b) regular periodic, (c) daily rhythmic, (d) irregular.

Where the *seasonal* change has been studied (21), it has been shown that there is a distinct three-phase pattern. In the winter, the water table is high and maintained by the winter rains. In the spring there is a fall in the water table which continues into the summer. This is associated with generally drier weather, but is probably more largely affected by the increasing transpirational demands of the plants. With the decrease in vegetative activity in autumn, and often an increased rainfall with reduced surface evaporation (air temperatures being lower), the water table commences to rise again. This type of behaviour is shown irrespective of the vegetation, though at Newborough the degree of change varied between the different types of vegetation. The water table movement in this particular dune system ranged from 70 to 100 cm. In the Winterton dunes on the east coast the range is about half this amount, and this can be correlated with the much lower rainfall there. There is, as one might anticipate, a correlation with monthly precipitation, and this is well shown for three dune sites at Newborough (Fig. 7.8). There the effect of the August rainfall is particularly obvious, also that of the later October dry period.

Periodic changes can occur in the water table of some dunes, especially if they are near the shore and the dunes are built upon shingle ridges. In these cases the changes are associated with the behaviour of the tides, the onset of spring tides bringing about a gradual elevation of the dune water table, with a subsequent fall during the neap tide period. Movements such as this only occur where the dunes have developed on shingle ridges (Blakeney, Scolt) which facilitate the influence of the tides (Fig. 7.9) (see p. 249). In dune systems based upon sand, periodic movements related to the tides have not been reported.

Sand movement, whether by accretion or erosion, at the surface of the dunes is

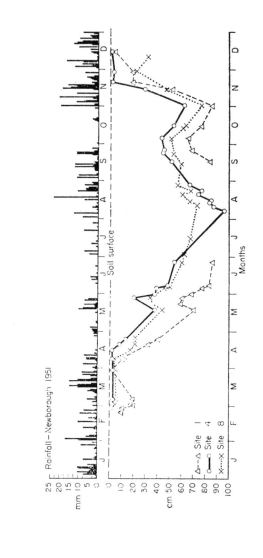

FIG. 7.8. *Effect of rainfall on water table at three dune sites in Newborough Warren (after Ranwell)*

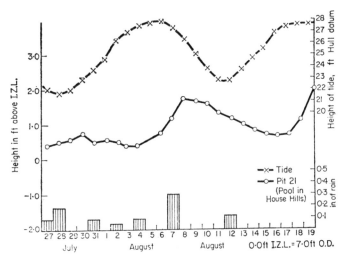

FIG. 7.9. *The relation of the change of water level in dunes (House Hills) on Scolt Head Island to that of the tide. The maximum height in the dunes is reached 48 hours after the highest spring tide (after Chapman).*

important because it can determine changes in the depth at which the water table occurs. To some extent this sand movement is responsible for the apparently *irregular* fluctuations of the water table because they are associated with wind of gale force rather than heavy rain. Some indication of the extent of this phenomenon is shown in Fig. 7.10 for a site where rapid accretion was taking place. The mean increase in depth of the water table between 1951 and

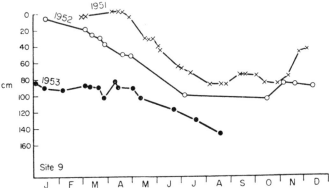

FIG. 7.10. *Sand accretion and the free water table at Newborough. The three curves show the depths of the free water table in centimetres below the soil surface in conditions of steadily increasing sand accretion from 1951 to 1953. The accretion from 1951 to 1952 was 8 cm and from 1951 to 1953 was 20 cm at this site (after Ranwell).*

1953 was of the order of 70-80 cm. *Daily rhythmic* movements have been recorded from the dunes at Newborough where the table fell 2-3 cm per day in summer
and rose again after sunset. This is clearly a transpirational effect, and
since the fall is generally greater than the rise in this period the overall
result is the summer lowering of the water table (Fig. 7.8).

The water table in the slacks may be very close to or even above the surface,
but in the dunes there is usually a considerable depth of sand above the water
table. This sand contains moisture available to the plants so the dune ecologist is greatly interested in the amount present. Normally moisture is expressed on a dry weight basis, but as Salisbury (26) has pointed out, if one
takes equal volumes of sand from young and old dunes and determines dry
weight, that of the old dune will be less because it contains more humus
which is lighter than sand. For sand dune soils therefore, the moisture content is more accurately expressed on a volume basis. The moisture content
can quite obviously vary with season but it can also vary with age of the
dunes, because older dunes with their greater amount of humus retain more
water. So far as seasonal variation is concerned, the water content will be
highest in winter and lowest in summer, but at any time it increases sharply
after rain.   In the Blakeney dunes 4 percent moisture by volume has been re-

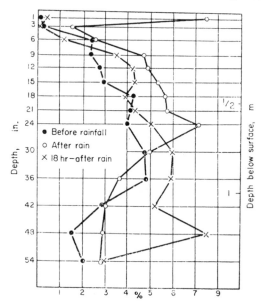

FIG. 7.11. *Water contents of yellow dunes before and after rain*
in summer, Blakeney Point, Norfolk. The surface water contents
are here represented as such, but in fact are averages for the
top inch of sand (after Salisbury).

corded in the spring but by the summer it has fallen to 1 percent or less.
In medium-aged and old dunes at Rye, Salisbury (26) records show that the moisture
content ranged from 4.6 to 7.7 percent by volume after rain.

The variation in moisture content that can occur with age of dunes can be
seen from Figs. 7.11 and 7.12 for yellow dune and young grey dune at Blakeney.

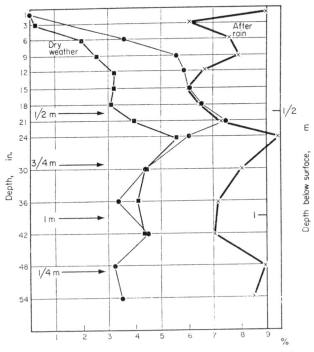

FIG. 7.12. *Water contents of grey dunes before and after rain.*
Early phase of grey dune in summer, Blakeney Point, Norfolk.
Compare with Fig. 7.11 (after Salisbury).

Figure 7.11 shows that in yellow dunes the water content increases with depth
and then falls off at about 0.75 m down. The effect of excess water from rain
is evident at the surface and 18 hours later the high peak is seen to have
percolated down to below 1 m. In the grey dunes (Fig. 7.12) the water content, which is greater than that of the yellow dunes, normally reaches a maximum at about 0.5 m below the surface, but this kind of profile is very dependent upon the amount of organic matter present in the surface layers. If it is
considerable the surface layers will tend to have higher values than shown
here. It has been demonstrated (16) that a considerable increase in water content of surface soil takes place between dunes with open vegetation (yellow)

but that little change occurs in the water content of soil at the 1 ft depth.

Further work will be necessary in order to show whether this is a universal
feature or not. In so far as open vegetation permits of sand movement and
consequent covering or removal of litter whereas closed vegetation promotes
the accumulation of litter, it is probable that the phenomenon is widespread.
After rainfall, however, the organic matter generally in the sand of grey
dunes results in higher values throughout the profile as compared with the
yellow dune phase. The effect of the organic matter in retaining this extra
moisture, even though it be only a few percent, is reflected in the greater
root development of the plants wherever such organically rich layers may
occur (Fig. 7.13).

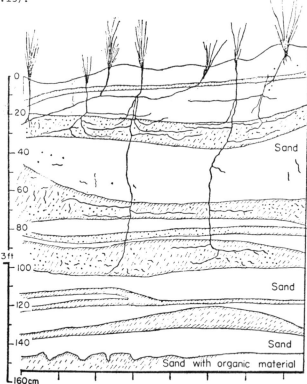

FIG. 7.13. *Semi-diagrammatic representation to scale of the root
system of the Marram grass* (Ammophila arenaria) *in the vertical
section of a dune on the Norfolk coast about 25 ft² in extent
(about 2.5 m²). Yellow sand is shown white and layers of dark
sand, containing considerable organic material, by diagonal shading. Roots, shown as black lines or as black dots where cut across
across, are seen to be most numerous in the originally enriched
and therefore moister strata (after Salisbury).*

The moisture content of sand dunes is obviously low, and if one considers it in relation to known transpiration rates of plants some interesting results emerge. The kind of observations which have been carried out are not diffi-cult, and comparable results could no doubt be obtained with the aid of quite a simple potometer for the transpiration experiments. Salisbury (26) has shown that if you take a plant such as Hare's foot (*Trifolium arvense*), it can have a total leaf area of 10.57 cm^2 and that such a plant will transpire 1 ml of water per day. The root system of such a plant will be distributed through a column of sand of about 95 cm^3 volume, so that if the water content of that sand is 4 percent by volume, the plant will have exhausted the entire water supply in 4 days. Plants of *Trifolium*, however, can be found growing appar-ently unharmed in sand and not showing signs of wilting even after 6 weeks of no rain. Similar calculations can be made for other dune plants which show that they ought to wilt within 1-4 days without rain. The explanation of their survival is provided by the process of internal dew formation which reg-ularly replaces the water used by the plants. Field studies have shown that even in June the internal temperatures of dunes drop below the dew point be-tween midnight and around 5.30 a.m. with a minimum value around 1.30 p.m., so that during this period dew will be steadily deposited within the dunes. A further demonstration of the phenomenon can be provided by actually determin-ing the increase in water content between the end of the day and towards the end of the following night. Table 7.2 gives data illustrating this phenomen-on for two different sites. Despite the information already available it is evident that further work on this subject is needed.

TABLE 7.2

Increase in Water Content (by weight) at Different Depths as a Result of Internal Dew Formation (after Salisbury)

	Site A	Site B
	percent	percent
3 in.	+ 0.18	+ 0.41
12 in.	+ 0.13	+ 0.64
36 in.	-	+ 1.86

SOIL ACIDITY

Apart from sand movement and water content, two other important features of
the dune habitat are the carbonate and humus contents of the soil, both of
which play a major part in determining the pH (acidity) of the soil. Humus
will accumulate so long as plants colonise the dunes, but the amount of carbonate present depends on whether shell sources are in the proximity or not.
Table 7.3 lists values for carbonate and pH in a number of dune systems.

TABLE 7.3

Percentage of Carbonate ($CaCO_3$) *and pH of Dunes*

Locality	Percentage of $CaCO_3$	pH
R. Camel (Cornwall)		
Shore	53.9	8.3
0-5 cm - fixed dune	55.6	8.4
0-5 cm - blow out	68.8	8.5
0-5 cm - blown sand 1 km from shore	51.7	8.0
Southport	2-3	7-7.4
Ayreland of Bride (Isle of Man)	0.75	6.9
Blakeney	Under 0.5	6.8
Dogs Bay, Galway	75	8.1
Rosapenna, Donegal	48	8.3
Holme, Norfolk	2-3	-
Walney, Lancashire	-	6-6.5
St. Cyrus	1.75	7.6 mean
Isle of Harris (Luskentyre banks)	(mean 58.6)	
South Haven (Dorset)	0.037	6.8 (young) to 4.4 (old)
North Carolina dunes	8.0	7.7 (fore) to 7.9 (hind)

As may be expected, non-calcareous dunes are more acid (have a lower pH), and
this is reflected in the ultimate character of their vegetation which is essentially acid grass heath (see p. 168). The average pH value for surface

soils of young dune systems is just above neutral (7.4-8.0) with a regular

tendency to become more acid with age. In the dunes on South Haven Peninsula,

where it has been possible to date the various ridges (32), the gradation of pH

with age is quite evident (Table 7.4), especially since in this siliceous

dune system the sand becomes highly acidic.

TABLE 7.4

Variation of pH with Age, South Haven Dunes (Dorset)

pH	Dune type	Age
		years
7.0-6.6	Fore-dune	0- 20
5.5-5.0	Dune grassland	0- 50
5.5-4.8	Late dune grassland	50- 80
4.6-3.9	Dune heath	80-110
4.5-3.9	Dune heath	110-230
4.5-3.6	Dry heath	240-350

Whilst sand dunes become more and more acidic with increasing age, when indiv-

idual profiles are examined it is found that they regularly become more alka-

line with increasing depth, a phenomenon which has been reported from several

dune systems (St. Cyrus, Newborough, South Haven).

These gradations in pH may depend upon the mobility or otherwise of dune sys-

tems, because at Newborough Warren (21) there is apparently no change in pH in

successive ridges. This can be accounted for in the mobility of the dunes

which would not give organic matter the opportunity to collect and so the

surface layers would not become more acid.

In dunes composed of sand containing a high proportion of carbonate, there is

generally a gradual leaching out of the carbonate with increasing dune age.

This has been very well demonstrated for dune systems by Salisbury (25) (Fig.

7.14), Gimingham(9),Van der Maarel and Westhoff (27)and Gorham(11). At Newbor-

ough(21) also the carbonate content decreased with distance from the sea but in

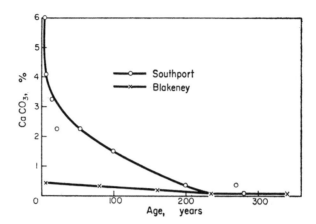

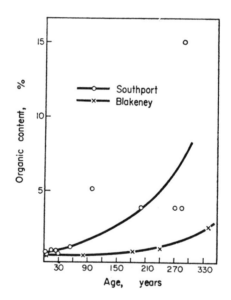

FIG. 7.14. *Carbonate and humus content of dunes at Southport and Blakeney Point. The diagrams show the regular variation of these contents with increasing age of the dunes. The soil changes are bound up with the occupation of the dunes by vegetation, which both induces the changes and indicates responses to them (after Salisbury).*

the wet slacks here, and possibly similarly in other dune areas, one can get local areas of high carbonate where molluscan shells have accumulated. In regions of high wind, where blown sand may be an important factor even at the grey dune phase, the gradual leaching out of the carbonate may not occur. This, at least, appears to have been the case at Luskentyre on the Isle of Harris. Gimingham (10) and his co-workers suggest that this dune system differs from those at Southport and Blakeney in that sand deposition can take place over all areas except the final dune pasture. It is evident, therefore, that further work on the carbonate content of dune soils is still necessary. Further work is also essential in order to demonstrate the effectiveness of the downward leaching.

The other factor which can affect pH is that of the humus. Here Salisbury (15) has shown that on the Southport and Blakeney dunes there is a steady increase in the humus content with increasing age (Fig. 7.14). This is perhaps to be expected because increasing vegetation cover should bring about more and more litter. However, this is apparently not always the case because on the St. Cyrus dunes the organic matter showed no significant increase until the vegetation became closed, and then the increase was only in the surface layers. Where the dune ridges are separated by slacks, and if such slacks carry a vegetation of Creeping willow (*Salix repens*), there will be a considerable increase in the organic matter from the decaying leaves and roots of the *Salix*.

MINERAL NUTRIENTS

The proximity of coastal dunes to the sea might lead one to think that the soil, particularly the surface layers, would have a higher than normal sodium content. This does not appear to be the case, and all investigators who have looked into the matter have reported low sodium chloride values, so that if spray is carried onto the dunes, as it certainly is in cases, then the salt must be rapidly leached down into the lower layers. The amount of aeolian (wind-borne) salt carried and deposited on the leaves of plants may be sufficient to inhibit some plants growing in areas of maximum deposition. The principal zone of deposition appears to be the windward slope and crest of the fore-dune and the crest of the rear-dune. On the coastal dunes of North Carolina the relative distribution of the grasses *Uniola* (tolerant) and *Andropogon* (relatively intolerant) can be explained on the basis of such salt spray distribution.

Apart from zonation, shrubs on dunes nearly always have a wind-swept appearance on the seaward side.   At least three alternative factors have been proposed in the past, e.g. salt spray, wind and sand blast.   A detailed study by
Boyce (2) showed that the latter produced only minor injuries and whilst high
wind speeds did injure leaf tips they were not responsible for the overall
appearance.   As may be expected the amount of salt spray deposited varies
with wind velocity and distance from the sea (Table 7.5).

TABLE 7.5

Salt deposited in relation to wind velocity and distance from sea in $mg/dm^2/hr$
(after Boyce)

Wind velocity	20 m.	45 m.	95 m.	120 m.	270 m. from sea
2.5 m/sec.	1.2	0.2	0.2	0.2	0.1
6 m/sec.	3.4	1.1	0.9	0.7	0.3
11 m/sec.	8.4	5.1	4.7	4.1	2.2

In sufficient quantity, and depending upon the species, salt deposition can
cause necrosis and death of leaves and twigs, but only on the exposed upper or
windward surfaces.   Boyce (2) was able to demonstrate that the canopy angle was
directly correlated with intensity of salt spray which in turn is related to
wind velocity.

In a detailed investigation of the fertility of the dune soils of Braunton
Burrows, it was found (31) that none were deficient in respect of minor nutrients, but that all were deficient in the major nutrients (nitrogen, phosphorus, potassium).   Because of this low fertility it has been suggested that the
growth of dune plants may be limited to some degree.   The major nutrients,
being very soluble, are probably leached out at an early stage in dune formation, though there may not be very much nitrogen and phosphorus from the
start.   In the case of potassium leaching may be compensated by sea spray (6).
Some support for early leaching is available from analyses of dune sands (11) at
Blakeney and of water in slacks at Sandscale (12) which showed the slack waters

representing the water table, to be rich in soluble salts and calcium (6).   The
cation exchange value for slack soils appears to depend upon age and soil
moisture.   In a dry slack it may be 2-3 me percent whereas in an old wet
slack it can be up to 15-20 me percent.

In the case of experiments at Braunton Burrows it was found that the addition
of the three major nutrients caused the grasses to assume dominance.   A very
similar phenomenon occurs on coastal cliffs in the presence of bird populations where, unless there is extensive rabbit grazing, grasses become over-
whelmingly dominant (see p. 256).   It is, therefore, highly probable that the
sparse growth and open character of the vegetation in the early stages of
dune development is at least partly associated with low nitrogen and phosphorus.

In the case of fixed grey dunes at Newborough Warren, Anglesey, dominated by
grassland it has been found that there was a significant correlation between
vegetation pattern and levels of exchangeable potassium, sodium, calcium and
magnesium.   This correlation was not, however, reflected in the plant tissues
and it appeared on further study to be related to the distribution of small
mammal (Vole, 5 shrew species) burrows which had resulted in the removal of
litter and nutrients through leaching (17).

In the case of dune slack plants a high water table can lead to an increase
of iron and manganese in some of the plants.   The latter may reach a point
where toxicity symptoms appear in *Festuca rubra*.   On the other hand increase
in manganese increases growth in the dune Carices (14).

On the Norfolk dunes Gorham (12) found that potassium, phosphate and ammonia
nitrogen increased with age of the dune, but that nitrate nitrogen decreased.
The latter may be related to the combined effect of absorption by plants and
leaching, and presumably the demand is so great that even the breakdown of
litter is not adequate to maintain the supply.   In the case of Carolina dunes
phosphorus decreases with age and potash does not change (28) so that further
studies are clearly needed.

SOIL MICROBIOLOGY

Relatively little attention has been paid to the biological properties of
dune soils, i.e. the microfauna and flora, and even less to the ecology of
the soil microflora that accompanies the plant communities. Gēhu has shown
that the principal bacteria belong to atmospheric nitrogen fixers, proteolyt-
ic, ammonifying, denitrifying, cellulolytic and amylolytic groups.

In communities with distinct dominant species, such as Marram (*Ammophila*),
Sand sedge (*Carex arenaria*), or Creeping fescue (*Festuca rubra*), these plants
can influence the flora as a whole through their own root microflora and also
by the effect their litter and humus may have upon the adjacent soil microflora. The rhizosphere of *Ammophila* contains abundant bacteria but as the
sand between plants is very poor bacterially, nitrogen can be limiting in open
dunes. A good example of this occurs on acid sand heaths carrying *Calluna*,
because the acid heath humus brings about a depression of the bacterial population but increases the fungal and Actinomycete (7) population. Soil algae are
apparently more abundant in the Hippophäe community. The micro-organisms of
the soil are also very important in so far as they materially contribute towards the general maturation of the habitat. Whilst at present we know practically nothing about the micro-organisms associated with the dune habitats
and their dominant species, even when we do we shall want to know how the
microflora and fauna varies with age of dune and depth of soil, and what is
the nature of the differences between the flora of the rhizosphere (portion
of the soil subject to the plant root system) and that of the root surface.
So far as depth is concerned the maximum density is in the surface layers,
except for the *Agropyron junceiforme* and *Corynephorus canescens* communities
are concerned where it occurs lower down (8).

Studies that have been carried out on the soil fungal population of dunes
(see p. 170) have shown that there appear to be three common soil genera,
Penicillium, Cephalosporium and *Coniothyrium*, both in respect of number of
species and frequency, and that *Penicillium nigricans* is the most widespread
species in British dunes (1). The available information indicates that the
fungal population is a rich one, but very few of the species can be considered as restricted to dunes. Indeed, many can only be regarded as casuals, and
quite a few are to be found associated primarily with rabbit pellets. There
is apparently no marked seasonal variation, but more work on this aspect is

really required. However, a very distinct difference is evident as between
the floras of acidic and alkaline dunes. Brown (1) compared two such dune systems (Sandwich and South Haven) and found that one yielded ninety-five species and the other ninety-nine, but only twenty-eight were common to the two
areas. In general the number of species and the frequency of their occurrence decreased with increasing depth of the soil (Table 7.6). The principal
exception to this was found in the fore-dunes, but one can perhaps account
for the greater numbers at the lower depths here by postulating their association with pockets of buried organic matter (drift). There was also some evidence of certain fungi being associated with specific stages in the phanerogamic succession. A similar phenomenon has also been reported in respect of
mycorrhizal infection. All this work is of the very greatest interest, but
it is evident that further studies of a similar nature on other dune systems
are greatly to be desired.

TABLE 7.6

No. of Fungal Species isolated at Different Depths on Sand Dune Soils (after Brown)

Soil depth (in.)	0-0.5	1.0	3.0	6.0	12.0
Sandwich (alkaline)					
Open sand	11	-	-	-	-
Fore-dune	10	14	12	7	14
Semi-fixed yellow	29	22	14	12	9
Fixed grey	20	17	13	14	12
Dune pasture	22	22	13	16	11
South Haven, Studland (acid)					
Open sand	9	-	-	-	-
Fore-dune	6	10	11	11	4
Semi-fixed grassland	20	13	10	14	8
Semi-fixed heath	25	22	7	14	20
Heath	22	22	14	14	12
Pteridium heath	23	20	15	16	10

Whilst a considerable volume of work has been carried out on the British sand
dune systems, it is also evident that it has been largely restricted to certain regions, and there is therefore plenty of scope for additional studies on
any of the numerous dune areas that have so far received no attention. It is

true that comparable work has been done on many continental and Scandinavian dune systems, and this mostly serves to confirm the results that have already been described.

DUNE BUILDING AND MAINTENANCE

Sand dunes in certain places form an essential feature of the natural coast protection system. This is particularly true in Norfolk when a major breach in the dunes can lead to disastrous flooding of the farmland behind, as happened in 1938 and 1953. Maintenance of the dune system is therefore of great practical importance, and, should it be breached, methods of rebuilding are equally vital. Much attention has been given to this problem in different parts of the world since Great Britain is not the only country that may depend on dunes to protect a part of the coast-line. Maintenance and repair of dune systems is essentially a job for the civil engineer, but since he makes use of plants it will not be out of place if some reference is made here to the principles involved. The agriculturist may also be concerned when a dune system becomes mobile and starts invading and swamping good agricultural land, as has happened with the Culbin sands. The immediate stabilisation of such mobile dune areas is therefore also very important.

It has already been seen that the development of coastal dunes results from sand meeting an obstacle (a plant), so that the effect of various types of obstacles upon sand drift is very important (2). If the obstacle is solid then the wind is reflected and an eddy is formed which scoops out the sand at the base of the obstacle and forms a mound in front (Fig. 7.15a). If the obstacle is low, e.g. buried paling or groyne, the mound increases in height until it is level with the top. No eddy can now occur and the sand is blown over the obstacle and collects on the leeward side as the wind velocity drops (see p. 186). Now that the eddy has ceased, sand falls into the scooped-out hollow, and as sand is also accumulating on the leeward side the obstacle is gradually buried. If the obstacle is flexible and open, e.g. tuft of Marram or Lyme grass, the sand is deposited first in the centre of the tussock and then it commences to accumulate on the lee side (Fig. 7.15b). If the obstacle is rigid and open, e.g. a brush fence, the wind is checked in its passage through it but as it is not reflected there is no eddy. As a result sand accumulates on both sides until the fence is finally buried (Fig. 7.15c).

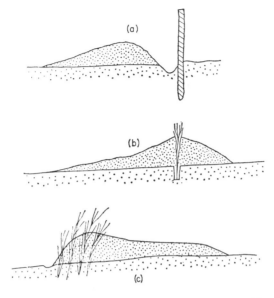

FIG. 7.15. a, *Effect of solid obstacle*. b, *Effect of an inflexible open obstacle*. c, *Effect of a flexible obstacle, for example, a bunch of Marram grass (after Cockayne)*.

Whether one is building new dunes, repairing breaches or immobilising mobile dunes, it is important to get plants established as quickly as possible because plant cover brings about sand stabilisation. The actual stabilisation of dunes is based upon certain principles which can be briefly enumerated as follows:

1. Elimination of sand movement by providing a cover to the sand. This may have to be artificial at first but a closed vegetation cover, preferably pasture or forest, is the ultimate objective.

2. Anything that can lead to secondary exposure of a bare sand surface should be prevented. Burning, over-grazing, excessive trampling by animals or human beings, can damage the plant cover and expose sand and then with undercutting the whole dune can erode away.

3. It is useless to try and establish on mobile sand plants that cannot survive sand covering. Sometimes the sand movement may be too great even for a plant such as Marram, and in these cases it is necessary to break the force of the wind by putting in brush fences or covering the sand surface with brush-

wood.

4. The most effective cover is given by trees because they have a long
life, improve the soil with their litter, and they require little attention
and are not likely to be damaged other than by fire. Adequate attention must
therefore be given to fire risk and also to the felling programme. The best
type of tree for this purpose is a softwood, and there are a number of pine
species that grow very well on the poor soil of sand dunes.

5. The most satisfactory way of establishing plants is through planting
rather than sowing. Marram is the grass usually planted and where areas are
extensive it can now be done by machinery, as at Muriwai in New Zealand. In
other parts of the world different dune grasses may be used. If a plant such
as Tree lupin (*Lupinus arboreus*) is to be used, it is best sown and then one
must select the best time of year for sowing, which is when the sand is wet
and not likely to travel, to give the seedlings a chance to become established.

6. The movement of sand should be stopped as near the source as possible.
On a beach, new dune should be formed as close to high water mark as possible.
In the case of mobile dunes, one should not try and stop the advancing edge:
measures have to be taken first at the source of the sand. When that has been
stabilised, attention can then be given to the advancing edge.

7. Since wind velocities are greatly affected by irregularities in the
dunes, gullies and embayments should not be allowed to develop in coastal
dunes. The smoother and more regular the sea frontage, the less chance of
erosion. Similarly, in interior dunes it is most desirable to build up hollows between hills. Because of the impact of surface irregularities on wind
behaviour, great care must be taken to see that no isolated artificial mounds
of sand are produced.

8. The initial fences must be located in relation to the prevailing or
dominant winds depending on which type is of major importance in sand movement.

9. If the land is sinking in relation to sea level, erosion may be a
continual menace unless the sand supply is very large, but if not dunes may
need artificial building up from time to time.

If the sand is not too mobile, it can be successfully stabilised by planting with Marram or sowing with lupin. In the former case, the Marram should be planted in rows at right angles to the incident wind, and plants in successive rows should alternate so as not to create wind channels. Lupin can be sown by scattering seed, but it is better to lay lupin branches on the sand and let the seed pods burst naturally. If the sand is highly mobile, it can be stabilised by burying brush fences at right angles to sand movement and planting in the leeward ridge dune that is formed.

When a fore-dune has to be repaired or a new dune created, there is a recognised process which should aim at producing a dune with a wide base, a low summit and relatively flat slopes. The general method is to establish two fence rows about 7 ft apart and 2½ ft high. When the sand reaches the top, two more fences, each a little to the seaward of the first pair, are set up. When these are nearly covered the sand can be planted, or if the dune is still not high enough a third set of fences can be put in (Fig. 7.16). The front of

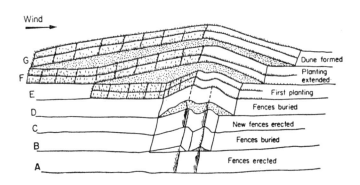

FIG. 7.16. *Stages in building of new fore-dune (after Steers).*

the dune is best planted in squares whilst rows can be used on the leeward slope. When the Marram is established lupin can be sown. Later, under the lupin, grass and clover or trefoil can be sown or young pine trees can be planted. Legumes are desirable plants to introduce at an early stage because of the nitrogen they add to the soil through the nitrifying bacteria in the root nodules. At this stage the dune has been stabilised and should form an effective part of the coast protection. Pines that can be used successfully include *Pinus maritima, P. austriaca, P. radiata* and *P. corsica,* whilst in wetter slacks birch, populars, alder and willows are readily established.

This brief account of the process of dune building and stabilisation will, it is hoped, serve to show how information gained from an ecological study of a particular habitat and the various communities it bears can be successfully applied to a major physiographic problem.

REFERENCES

1   BOERBOOM J.H.A., Microklimatologische Waarnemingen in de Wassenaarse Duinen. *Mededel. Landbouw. Wagen.*, 64, 322 pp. (1964).

2   BOYCE S.G., The Salt Spray Community. *Ecol. Monog.*, 25, 29-64 (1955).

3   BROWN J.C., Soil fungi of some British sand dunes in relation to soil type and succession. *J. Ecol.*, 46(3), 641-664 (1958).

4   CHAPMAN V.J., The stabilization of sand-dunes by vegetation. *Proc. Conf. Biol. & Civil Engin.* (Inst. of Civil Engineers), 1948. 142-157 (1949).

5   EASTWOOD D.J., FRASER G.K. and WEBLEY D.M., Microbiological factor in the Culbin Sands afforestation scheme. *Nature, London*, 165, 980 (1950).

6   ETHERINGTON J.R., Studies of nutrient cycling and productivity in oligo-trophic ecosystems. 1. Soil potassium and windblown sea spray in South Wales dune grassland. *J. Ecol.*, 55, 743-52 (1967).

7   GÉHU J.M., Activité microbiologique des sables de quelques groupements végétaux du littoral du Pas-de-Calais. *Ann. Inst. Pasteur*, 100, 638-655 (1961).

8   GÉHU J.M., Importance de certains facteurs dans la microbiologie des Sables de Dunes. *Ann. Inst. Pasteur*, 105, 209-17 (1963).

9   GIMINGHAM C.H., Contribution to the maritime ecology of St. Cyrus, Kin-cardineshire. II. The Sand Dunes. *Trans. Bot. Soc. Edin.*, 35(4), 387-414 (1951).

10   GIMINGHAM C.H., GEMMELL A.R. and GREIG-SMITH P., The vegetation of a sand-dune system in the Outer Hebrides. *Trans. Bot. Soc. Edin.*, 35(1), 82-96 (1948).

11   GORHAM E., Soluble salts from dune sands from Blakeney Pt. in Norfolk. *J. Ecol.*, 46, 373-379 (1958).

12   GORHAM E., The chemical composition of some waters from dune slacks at Sandscale, north Lancashire. *J. Ecol.*, 49(1), 79-82 (1961).

13   JONES R. and ETHERINGTON J.R., Comparative studies of plant growth and distribution in relation to water-logging. IV. The growth of dune and dune slack plants. *J. Ecol.*, 59, 793-801 (1971).

14   JONES R. and ETHERINGTON J.R., Ibid. V. VI. The uptake of iron and mang-
      anese by dune and dune slack plants. *J. Ecol.*, 60, 131-145 (1972).

15   LAING C.C., Studies in the ecology of *Ammophila breviligulata*. 1. Seed-
      ling survival and its relation to population increase and dispersal.
      Bot. Gaz., 119, 208-216 (1958).

16   MARSHALL J.K., *Corynephorus canescens* (L.) P. Beauv. as a model for the
      Ammophila problem. *J. Ecol.*, 53, 447-463 (1965).

17   MORTON A.J., Ecological studies of a fixed dune grassland at Newborough
      Warren, Anglesey. II. Causal factors of the grassland structure.
      J. Ecol., 62, 261-278 (1974).

18   NICHOLSON T.H., Mycorrhiza in the Gramineae. II. Development in differ-
      ent habitats, particularly sand dunes. *Trans. Brit. Mycol. Soc.*, 43(1),
      132-145 (1960).

19   ONYEKWELU S.S.C., The vegetation of dune slacks at Newborough Warren.
      J. Ecol., 60(3), 887-898 (1972).

20   RANWELL D., Movement of vegetated sand-dunes at Newborough Warren, Angle-
      sey. *J. Ecol.*, 46(1), 83-100 (1958).

21   RANWELL D., Newborough Warren, Anglesey. I. The dune system and dune
      slack habitat. *J. Ecol.*, 47(3), 571-601 (1959).

22   RANWELL D., *Ecology of Salt Marshes and Sand Dunes*. Chapman & Hall (1972).

23   ROBERTSON E.T. and GIMINGHAM C.H., Contributions to the maritime ecology
      of St. Cyrus, Kincardineshire. *Trans. Proc. Bot. Soc. Edin.*, 35(4), 370-
      412 (1951).

24   SALISBURY E.J., The soils of Blakeney Point: a study of soil reaction
      and succession in relation to plant covering. *Ann. Bot.*, 36, 391-431
      (1922).

25   SALISBURY E.J., Note on the edaphic succession in some dune soils with
      special reference to the time factor. *J. Ecol.*, 13(3), 322-328 (1925).

26   SALISBURY E.J., *Downs and Dunes*. G. Bell (1952).

27   VAN DER MAAREL E. and WESTHOFF V., The vegetation of the dunes near Oost-
      vorne (The Netherlands) with a vegetation map. *Wentia*, 12, 1-61 (1964).

28   WAGNER R.H., The ecology of *Uniola paniculata* L. in the dune-strand hab-
      itat of North Carolina. *Ecol. Monog.*, 34, 79-96 (1964).

29   WEBLEY D.M., EASTWOOD D.J. and GIMINGHAM C.H., Development of a soil
      microflora in relation to plant succession on sand dunes, including the
      rhizosphere flora associated with colonising species. *J. Ecol.*, 40(1),
      168-178 (1952).

30   WILLIS A.J. and JEFFRIES R.L., Investigations on the water relations of

sand-dune plants under natural conditions in *The Water Relations of Plants*. Blackwell. pp. 168-88 (1963).

31   WILLIS A.J. and YEMM E.W., Braunton Burrows: mineral nutrient status of the dune soils. *J. Ecol.*, 49(2), 377-390 (1961).

32   WILSON K., The time factor in the development of dune soils at South Haven Peninsula, Dorset. *J. Ecol.*, 48(2), 341-360 (1960).

33   WRIGHT T.W., Profile development in the sand dunes of Culbin Forest, Morayshore. I. Physical properties. *Soil Sci.*, 6, 270-283 (1955).

34   WRIGHT T.W., Profile development in the sand dunes of Culbin Forest, Morayshore. II. Chemical properties. *Soil Sci.*, 7(1), 33-42 (1955).

CHAPTER 8

MANGROVE SWAMPS

These represent the tropical equivalent of salt marshes and in subtropical regions the two types of vegetation may intermingle. Like salt marshes mangrove swamps are subject to total inundations during which mud is deposited so that there is a gradual elevation in land height. Physiognomically mangrove differs from salt marsh in that the dominant plants are trees and not herbs.

OCCURRENCE

Mangrove swamps like salt marshes, occur on coast-lines that are stable, rising or falling and in Florida there is evidence that the swamps there have developed on a subsiding coast-line. Ecologically mangrove develops in the same physiographic areas as salt marsh, namely in estuaries, behind spits or off-shore islands and in protected bays with shallow water. In addition, since they are tropical, they also develop, although in an attenuated form, on coral cays, e.g. the Florida Cays. Mangrove vegetation does not occur in Europe, the nearest examples being in the Red Sea or on the west coast of Africa south of Dakar (2).

The mangrove swamps of southern Florida are very extensive and are representative of all the physiographic features mentioned above. There is a considerable literature on the Florida mangroves (4-9) including an account of their sediments by Scholl (16). Mangrove swamp formation follows closely the pattern of salt marsh formation (see pp. 88, 89) though laterals associated with spits and off-shore islands are not perhaps so common. Similarly the extent of mangrove forest is related to the nature of the coast. If it is a rising coast mangrove tends to form a fringe zone only: if the coast is stable the extent of the forest is related to whether the sea bed shelves gently or sharply. On a subsiding coast mangrove tends to be extensive.

Sedimentation rates can be determined in mangrove forest in the same way as they can on salt marsh (see p. 95) and the same factors affect sedimentation

as those on salt marshes (2). Depressed areas in the mangrove swamps can be
found but pans, as recognised on salt marshes, do not exist. These depressed
areas are important since they form breeding areas for mosquitoes. Creeks
are as much a feature of mangrove swamps as they are of salt marshes, the
banks either showing evidence of erosion or of build up.

The species forming the mangrove forests grow on a variety of substrates.
The great bulk of mangrove forest is developed on muddy soils and such soils
are common in Florida where much mud is brought down by the rivers. Where
protection is afforded by sand spits or off-shore sand islands mangrove species, e.g. *Laguncularia racemosa*, can be found growing in sand. This may also
happen in lagoons associated with coral cays (7). The cays with their coral
structure provide yet another substrate and, providing seedlings can become
stranded, isolated mangrove plants can be found growing on the coral itself.
Where there is little silt carried in the water but physiographic conditions
are favourable mangrove still develops, and in such cases the soil is a peat
formed from the roots (6). This is comparable to salt marshes forming a peaty
soil (c.f. as in New England or south-west Eire).

THE VEGETATION

The Florida mangroves, like those of the rest of the New World, are not rich
in species (6). The four principal trees are *Rhizophora mangle* (red mangrove),
Avicennia germinans (black mangrove), *Laguncularia racemosa* (white mangrove)
and *Conocarpus erecta* (button mangrove). The first three species are characterised by the presence of special roots which have an aerating function. In
the case of *Rhizophora mangle* they take the form of the so-called "prop"
roots, which not only give mechanical rigidity (Fig. 8.1) but, because of
their abundant lenticels, they provide gaseous exchange with the atmosphere.
In *Avicennia* and *Laguncularia* the special roots emerge like telegraph poles
from the soil. They are negatively geotropic and the abundant lenticels
communicate via aerenchymatous tissue (Fig. 8.2) with the underground roots
thus providing a system of gaseous exchange (1,2). These special roots, known
as pneumatophores, often bear an algal flora or a fauna of oysters (*Ostrea
rhizophorae*), barnacles and molluscs (*Perna alata*).

Apart from the pneumatophores there is an extensive system of horizontal or

FIG. 8.1. Rhizophora mangle *showing prop roots.*

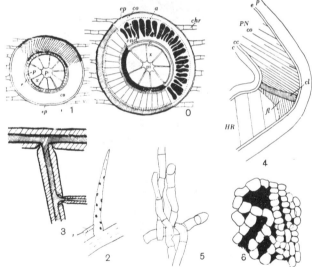

FIG. 8.2. Avicennia germinans *showing aerenchymatous tissue* (a).
0 = *T.S. base of pneumatophore. Shading in half of section indicating resistance to gaseous diffusion based on air space extent.*
Co = *cortex*, end = *endodermis*, ep = *epidermis*, p = *phloem*, pi =
pithy, x = *xylem. 1. T.S. pneumatophore in cortex of horizontal
root. Shading as for 0. 2 = pneumatophore with absorbing root
arising from horizontal root. 3. L.S. of same roots. Shading as
for 0. 4. Diagram of base of pneumatophore* (FN) *from cork* (C) *to
phloem* (P). *Shading as for 0.* Cl = *closing layer*, CC = *cork camb-
ium*, HR = *horizontal root. 5. Cells from fibre zone of 4* (fl).
6. *Cells of "closing layer". (after Chapman).*

cable roots from which the erect roots arise as well as a system of vertical anchoring roots, which are positively geotropic. Finally there are small absorbing rootlets which are generally attached to the pneumatophores at about 5-10 cm below the surface. As the soil level rises so new absorbing rootlets are produced and their level on the soil appears to be related to the presence of soil aeration (2) (Fig. 8.3). On coral where horizontal roots may lie on the surface the absorbing rootlets emerge from the vertical anchoring roots.

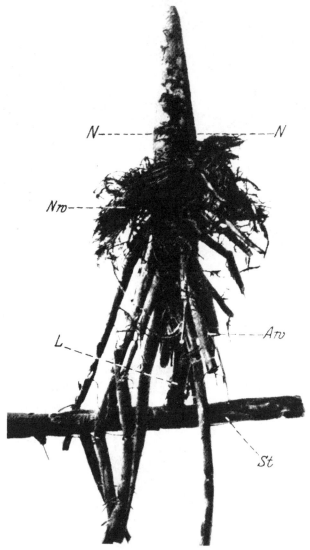

FIG. 8.3. *Pneumatophore* (L) *showing distribution of absorbing rootlets* (Nro) *in relation to soil surface* (N-N) *and cable root* (st). Arv = *anchoring roots (after Troll).*

Apart from the pneumatophores the other outstanding feature of mangrove trees
are the viviparous seedlings of *Rhizophora* and *Avicennia*. These develop on
the trees directly after fertilisation. In the case of *R mangle* the seedlings are long and torpedo-like and in the case of *Avicennia* they are bean-
like (Fig. 8.4). These seedlings when they drop, either become sufficiently
fixed in the mud so that they are not washed away or they float off in the
sea water and in this way distribution takes place. Davis (6) estimated that
some 10 000 seedlings annually floated around the southern tip of Florida.

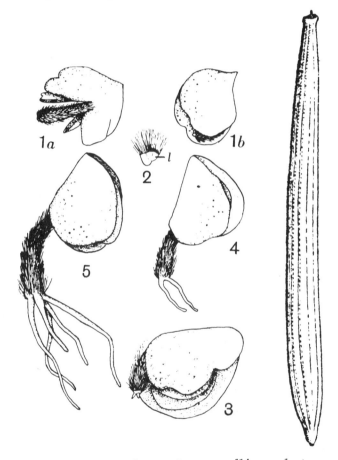

FIG. 8.4. 1-5 Avicennia germinans *seedling and stages of development after falling*. 6. Rhizophora mangle *seedling (after Chapman)*.

With the gradual change in land level so there are changes in the environmental conditions and as a result one mangrove species is replaced by another
(see p. 224). The vegetation is therefore dynamic, as on a salt marsh, and
the zonation to be observed represents a succession (Fig. 8.5).

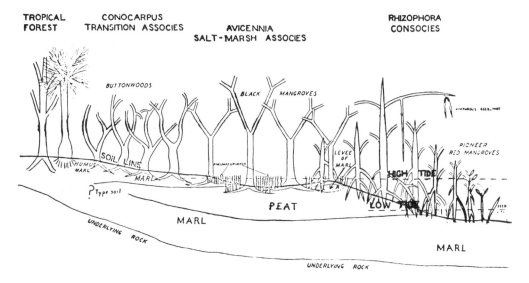

FIG. 8.5. *Diagrammatic transect of Florida mangrove communities from the pioneer* Rhizophora *family to the tropical hammock forest (after Davis).*

There has been considerable debate about the role of mangrove in the production of new land (2,5,6). It is quite clear that until the sea bed reaches a level where mangrove seedlings can survive the frequency and depth of floodings no mangrove swamp can develop. Once there, however, the presence of the plants and the existence of their mass of pneumatophores hastens silt deposition and land elevation takes place more rapidly. Once established with seed parents, slow seaward migration takes place and so it can be said that mangrove do produce new land.

At the rear of the mangrove swamp the vegetation either abuts onto upland or where it is bordering a river it passes into fresh water swamp or riverine forest. One of the features of the Floridan mangrove swamps are the "hammocks" of upland scattered through them on which terrestrial forest trees, such as *Magnolia*, can be found (Fig. 8.5).

On the Atlantic coast of the U.S.A. mangrove extends north until it is halted by killing frosts of about -4°C (2). Around Cape Kennedy the mangrove is low and forms a fringe along creeks with salt marsh behind. *Rhizophora mangle* has more or less disappeared and one finds low bushes of *Avicennia* and *Lagun-*

cularia. Similar low bushes of *Avicennia* occur as fringe vegetation on the
Louisiana marshes.

A study of the soil deposits (Fig. 8.6) in the Florida mangrove using the
technique of radio-carbon dating, has shown that they have been formed since
about 3000 BP (Before Present) and this would mean that the mangrove colonisation probably began around 2000 BP.

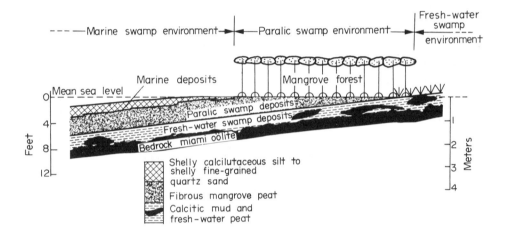

FIG. 8.6. *Transgressive stratigraphic section under edges of bays,
swamps and marshes of southern Florida (after Scholl and Stuvier).*

Earlier data (16) suggests that the land was sinking, relative to sea level,
originally at about 0.55 ft/100 yrs, then decreasing to 0.14 ft/100 yrs at
2000 BP, and reducing still further to 0.05 ft/100 yrs at 1000 BP. Where the
land is sinking like this the mangrove is essentially invading and replacing
upland vegetation as it becomes killed by the advent of salt water. At the
same time there is also some seaward spread as silting takes place.

At present the mangrove belt is from 0.3-3 miles wide with bands extending
landwards (15) giving a honeycomb appearance from the air. In south-west Florida the mangrove extends up to 6 miles inland and the three are growing on a
deep peat soil (10).

MANGROVE COMMUNITIES

The lowest phanerogam communities are beds of sea grasses, *Zostera*, *Thalassia*, *Cymodocea* (5) but there is generally a bare zone between them and the lowest mangrove as *Zostera* is the only genus that will tolerate any degree of exposure at low tide.

The primary mangrove species is *Rhizophora mangle*, which appears as scattered pioneers. If there are depressed areas where water lies at low tide *Thalassia testudinum* or *Cymodocea manatorum* can be found. The *Rhizophora* prop roots carry an algal flora of the small turfy red seaweeds *Bostrychia*, *Catenella* and *Caloglossa* (p. 49) as well as the blue-green *Microcoleus tenerrimus*, *Lyngbya maiuscula* and *Sirocoleum guyanense* (9). Additional algae form communities on the mud between the plants: these include *Caulerpa cupressoides*, *Acetabularia crenulatum*, *Gracilaria cornea*, *Halimeda tridens*, *Sargassum natans* (the famed Sargasso weed) and *Batophora oerstedii*.

The pioneer zone is generally followed by a belt of pure *Rhizophora* trees 10 m or so in height with the same associated algal communities. The next zone is commonly dominated by *Avicennia germinans* which, as one goes northwards, becomes replaced by an *Avicennia*-salt marsh associes (6,9) with the composition given in Table 8.1. It is in this community that the salt marsh mosquito can be found feeding on the nectar of the *Avicennia* flowers (18).

Where mangrove is extensive the main area is occupied by the mature mangrove associes (6) in which *Rhizophora* and *Avicennia* are predominant, but both *Laguncularia* and *Conocarpus* are also present. *Batis maritima* forms the principal ground cover. Where streams meander through the community there is a narrow frontal fringe of *Rhizophora* trees. Hurricanes often sweep through these forests and in such cases *Rhizophora* comes to predominate because it survives better than *Avicennia* (3,9).

The most landward and highest community is dominated by trees of *Conocarpus erecta* (Fig. 8.5). It is an open type of community and generally contains isolated specimens of trees from adjacent upland forest, or from the hammocks. Davis (6) listed forty trees and shrubs, 16 herbs, 6 epiphytes and the fern *Acrostichum aureum*.

TABLE 8.1

Presence and relative abundance of the most important species of the
Avicennia *salt marsh associes and the scrub mangrove facies (from Davis)*
(scale 1 to 10)

Species	Avicennia salt marsh associes: stations					Scrub mangrove facies: stations		
	Gen-eral	KL3	KW7	FB18	SB1	KL3	KW1	SB9
Trees and shrubs:								
Avicennia germinans	9	10	8	9	10	1	2	3
Rhizophora mangle	2	2	1	1	1	4	1	3
Laguncularia racemosa	1	1			1	2	1	2
Conocarpus erecta	1			1			1	1
Batis maritima	7	7	9	3	7	1	2	2
Salicornia perennis	3	3	1	4	1	6	5	3
Borrichia frutescens	1			2	1	1		1
Lycium carolinianum	1	1		1	1			1
Bumelia angustifolia	1			1		1		1
Ecastophyllum brownei	1	1						
Coccolobis uvifera	1				1		1	1
Rhabdadenia biflora	1		1			1		
Herbs and ferns:								
Sporobolus virginicus	2	1	2	1	3		1	2
Monanthochloe littoralis	2		5	7			4	
Dondia linearis	1	1			1		1	1
Sesuvium portulacastrum	1	2	1		1		1	1
Acrostichum aureum	2				1			
Spartina alterniflora	1		1		2			1
Spartina spartinae	1			1			3	
Spartina cynosuroides	1		1					
Juncus roemerianus	1				1			1
Fimbristylis castanea	1			1			1	
Cyperus ottonis	1							1
Chloris glauca	1							1

The transition to fresh water sawgrass prairie (*Mariscus jamaicensis*) is marked by isolated *Rhizophora* trees mixed in the sawgrass. Several variations of
this *Rhizophora* locies have been described by Davis (6) and Egler (9), but essentially they appear to be the same. With increasing fall in land level the
Rhizophora continues to push landward into the sawgrass. This process is
further facilitated by the occasional Indian sawgrass prairie trees which
open up the vegetation but do keep the *Rhizophora* stunted. In this type of

community *Mariscus* has a 100 percent frequency, *Rhizophora* 76 percent and *Eleocharis* 83 percent (9). On the hammocks scattered through this type of community the palmetto palm, *Sabal palmetto*, is the dominant species.

Whilst Davis (6) has argued that one can recognise a complex succession leading to tropical forest and Egler (9) has agreed that because of fires and hurricanes succession is impossible, the present author (2) has argued that one is really dealing with a succession of successions (Schema A). In this stages can be repeated any number of times before there is progress to the next major stage.

SCHEMA A

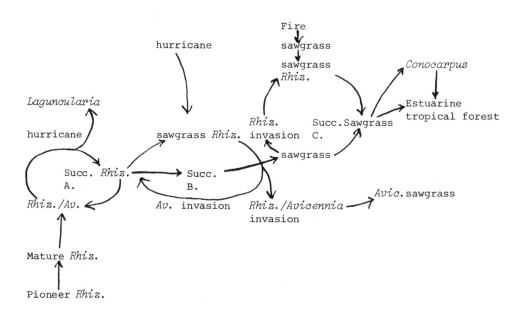

Where mangrove is felled or destroyed by hurricanes invasion by the fern *Acrostichum aureum* commonly takes place. This rapidly becomes so dense that invasion by the light-demanding mangrove seedlings is almost impossible and regeneration is difficult. This is a feature that occurs elsewhere in the world (2). One may also encounter a *Laguncularia* consocies but it does not seem to be restricted to any particular habitat.

On the cays the mangrove, as might be expected, develops either on the protected leeward side or in the central lagoon (6,7). Generally only two belts

can be distinguished, a seaward one of *Rhizophora* and a landward one of *Avi-*
cennia (Fig. 8.7). On the edge of the beach at the back of the mangrove
there can be a border of *Conocarpus*. Salt marsh plants such as *Sesuvium*
portulacastrum, Borrichia frutescens, Iva ovaria can also occur at the landward edge. Schema B below indicates the nature of the succession.

SCHEMA B

L.W.M................................. Pioneer *Rhizophora*

H.W.M. .... Mixed mature mangrove (*Rhizophora &*
                                         Avicennia)

Avicennia consocies

(+ *Laguncularia* on strand fringe)

H.W.M. .... Salt marsh   *Conocarpus* border
                                                             (indistinct)

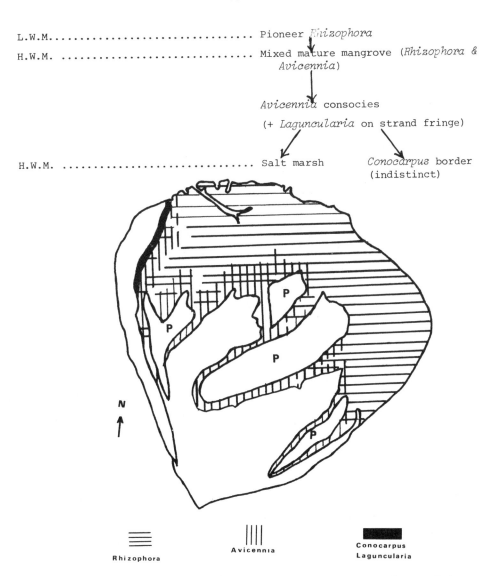

Rhizophora   Avicennia   Conocarpus
                                        Laguncularia

FIG. 8.7. *Distribution of mangrove on Boca Grande Key (after*
Davis).

Some quite considerable work has been carried out on the marine fungi of mangroves in Florida (11,13). Some of these fungi must be regarded as essentially
terrestrial because they occur on the trees above high water mark. Others
have been recorded from mangrove soils where their distribution may be related to salinity. However, insufficient work has been carried out on the mangrove fungi to lead to any general conclusions.

ECOLOGICAL FACTORS

Level, salinity, drainage and soil composition have all been regarded as
major factors (2,14), but level is probably really only of significance in so
far as seedling establishment is concerned. Salinity, drainage and soil composition are all factors that can affect mature trees. *Laguncularia racemosa*
appears to be a species that is favoured by well-drained areas and *Avicennia*
trees also tend to grow taller near to creeks. In Florida hurricanes and
fires are significant local factors.

Although Watson (21) initiated the concept of inundation classes for mangroves,
which was later modified by de Haan and used by the present author in the
Caribbean (1), it seems that their use does not really provide much useful information and they can be abandoned. Chapman (2) points out that the most important aspect of the tidal phenomena is the number of consecutive days at
any one level when there are no floodings. In the Caribbean, and probably
also in Florida, these are 0-10 days in the *Rhizophora mangle* belt, 10-110
days in the *Avicennia germinans* belt and up to 157 in the *Laguncularia* belt.
These periods are particularly important in respect of seedling survival. If
a seedling falls just before a long exposure time it may not become established unless the ground remains moist through rainfall. The tidal movements are
also responsible for distribution of the viviparous seedlings. Normally
seedlings after floating will become stranded horizontally (6,8), and radicle
growth only takes place near the base of the hypocotyl, until the hypocotyl
has bent into a vertical position. However, root growth can be sufficient
after two days to retain the seedling. Egler (8) argues that seedlings of *R.*
mangle are usually not borne high enough to penetrate the soil when they drop.
La Rue and Muzik (12), however, report that 24 cm long *R. mangle* seedlings if
dropped from a height of 2 m will penetrate a soft mud and will have become
well-rooted within two weeks. Seedlings of *R. mangle* are susceptible to

water depth for successful establishment. Daily submergence of more than 10-20 cm seems to be inhibitory (8,12).

TABLE 8.2

Salinity analyses of flooding or standing water in mangrove swamps of Florida and Jamaica

	% NaCl Florida	% NaCl Jamaica
Atlantic Ocean	3.7	–
Pioneer *Rhizophora mangle*	3.13	–
Mature *Rhizophora mangle*	3.49	3.54
Avicennia germinans	3.68	2.03–4.26
Brackish mangrove	1.56	0.31–1.09
Freshwater mangrove	0.01	0.0
Scrub mangrove	4.58	1.73–2.09
Laguncularia	1.29	4.14

Salinity may not be so important as previously thought, because it has been shown that some species, especially those of *Rhizophora*, can ultra-filter sodium chloride out of the water in the absorbing roots. In any case there do not appear to be high salinity values other than in regions of monsoonal rainfall, where the dry periods may produce excessive evaporation. Analyses of flooding or standing water in Florida (6) and Jamaica (1) are set out in Table 8.2. Studies of salinities in coral, peat, sand and mud soils of Jamaica showed considerable variation in relation to soil type (Fig. 8.8) and also made it clear that both sodium and chloride need to be determined. The soluble chloride reaches high values in mud soils. The mud soils occasionally are black on the surface but they are almost invariably black beneath. The black colour is a result of the production, by anaerobic bacteria, of iron sulphide from the sulphate present in the water (20).

The general soil structure of mangrove swamps always needs to be studied because only then can water movements be properly appreciated. In south-west Florida Scholl (16) found that the marine silts overlaid a fresh water mud that

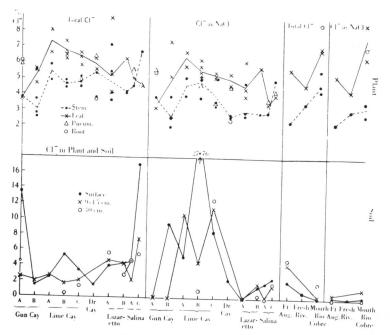

FIG. 8.8. *Total Cl⁻ and Cl⁻ equivalent of Na⁺ in plants and soils of Jamaican mangrove swamps. The continuous and dotted lines for stem and leaf = average values (after Chapman).*

itself was deposited either on bed rock or on a freshwater peat, which was identified as being about 4000 years old (Fig. 8.6). In Florida the fibrous mangrove peat is mainly formed in the upper half of the tidal range but if the tidal range is not more than about 30 cm *Rhizophora mangle* peat can form over the whole range (6).

Detailed mechanical analyses of soils have been made for mangroves in various parts of the world. Table 8.3 sets out the values for mangrove in Florida(6) and Jamaica (1). The important feature is the relative proportions of sand fractions to those of clay and silt because the drainage capacity of the soil depends upon this. Note should also be taken of the considerable variations in carbonate and humus content, the former being primarily related to the soil molluscan content.

As might be expected the mean depth of the water table increases with distance from the sea (5) and this has relevance with respect to soil aeration. It has been demonstrated, not only from the anaerobic nature of the black mud and the mean depth of water table, but also experimentally that an aerated

TABLE 8.3

Mechanical analyses of Floridan and Jamaican mangrove soils

	Coarse sand %	Fine sand %	Clay %	Silt %	Humus %	CO_3^-
Jamaica peat						
surface	1.7–17.3	1.1–27.2	9.0–20	5.1–24.4	19.4–54.4	0–1.85
subsurface	3.5–13.8	0.7–20.3	12.7–54.7	5.6–44.9	21.8–48.4	0–0.2
Jamaica siliceous sand						
surface	34.7–93.5	0.7–30.93	0–2.2	0.03–2.02	0.74–13.8	1.85–47.4
subsurface	30.5–93.7	0.8–27.86	0.1–1.42	0.2–1.85	1.21–8.56	1.76–53.22
Florida						
peat					65.2	7.1
mud					29.83	67.26
sand					9.21	9.36

layer exists in the upper regions of mangrove soils (1). In such aerated layers the occluded atmosphere is commonly very poor in oxygen and high in CO_2 and H_2S, and it is this that renders the existence of the pneumatophores so important. In areas associated with *R. mangle* oxygen concentrations tend to range from 2.45–11.02 percent whereas in *Avicennia germinans* they range from 0–9.6 percent but with a higher average. The highest CO_2/H_2S values were also recorded in *Avicennia* soils (1).

Since mangrove is essentially tropical, regional temperature and humidity play a major part in determining the evaporation power of the air. In Florida mangal Davis (6) recorded very high evaporation rates, e.g. 20.5 cc/day in *R. mangle*, 21.5 cc/day in *Avicennia*. During periods of continuous exposure (see p. 124) these rates could be significant in reducing soil moisture content.

So far as fauna is concerned it would seem that there are six distinct habitats: (1) tree canopy which is essentially terrestrial and occupied by animals from adjacent terrestrial forest but it can include mosquitoes, egret and herons; (2) rot holes in branches wherein mosquito larvae can develop; (3) soil surface and (4) subsoil where one can find climbing snails, barnacles,

oysters and crabs, etc.; (5) permanent and semi-permanent pools; (6) channels
with alligators, mudskippers and jelly fish (5). It seems (14) that there is
really no specific mangrove fauna, most of the animals recorded coming either
from adjacent terrestrial vegetation or else being typical of saline mud
flats whether or not they are covered by vegetation.

REFERENCES

1   CHAPMAN V.J., 1939 Cambridge University Expedition to Jamaica. *J. Linn.
     Soc. Bot.* (Lond.), 52, 407-533 (1944).

2   CHAPMAN V.J., *Mangrove Vegetation.* Cramer, Lehre (1975).

3   CRAIGHEAD F.C., Land, mangroves and hurricanes. *Fairchild Tropical Gard.
     Bull., 19,* No. 4, 1-18 (1964).

4   DAVIS J.H., Mangroves, makers of land. *Nature Mag.,* 31, 551 (1938a).

5   DAVIS J.H., The role of mangrove vegetation in land building in Southern
     Florida. *Amer. Phil. Soc. Yr. Bk.,* 1938, p. 162 (1938b).

6   DAVIS J.H., The ecology and geologic role of mangroves in Florida. *Pap.
     Tortugas Lab.,* 52 (*Publ. Carn. Inst.,* No. 517), 303-412 (1940).

7   DAVIS J.H., The ecology of the vegetation and topography of the sand
     keys of Florida. *Publ. Carn. Inst. Wash.,* No. 524, 117-195 (1942).

8   EGLER F.E., The dispersal and establishment of red mangroves, *Rhizophora,*
     in Florida. *Carib. Forest.,* 9(4), 299-319 (1948).

9   EGLER F.E., Southeast saline Everglades vegetation, Florida, and its
     management. *Vegetatio,* 3(4/5), 213-65 (1950).

10   GIFFORD J.C., *The keys and glades of South Florida.* N.Y. Books Inc.

11   KOHLMEYER J., Marine fungi from the tropics. *Mycologia,* 60, 252-270
     (1968).

12   LARUE C.D. and MUZIK T.J., Growth, regeneration and precocious rooting
     in *Rhizophora mangle. Pap. Mich. Acad. Sci. Arts Lett.,* 39, 9 (1954).

13   LEE B.K.H. and BAKER G.E., An ecological study of the soil microfungi in
     a Hawaiian mangrove swamp. *Pac. Sci.,* 26, 1-10 (1972).

14   MACNAE W., A general account of the fauna and flora of mangrove swamps
     and forests in the Indo-West-Pacific region. Adv. Mar. Biol., 6, 73-269
     (1968).

15   PRICE W.A., Development of the basin-in-basin honeycomb of Florida Bay
     and the north-eastern Cuban lagoon. *Trans. Gulf Coast Ass. Geol. Soc.,*
     17, 368-399 (1967).

16   SCHOLL D.W., Recent sedimentary record in mangrove swamps and rise in
     sea level over the south-western coast of Florida. I. *Mar. Geol.*, 1, 344–
     66; II. *Ibid*, 2, 343-364.

17   SCHOLL D.W. and STUVIER M., Recent submergence of southern Florida: a
     comparison with adjacent coasts and other eustatic data. *Geol. Soc. Amer.
     Bull.*, 78, 437-454 (1967).

18   STEWART I.E., Biologists invade Florida. *Science* 120, 874-876 (1954).

19   TAYLOR W.R., Associations algales des mangrove d'Amérique. *Colloques
     Inter. C.N.R.S.*, 81, 143-52 (1959).

20   TOMLINSON T.E., Changes in sulphate-containing mangrove soil on dying
     and their effect upon the suitability of the soil for the growth of rice.
     Emp. J. exp. Agric., 25, 108-118 (1957).

21   WATSON J.G., Mangrove forests of the Malay Peninsula. Malay. For. Rec.
     6, 275 pp.

CHAPTER 9

SHINGLE BEACHES

FORMATION

Whilst shingle beaches occur from place to place around coasts, in most cases the stones and pebbles are so mobile that vegetation is quite unable to become established. The large shingle beaches, where portions have become stabilised and bear vegetation, are relatively few. Stones varying in size form the basic materials of which they are composed. Quite a proportion of these stones are derived from glacial deposits and have come from cliff erosion.

In other cases they have been brought down by rivers, especially where there is an adjacent high upland. A third source of material is the off-shore sea bed. The shingle from any one of these sources may be built up to form a beach in the immediate vicinity, or the material may be transported along the coast (see p. 235) to form a shingle beach some distance away. Some of these shingle beaches subsequently acquire a partial covering of sand dunes (e.g. Blakeney, Scolt Head Island) and so it is necessary to consider both habitats (see Chapter 6) in order to obtain a comprehensive picture.

The main factors responsible for beach building are fourfold: first, there is the beach material and here size and quantity is important; secondly, the strength and direction of the waves, which in turn are influenced by a third factor, the wind, and finally there is the extent of the tidal rise and fall. On some beaches, e.g. the Chesil in Dorset, the structure may also be determined to some extent by water percolation (see p. 239).

In the construction of shingle beaches, the most important factor is that of wave action. The size of the waves is, of course, determined by wind velocity and duration, associated with the distance or *fetch* over which the waves are generated, the greater the fetch the larger the waves. Waves can approach the beach either directly or obliquely. In either case they can throw up material, but if oblique they can also bring about beach drift as well as generate longshore currents that will produce movement of material. Dependent upon the degree of wave action, there may be mass transport of water that in shallow

234

depths can result in landward movement of material on the sea bottom.

The tides are obviously less important than wave action, though abnormal high tides can have a major effect on a shingle beach, particularly in raising its elevation and causing landward movement. Associated with the tides there are the tidal currents, which can move the lighter material on the sea bottom. These currents exist during ebb and flow periods and are non-existent at slack low and high water.

LONG-SHORE MOVEMENT

Long-shore movement of beach material takes place either at the upper limit of the waves or else in the surf and breaker zone. In the former case the swash moves pebbles obliquely up the beach and the backwash takes them down vertically (Fig. 9.1). The angle of wave incidence is therefore important,

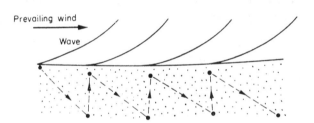

FIG. 9.1. *Diagram illustrating beach drift with waves caused by prevailing wind approaching obliquely. The broken line represents successive movements of a pebble (after Steers).*

though movement is also greater on a more steeply shelving coast. In the surf and breaker zone, it is mostly smaller material in suspension that is moved, such movement also being contributed to by any long-shore tidal and wind currents. The actual rate of beach material movement can be followed by the use of marked pebbles. On the beach proper paint can be used, whilst below low water stones tagged with radio-active barium or lanthanum have been employed successfully, the course of movement being followed by means of detectors. Movement does not take place in deep water, but in shallow water stones may travel from 50-550 m over a period of 4 weeks (7).

Long-shore growth of shingle beaches, especially when they form a spit or off-

shore barrier island, normally takes place in one direction depending on the
prevalence of the factors mentioned above. From time to time, however,
storms come from the opposite direction to the winds and waves that promote
normal growth. When this happens the growing point can be turned at right
angles and a lateral is formed. It is not uncommon, therefore, for spits to
show a series of such laterals with a hook at the end (Fig. 4.1). At the
growing point, movement can be considerable and this is reflected in the
changes over the years. Under such conditions any vegetational growth is
likely to be of an ephemeral nature.

BEACH MATERIAL

It should be evident that, in general, shingle beaches normally develop at
right angles to the incident waves (7,8) and that the "pile-up" to form our
shingle beaches is due to the action of direct onshore waves. On the beach
itself it is usual to find the coarsest stones on the crest. This is because
the beach profile is often such that it allows the waves to break close in-
shore at high tide, and the energy liberated by these waves moves the larger
material. This is particularly true of storm waves operating at high tide
periods. These are, in fact, the principal beach builders and profile mould-
ers.

On some beaches, such as the Chesil in Dorset, the stones show a gradation in
size from large ones at the Portland end to small ones at Abbotsbury. At the
former place the beach is 185 m wide and 13 m above high water, and the stones
are 5-7.5 cm in diameter. At the latter, the width is 160 m and the height is
about halved and the stones are only about 1.5 cm in diameter. This gradation
of material has resulted in argument concerning the origin of the beach and
whether it has grown from the east or the west. There is no doubt that in
relation to its physiography the waves at the Portland end have more energy
and have therefore built a wider and higher beach with the coarser materials.

Scott's study (1963) (17) of shingle beaches has shown that plants only produce
extensive fine absorption roots when fine silty material is present with the
stones. The regression coefficient of plant density to fine material was also
highly significant. Scott suggests that the following four types of shingle
beach substrate can be recognised:

(a) No matrix - lichens only on boulders.

(b) Sand matrix - species of yellow and grey dune, e.g. *Festuca rubra, Sedum acre, Agropyron junceiforme, Poa pratensis.*

(c) Wrack (seaweed debris) matrix - rich flora varying with drainage and salinity conditions but species of *Atriplex* prominent.

(d) Silt matrix - a rich flora varying with degree of inundation. Typical species include *Glaux maritima, Artemisia maritima, Spergularia media, Halimione* and *Puccinellia maritima,* mainly from adjacent salt marsh.

WAVE ACTION

It is not necessary in this little book to embark on a detailed discussion of waves and wave action, but in so far as shingle beaches are concerned it should be noted that waves are either constructive or destructive (8). The former have an elliptical motion, and when breaking or spilling the wave front is not at a steep angle (Fig. 8.2b). The energy contained in such waves resides mainly in the swash, which therefore carried pebbles up the beach. Destructive waves have a plunging motion and a steep front when breaking (Fig. 8.2a), and because they plunge more vertically downwards their energy is mainly contained in the backwash, so that the beach is combed down and a steep head bank is formed around high tide mark. The two kinds of beach profiles are shown in Fig. 8.2c, AB representing the profile formed by destructive waves and CD that formed by constructive waves. In Fig. 8.2d, we see the effect of destructive waves upon the beach profile CD that has been built up. At low tide the backwash removes material below E resulting in a new profile. As the tide rises, more and more material is removed by the backwash (e.g. FB). At or near high water, the top of the beach at C will be cut back and the final stage will be a beach profile resembling the curve AB. In Fig. 8.2e, we follow the effect of constructive waves on a profile formed after a series of destructive waves as above. Here the swash carried up more pebbles than the backwash removes, and a small ridge CD is formed. As the tide rises, this ridge travels up the rising shore (e.g. E) until around high water the final ridge AGHK is produced. In a series of tides from neaps to springs, a new ridge will develop at each new high tide. In Fig. 8.2f the same beach is seen on a falling tide when material is still being added to the beach, so that there is a slight ridge at C which may travel slowly down the beach as the tide recedes. In Fig. 8.2g, AL represents a beach profile resulting from

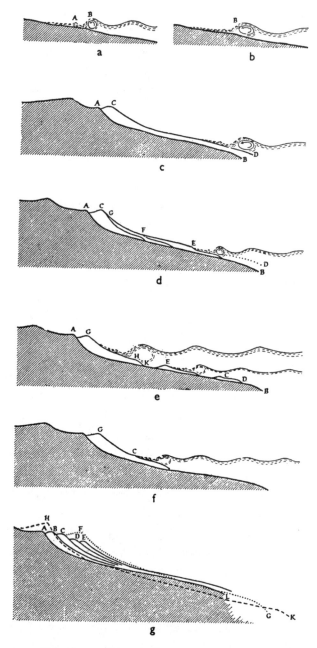

FIG. 9.2. *Beach profiles and wave action. For explanation, see text (after Lewis).*

destructive waves at spring tides. If a period of constructive waves sets
in, then ridges such as B, C, D, E will be formed, falling in height as successive tides decrease. If these are then followed by another series of
spring tides a new major ridge F would be formed with the profile FLG. If,
however, destructive storm waves are at work they will cut down all these
ridges, carrying the shingle below low water mark and result, at low water,
in the profile represented by HLK. It should be sufficiently clear now that
the profile of shingle beaches is likely to be extremely variable and therefore inhospitable to vegetation of any kind.

Storm waves at high tide, and particularly at spring high tides, are of paramount importance because at such times pebbles can be thrown right over the
beach. It is indeed through the action of such storms that shingle beaches
gradually move landwards, and, if salt marsh had previously developed behind,
old marsh mud can be exposed on the foreshore. Such landward movement is not
a regular process along the whole length of the beach and is generally represented by shingle fans on the landward side. These may remain mobile or they
may become stabilised by vegetation and new fans develop elsewhere. Whilst
movement for any given storm is therefore represented by specific points of
mobility, over a long period the whole beach exhibits landward movement.

On a large, high beach, such as the Chesil, the development of shingle fans on
the landward side is associated with the percolation of sea water, which takes
place under storm conditions, and which is of course easy with shingle. As
drainage water percolates out on the landward side, usually between fans,
shingle is removed and small ravines are formed. On the Chesil these ravines
are known as "cans" and together with their two side buttresses they form a
"camm" (13) (Fig. 8.3). These camms are quite important physiographic features
in relation to the distribution of the vegetation, particularly of Shrubby
seablite (*Suaeda fruticosa*) (p. 243). The shingle forming the back and walls
of a camm is usually just at the angle of repose (34°) for shingle of that
size.

Whilst the main beach material is clearly shingle or pebbles, in certain
areas either material is mixed with sand so that dune plants become associated
with the shingle plants in the same way as they do when dunes on a shingle
ridge erode away (see p. 246). This kind of phenomenon can be seen at the
Ayreland of Bride in the Isle of Man, where there are low dunes lying on

FIG. 9.3. *Shingle ravines on the Chesil Bank as seen from the terrace. Sketch by Mr T.G. Hill (after Oliver and Salisbury).*

shingle, and shingle ridges can be seen in the dune lows of Winterton Ness (20).

On the Norfolk coast the shingle is commonly associated with sand, but as a result of landward movement the beach may rest on salt marsh mud (see p. 92), though in other localities it lies on a sand base. Where a shingle beach protects salt marsh, one can expect to find some salt marsh plants at the lower levels on the landward side. It has been suggested that a true shingle beach flora only develops where there is pure shingle overlying a sand base. Even here, however, the presence of drift-line plants adds a complicating element. Indeed it can be argued that there are no true shingle species, and that all those plants which do occur have come in from other habitats.

TYPES OF BEACH

Shingle beaches can be placed in one of five different categories. The first type of beach, which is associated directly with cliff, has been called a *fringing beach* (22) and generally carries only drift-line vegetation. The second type of shingle beach is the *spit* which is represented by Hurst Castle spit, Calshot, Northam and Blakeney Point (Fig. 4.1).

Very comparable to the spit, but differing from it in that it unites two areas of upland, is the shingle *bar*. The outstanding example of this type is the

seven-mile-long Chesil Beach in Dorset. The fourth type of shingle area is
represented by a place such as Dungeness where a whole series of parallel
shingle ridges have been thrown up. This forms what is known as a *cuspate
foreland*. The inner ridges soon become isolated from the sea and in the absence of drift and seeds they remain sterile for a long period. Finally,
there are shingle *off-shore barrier islands* represented by Scolt Head Island.
Of these various types of shingle beach only Blakeney, Scolt and the Chesil
have had any detailed botanical examination. Therefore any other shingle
beach that carries vegetation provides, at present, a significant field for
study.

Blakeney Point, Scolt Head Island, Dungeness and the Chesil are such major
physiographic features that geomorphologists (8,9,10,19) have devoted considerable attention to their origin and development. At Blakeney and Scolt Head,
growth westwards has been interrupted by the formation of laterals formed as
described above. Between the laterals, salt marsh has developed, and on the
shingle, sand dunes have formed and in some cases have subsequently been
eroded away.

At Dungeness, Lewis and Balchin (10) have argued that the various heights of the
successive groups of ridges are related to past changes in land-sea levels.
Whilst this may indeed be the correct interpretation one must express the hope
that future physiographers will have a further look at the problem here and
elsewhere, in particular making use perhaps of ^{14}C methods for dating ridges.
After a careful study of the ridges, Lewis (9) has worked out the probable
course of development (Fig. 9.4). Early successive beaches are thought to
have existed along the lines AB, AC, AD, AE, AF and then later a change of
direction took place represented by HK, MN and BQ. At present Dungeness is
growing outwards as a result of on-shore waves from the south-west and from
the east forming shingle beaches on two sides.

The account given above of the nature of shingle beaches and the factors involved in their formation does not pretend to be exhaustive. There are other
facets and details that could be elaborated, and for those who are interested
reference should be made to King's (7) book - *Beaches and Coasts*.

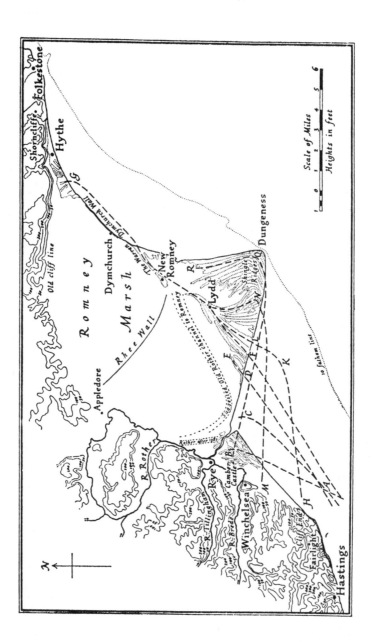

FIG. 9.4. Dungeness, showing lines of probable previous shingle beaches. AB is the oldest and BNQR the stage not very different from that of the present day (after Lewis)

VEGETATION

The vegetation can conveniently be placed into five stability groups (17).

1.   Beach very unstable and lacking vegetation.

2.   Summer annuals on beaches that are stable between spring and autumn.

3.   Short-lived perennials where beaches are stable for 3-4 years, e.g. *Catopodium marinum*, *Sedum acre* and the long-lived perennial *Suaeda fruticosa*.

4.   Long-lived perennials on stable shingle, e.g. *Crambe maritima*, *Rumex crispus*, *Silene maritima* (see p. 247).

5.   Heath vegetation with *Arrhenatherum elatine*, *Festuca rubra*.

It is clear that vegetation of shingle beaches is not rich floristically, but in the light of their mobility this is not surprising, nor has it been studied in any great detail except at Blakeney, Scolt, the Chesil and North Brittany (4). On the first three areas, the Shrubby seablite *Suaeda fruticosa*, which can grow to a height of 4 feet, is a most important plant(1,15) and originates as a drift-line plant (p. 155), the seeds being brought with the flotsam and jetsam. When the seeds germinate, long tap roots rapidly grow down and enable the plants to become established.

Once plants have established, sooner or later they become overwhelmed by a shingle fan (p. 239); the now horizontal shoots put out new roots and new vertical shoots (Fig. 9.5). This process is repeated again and again as each succeeding shingle flow increases the amount of shingle over the original spot, so that the *Suaeda* appears to mount the shingle beach (Fig. 9.6), though really the beach is very slowly being moved backwards.

As the shingle becomes deeper and deeper, the older parts of the plant decay. Also since each line of *Suaeda* establishes during the same quiescent period and it is the same storms that generally bring about the overwhelming process, the plants appear to move up as a zone (Fig. 9.7).

The response of *Suaeda* to shingle covering is not the only factor controlling its growth. Thus, experiments have shown that the seedlings are very susceptible to water-logging of the roots though the adult plants are not so sensitive.

FIG. 9.5. *Prostrated branch of Shrubby seablite* (Suaeda fruticosa) *rejuvenating in the shingle from lateral buds; to show habit. One-third natural size (after Oliver and Salisbury).*

On a relatively low beach, such as Blakeney, where there may be some mobility on the landward side, the plants of *Suaeda* are more common in the bays between successive shingle fans, since it is noticeable that successive shingle flows tend to move along the same lines. The shingle on the Blakeney beach is sufficiently mobile for it to be thrown right over the beach. When such thrown shingle encounters lines of *Suaeda* bushes, a heaping up of the shingle occurs (Fig. 9.7).

Apart from the shrubby seablite, a number of other species occur on the more stable portions of shingle beaches. More than sixty species have been listed for the main beach and laterals at Blakeney, of which at least twenty are very rare and a further sixteen rare. Among the more important and common species are Sand couch grass (*Agropyron junceiforme*) (drift-line plant), Sea couch grass (*A. pungens*) (dune plant), Creeping fescue (*Festuca rubra*) (dune plant), Yellow horned-poppy (*Glaucium flavum*), Sea sandwort (*Honkenya peploides*) (drift-line and embryo dunes), Curled dock (*Rumex crispus*), Wall-pepper

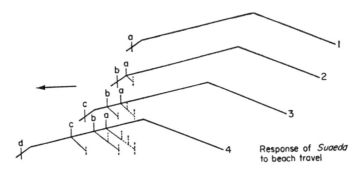

Response of *Suaeda*
to beach travel

FIG. 9.6. *Diagram illustrating the mode of ascent of Shrubby sea-blite* (Suaeda fruticosa) *from the place of establishment on the lee fringe up to the crest of a travelling beach. Four profiles (1, 2, 3, 4) in the travel of the beach are shown and four* Suaeda *plants (a, b, c, d) successively establishing at each stage are considered. The existing portions of the* Suaeda *are represented by continuous lines, the parts which have disintegrated by broken lines. The direction of travel is from right to left (after Oliver and Salisbury).*

(*Sedum acre*), Groundsel (*Senecio vulgaris*), Sea campion (*Silene maritima*), Sowthistle (*Sonchus oleraceus*) and Field milk-thistle (*S. arvensis*). Sea sandwort is normally found where the shingle is mixed with sand and nearly all the above species are associated with the drift-laden portion of the beach. An interesting plant found only locally but characteristic of shingle beaches, is the Northern shore-wort (*Mertensia maritima*). This is found at Blakeney and on shingle beaches in northern England and Scotland, as well as in Ireland.

On the landward side where the shingle abuts on to salt marsh both at Blakeney and Scolt, one can find Sea purslane (*Halimione*), Sea aster (*Aster*), Sea wormwood (*Artemisia*), Sea poa (*Puccinellia*), Sea plantain (*Plantago maritima*) and Sea lavender (*Limonium vulgare*). Where sand is mixed with shingle, either be-

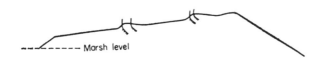

Marsh level

FIG. 9.7. *Profile of Blakeney Main Beach showing how the* Suaeda *bushes cause a heaping up of the shingle. Only two of the* Suaeda *zones are represented (after Oliver and Salisbury).*

cause it is blown there or because former dunes have been removed by erosion
(see p. 155), plants of Sand sedge (*Carex arenaria*), Sea convolvulus (*Calystegia soldanella*), Lyme grass (*Elymus*), Sea holly (*Eryngium*) and Ragwort
(*Senecio jacobaea*) may occasionally be found. Nearly all these plants have a
lower growth habit than their counterparts in the other habitats that they
normally occupy.

On the laterals at both Blakeney and Scolt Head, where conditions are very
much more stable, a wider variety of plants can be found. Species additional
to those listed above are Rock sea lavender (*Limonium binervosum*) (a plant
which will not tolerate covering by sand or shingle), Darnel poa (*Desmazeria
marina*), Sea pink (*Armeria maritima*), Thyme-leaved sandwort (*Arenaria serpyllifolia*), Sea heath (*Frankenia laevis*) and Buck's-horn plantain (*Plantago coronopus* var. *pygmaea*). These stable laterals frequently exhibit a distinct
zonation. This zonation may be related to inundations but is more likely to
be related to gradations of salinity in the soil water or decrease in the
amount of soil. It must, however, be admitted that at the present time no
work has been carried out on such zonations, and until it has been, it is
probably premature to suggest possible factors.

The lowest zone on these stable shingle laterals of the Norfolk coast is dominated by Shrubby seablite (*Suaeda fruticosa*), but associated with it one
finds Sea purslane (*Halimione portulacoides*), Sea poa (*Puccinellia maritima*),
Scurvy-grass (*Cochlearia*), Matted sea lavender (*Limonium bellidifolium*),
Annual glasswort (*Salicornia stricta*) and Seablite (*Suaeda maritima* var. *flexilis*) - the whole group being strongly representative of the salt marsh flora.

At Blakeney (14) there is a zone above this with Sea couch grass (*Agropyron pungens*) and Creeping fescue (*Festuca rubra*), the latter being the dominant. The
zone next above is found in both localities, and can well be termed the *Limonium binervosum* zone. Associated with the lavender, there is sea pink, sea
heath, sea poa, and the dwarf form of buck's-horn plantain. On the crest,
Fiorin (*Agrostis stolonifera*), Wall-pepper (*Sedum acre*), Sea campion (*Silene
maritima*) and some of the species from lower down form the final cover.
Should the lateral have a curved tip, the elbow of the bend is commonly higher
than the crest of the lateral, and on the elbow additional species such as
Bird's-foot trefoil (*Lotus corniculatus*), Sheep's sorrel (*Rumex acetosella*),
Ribwort (*Plantago lanceolata*), Lady's bedstraw (*Galium verum*), Crested hair-

grass (*Koeleria gracilis*) are to be found. These are all species of gravelly
heaths and light inland soils, and their presence indicates more or less complete freedom from strictly maritime conditions. Such zonation as has been
described above is essentially a static one. A comparable zonation can be
found on the Chesil, but of course there are no laterals. The crest of the
Chesil is dominated by the Sea pea (*Lathyrus maritimus*), which is not present
in Norfolk, and there may also be much *Geranium purpureum*.

Information about the vegetation of the other main shingle areas is very
scanty, and no detailed accounts have appeared. Golden samphire (*Inula crithmoides*) is reported as occurring on stable shingle at both Dover, Hamstead and
Hurst Castle. At Dungeness whilst there is a fringe of rather fine and extensive *Crambe maritima*, the ridges, known as "fulls", generally bear Curled dock
(*Rumex crispus*), and Sea campion (*Silene maritima*) in the younger stages;
later a whole collection of herbs and grasses cover them, so much so that some
areas have been incorporated as pasture. If no grazing takes place, a scrub
develops with bramble, gorse, hawthorn, blackthorn and elder. It is considered that this scrub would give way to a forest climax of *Ilex aquifolius* (Fig.
9.8). The hollows between ridges, which are known as "lows" or "swales", are
bare in the early stages and later may carry marsh plants such as Marsh arrow-
grass (*Triglochin palustris*).

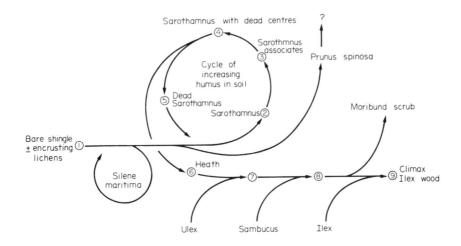

FIG. 9.8. *Summary of zerosere at Dungeness; numbers are those of
seral stages (after Scott)*

The ridges at Winterton Ness are less obvious than those at Dungeness, and there is a considerable amount of sand mixed in the soil. According to Steers and Jensen (20), the youngest ridges are characterised by a covering of the grass *Corynephorus canescens* with two species of the lichen genus *Cladonia.* Older ridges, which are farther inland, are still dominated by *Corynephorus* but plants of Sand sedge (*Carex arenaria*) are evident, and this becomes more and more abundant with increasing distance from the sea.

On the shingle beaches of Talbert Géhu (4) recognised two communities. The lowest was dominated by *Atriplex glabriuscula* (= *A. Babingtonii*) together with *Beta maritima*, *Atriplex hastata* and *A. arenaria*. This community was associated with the drift-line and all species are nitrophiles. The higher belt was dominated by *Crambe maritima* with *Rumex crispus*, *Solanum dulcamara* and *Crithmum maritimum*. A subassociation of *Silene maritima* was also recognised.

Mosses and lichens have been studied at Scolt (2,3), Blakeney (11,16) and on the Chesil (23). As may be expected they are confined to the stable areas of shingle, namely near and on the crest of the beaches. At Blakeney there is some difference between the moss species (nine) that occur on the more mobile main bank in comparison with those on the more stable laterals. On the Chesil the most important species are *Bryum capillare*, *Ceratodon purpureus* and *Hypnum cupressiforme*. Because of the stony substrate, lichens are really more important than mosses. Since there are lichens that tolerate immersion in salt water (p. 36), it is not surprising to find *Verrucaria maura* and *Placodium lobulatum* occupying the lowest part of the beach where there will be occasional submergence. On the stable laterals of Scolt and Blakeney, crustose lichen species form the characteristic element at the lower levels, whilst below and on the crest where there are grasses, the non-crustose *Cladonia furcata*, *C. pungens* and *Cetraria aculeata* give a greyish colour to the ground. The nature of the habitat does not, of course, provide encouragement for any growth of algae.

On the western Atlantic coast practically no information is available about the vegetation of maritime shingle beaches, though some is available about raised beaches. On Long Island shingle beaches have a flora of *Rhus toxicodendron*, *Spartina juncea*, *Juniperus virginiana*, *Myrica cerifera* and *Puccinellia maritima*. All of these except the last are species of dune habitats (Chapter 6) and the *Puccinellia* of salt marsh (see p. 108). There are therefore no characteristic species (45).

FACTORS

When we turn to consider the factors of the environment, it will be evident from what has been said that the seaward side of the beach is substantially different from the landward. There will clearly be variations in the soil environment and also the microclimate, as between each of these. Unfortunately at present no information is available and a detailed study of the environment of shingle beaches is greatly to be desired. Any humus present comes essentially from the drift, and on old laterals at Blakeney it can amount to 3.1 percent of the soil, sufficient to give a hydrogen ion concentration slightly on the acid side of neutral.

Water Table

When pits are dug into the shingle, standing water can be encountered at not too great a depth. In many cases this water is fresh, or at the most brackish. Values have been recorded from the Blakeney beach at 5 cm depth with a chloride content of 0.07-0.44 percent. Lower down at 5-9 ft, which was equivalent to the level of the adjacent salt marsh, the chloride in the water did not exceed the same range. The whole question of fresh water in shingle beaches has been carefully examined by Hill and Hanley (6), though further work would be desirable in order to substantiate their conclusions. Figure 9.9 shows a composite profile of the Blakeney main beach derived from digging a series of pits. The position of the water table in relation to the soil surface is also shown. There is no doubt that in such shingle beaches the water table fluctuates in relation to the tides (see also p. 195). There will be irregularities in tide heights, since the tides only rarely conform to their exact predicted heights (Fig. 9.9).

The water that is present is regarded as coming essentially from three different sources. Because of the nature of the substrate, rain water penetrates rapidly and comes to lie on top of any underlying salt water table, if there is one (and further work here would be desirable). Ordinary dew forms and water from this source also readily runs down between the shingle. There is, however, the special process known as internal dew formation (see p. 201) which could be responsible for some of the water, and which keeps the stones moist to just below the surface (this cannot be capillarity as the rise is

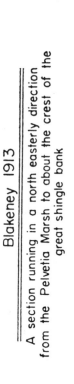

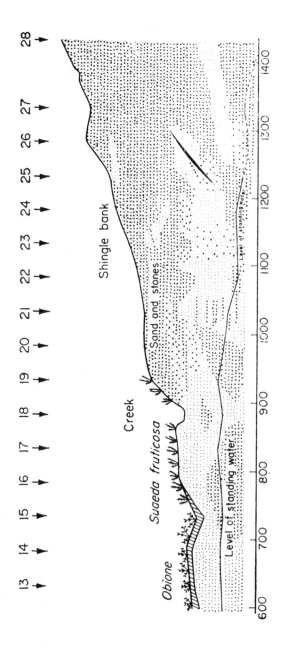

FIG. 9.9. *Section of part of Blakeney Beach to show structure (after Hill and Hanley).*

often too high above the water table). Further work is wanted on this subject as Scott (17) believes there is no more condensation in shingle soils than in any other type.

From the above account it will be seen how relatively scanty is our knowledge of shingle beaches, and it is clear that in the case of cuspate foreland and fringing beaches in particular there is scope for plenty of study, both descriptive and experimental.

REFERENCES

1   CHAPMAN V.J., *Suaeda fruticosa* Forsk *in* Biological Flora of the British Isles. *J. Ecol.*, 35, 303-310 (1947).

2   DUCKER B.F.T., The Bryophytes of Scolt Head Island, in *Scolt Head Island*. Ed. J.A. Steers. Heffer, Cambridge (1960).

3   ELLIS G.A., The Lichens, in *Scolt Head Island*. Ed. J.A. Steers. Heffer, Cambridge (1960).

4   GÉHU J.M., Un site célèbre de la côte Nord Bretonne: Le Sillon de Talbert (C-du-N). Observations phytosociologique et écologiques. *Lab. Mar. Dinard*, Fasc. 46, 93-113.

5   HARSHBERGER J.W., Phytogeographical survey of North America. 2nd repr. Ed. Weimar (1958).

6   HILL T.G. and HANLEY J.A., The structure and water content of shingle beaches. *J. Ecol.*, 2, 21-38 (1914).

7   KING C.A.M., *Beaches and Coasts*. Arnold (1959).

8   LEWIS W.V., The effect of wave incidence on the configuration of a shingle beach. *Geog. J.*, 78(2), 129-148 (1931).

9   LEWIS W.V., The formation of Dungeness Foreland. *Geog. J.*, 80(4), 309-524 (1932).

10 LEWIS W.V. and BALCHIN W.G.V., Past sea-levels at Dungeness. *Geog. J.*, 96 (4), 258-285 (1940).

11 MCLEAN R.C., The ecology of the maritime lichens at Blakeney Pt., Norfolk. *J. Ecol.*, 3, 129-148 (1915).

12 OLIVER F.W., The shingle beach as a plant habitat. *New Phyt.*, 11, 73-99 (1912).

13 OLIVER F.W., Some remarks on Blakeney Pt., Norfolk. *J. Ecol.*, 1, 4-15 (1913).

14   OLIVER F.W. and SALISBURY E.J., Topography and vegetation of Blakeney
      Point. *Trans. Norf. Norw. Nat. Soc.*, 9 (1913).

15   OLIVER F.W. and SALISBURY E.J., Vegetation and mobile ground as illust-
      rated by *Suaeda fruticosa* on shingle. *J. Ecol.*, 1, 249-272 (1913).

16   RICHARDS P.W., Notes on the ecology of the bryophytes and lichens at
      Blakeney Pt., Norfolk. *J. Ecol.*, 17, 127-140 (1929).

17   SCOTT G.A.M., The ecology of shingle beach plants. *J. Ecol.*, 51(3), 517-
      527 (1963).

18   SCOTT G.A.M., The shingle succession at Dungeness. *J. Ecol.*, 53(1), 21-
      31 (1965).

19   STEERS J.A., *The Coastline of England and Wales*. C.U. Press (1946).

20   STEERS J.A. and JENSEN H.A.P., Winterton Ness. *Trans. Norf. Norw. Nat.
      Soc.*, 17(4), 259-274 (1953).

21   TANSLEY A.G., *Types of British Vegetation*. C.U. Press (1911).

22   TANSLEY A.G., *The British Islands and their Vegetation*. C.U. Press
      (1939).

23   WATSON W., List of lichens from Chesil beach. *J. Ecol.*, 10, 255-256
      (1922).

CHAPTER 10

COASTAL CLIFF VEGETATION

The vegetation that is to be found above high water mark on coastal cliffs
has been the least studied of all maritime vegetation types. One reason is
probably that it does not normally form the clearly demarcated communities
that are to be found on salt marshes, sand dunes and shingle ridges. Whilst
undoubted maritime species occur, there is a considerable admixture of non-
halophytes and the transition from what may be termed true maritime to non-
maritime is not readily observable. Cliffs of any nature are also dangerous
places on which to work, and in many cases, unless the investigator is also an
experienced rock climber, effective study of the plant cover is not possible.
Relatively few areas of coast have therefore been subject to investigation,
but there is a classical work on the subject in the series of papers by M.E.
Gillham (5-10). Vegetation changes over a period of years emerge from the series of papers on St. Kilda by Petch(17), Poore and Robertson(18) and McVean(15)
whilst accounts have also been published on Ailsa Craig in the Firth of Clyde
(23), on Cornish cliffs (13,16), on Sussex cliffs (22), on the cliffs of Clare
Island and western Eire (19) and on the North Breton coast (2-4).

CHARACTERISTIC PLANTS

Tansley (21), in his monumental work on the vegetation of the British Isles, considered that the only plants which could be regarded as characteristic of
cliffs were Seakale (*Crambe maritima*), Rock samphire (*Crithmum maritimum*), Sea
beetroot (*Beta vulgaris* ssp. *maritima*), Fennel (*Foeniculum vulgare*), Wild
cabbage (*Brassica oleracea*), Stock (*Matthiola incana*) and Sea spleenwort
(*Asplenium marinum*). *Lavatera arborea* should perhaps also be considered here
(2). To this list Petch (17) added the following as characteristic cliff-dwelling
plants on St. Kilda: Long-leaved scurvy grass (*Cochlearia anglica*),* Scentless
mayweed (*Matricaria maritima* ssp. *inodora* var. *salina*), Sea pink (*Armeria maritima*), Sea campion (*Silene maritima*) and Dark green mouse-ear chickweed (*Cer-

* Dr Gillham (personal communication) considers that *C. officinalis*
is more characteristic of cliffs.

253

astium tetrandrum). It seems evident that some of the species, e.g. *Armeria maritima, Silene maritima, Plantago maritima,* though occurring elsewhere, e.g. salt marsh, shingle, are nevertheless characteristic species of sea cliffs. Indeed, it is not surprising to find salt marsh and other species finding a niche in rock face communities. The general sequence most likely in any suit- able place at low levels, is first of all for mats of vegetation to occur in which halophytes are predominant.

With increasing height or distance from the sea these mats are replaced by submaritime grassland or heathland, or in Scotland, by a community with pro- nounced alpines such as Least willow (*Salix harbacea*) and Rose-root (*Sedum rosea*). In some places, perhaps surprisingly, one may even find woodland plants, e.g. Wild angelica (*Angelica sylvestris*), Lady fern (*Athyrium felix- foemina*), Broad buckler-fern (*Dryopteris austriaca*), which may be present as relics of former woodland or, perhaps more likely, because of reduced compet- ition.

Cliff vegetation of the western Atlantic has been but little studied. In New- foundland *Alnus viridis, Viburnum pauciflorum, Ribes prostratum, Empetrum nigrum* have been reported, and the last named, together with *Juniperus sabina* and *Solidago sempervirens* have been recorded from New England cliffs (12).

SPECIAL FEATURES

Maritime cliffs are often the haunt of sea birds, either as nesting areas or as "sitting out" places. If the bird population is considerable and the area repeatedly used, then the amount of bird droppings can exert a considerable influence upon the plant life. Indeed, vegetation altered in this way by in- tense animal occupation has been termed zooplethismic, and any account of coastal cliff vegetation must pay particular attention to examples of such vegetation. Apart from bird populations, which, around the coastal cliffs of Great Britain, essentially comprise colonies of gulls, puffins, fulmars, storm petrels, shearwaters and others, there is no doubt that sheep-grazing also has exerted as much effect on the vegetation as it does on the grassy salt marshes of the western coasts (see p. 101). Until the advent of myxomatosis, rabbit populations were also highly significant, not only because of the grazing but also because their burrows were used by the puffins and shearwaters. In certain isolated places, such as Skokholm, where the virus has not penetrated, rabbits still remain a most important factor (7).

Some of the best coastal cliff vegetation is to be found on the off-shore islands around the coast, and indeed much of the published work relates to the Pembrokeshire Islands, St. Kilda and Ailsa Craig. Here, whilst one may observe the effects of animal grazing from introduced domestic animals, there are places where no grazing occurs and then one can see the difference between grazed and ungrazed vegetation (see p. 257).

As with other types of plant communities it is possible to compile biological spectra based on Raunkaier's Life Form System. So far this has only been done for the Pembrokeshire Islands (11) where the spectrum is as follows:

Nph.	Ch.	H.	G.	Hh.	Th.
2.5	6.0	45	11	7	28.5

It will be evident that there is a close similarity to the kind of biological spectrum found for salt marshes (see p. 115) and sand dunes (p. 171) with Hemicryptophytes as the dominants and Therophytes as the next most important group. The absence of tree vegetation is essentially related to the impact of grazing and the susceptibility of British native trees to the effect of salt spray. However, in other parts of the world trees may form a component of the sea cliff vegetation. In northern New Zealand the Christmas tree or Pohutu-kawa (*Metrosideros excelsa*) is the characteristic tree of coastal cliffs, though it will also occur on maritime volcanic lava and maritime sand dunes.

PLANT COMMUNITIES

A number of communities have been described from coastal cliffs and a brief account of these will follow. The height at which these communities commence above mean high water mark depends very largely on the exposure of the coast to wind and wave action. The more exposed the coast the higher up the cliff face the vegetation will begin. In Cornwall Hepburn (13) records it as commencing about 6 m above M.H.W.M., though in sheltered coves the plants may descend to high tide level. Tansley (21) recorded Rock samphire (*Crithmum*), Sea beet (*Beta*) and Sea purslane (*Halimione*) at a height of 6 ft on the Sussex cliffs with Sea poa (*Puccinellia maritima*), Sea lavender (*Limonium vulgare*) and *Spergularia marginata* at 10 ft.   In most places it is the Sea pink (*Armeria*) that descends closest to sea level.

In areas where grazing is not a pronounced feature, one of the most extensive communities is the Festucetum rubrae.   Gillham (5) believes that it is indeed the climatic climax for the majority of exposed coastal regions in Great Britain.   In those places where there is no grazing or trampling, the *Festuca* grows luxuriantly with leaves up to 30 cm long.   Under such conditions other plants are not able to compete and very few species are associated with the dominant.   The same situation has also been recorded from sand dunes (see p. 178).   On Grassholm, off the Pembrokeshire coast, Gillham recorded only eight species in the Festucetum.   Similar dense *Festuca* is recorded (18) on the Island of Dun off St. Kilda and on sea stacks off the west coast of Eire.   The extreme competition provided by the fescue is not only through nutrients but also in respect of light, since the species likely to be associated with it in such a habitat are the low-growing maritime ones, e.g. the sea pink, sea plantain and sea campion.   On Fair Isle, Red campion (*Melandrium rubrum*) grows well in the fescue swards, probably because being a woodland species it is shade-tolerant.   Where there is some grazing, additional species enter and one may find from sixteen to twenty-two species or more.   At the same time the Festucetum as a community is not so ubiquitous, and other communities are also to be found covering rather greater areas than in ungrazed places.   When grazing becomes even more intense, a still greater variety of species are able to enter and one may find up to fifty species present.   The effect of grazing is illustrated very well in Table 10.1 (p. 260) for three islands off the Pembroke coast.

Another very widespread community in exposed places is the so-called "Plantago sward"; this covers large areas with smooth, shining sheets where there is heavy grazing by sheep and/or rabbits, and where conditions farther inland favour the development of moorland rather than grassland.   The soil of this community becomes soaked regularly in spray during the winter gales.   The existence of the Plantaginetum relative to exposure and spray means that it plays a large part in western Ireland and also on the coastal cliffs of Scotland, whilst on St. Kilda, where the winter spray can be terrific, the community occurs up to a height of 180 m above sea level.   The dominant is generally Sea plantain (*Plantago maritima*) but in places *Festuca* may become almost co-dominant. Other species found in this sward include Buck's-horn plantain (*Plantago coronopus*), Ribwort (*P. lanceolata*), Sea pink (*Armeria maritima*), Dark green mouse-ear chickweed (*Cerastium tetrandrum*), Early hair-grass (*Aira praecox*), Sea pearlwort (*Sagina maritima*) and Creeping fescue (*Festuca rubra*).

In the presence of heavy grazing, this community probably represents the plagioclimax (see below) on cliffs of western Ireland and the western and northern Scottish coasts, where the climate generally favours the development of peat. In the southern portion of its range the community, as one might expect, is floristically much richer. This has been referred to by those who have compared the same sward in western Ireland with that on St. Kilda. Poore and Robertson (18) record the community as occurring on 3 ft deep peat on St. Kilda, the peat being formed under the prevailing climatic conditions from the remains of the plants. Since the Festucetum rubrae appears to be the climatic climax in the absence of grazing, one must regard the Plantaginetum maritimi as either a post-climax or more properly as a *Zooplethismic* or deflected climax (plagioclimax) brought about by grazing. Thus on St. Kilda the probable succession is regarded as bare -----> Armerietum -----> Festucetum (grazed)-----> Plantaginetum maritimi.

The transition from the "Plantago sward" to adjacent communities can be extremely sharp, often a matter of 2-3 ft. On the islands off the Welsh coast, the Plantaginetum is more commonly dominated by Buck's-horn plantain (*Plantago coronopus*) rather than the Sea plantain (*P. maritima*), and the community does not occupy extensive areas, occurring mainly on rock outcrops, ledges and in shallow depressions. The presence of *P. coronopus* rather than *P. maritima* is probably the result of very severe grazing, because in places where grazing is less severe *P. maritima* may become co-dominant or even locally dominant. When, however, grazing is completely removed, *P. maritima* is not able to compete with the lush growth of Creeping fescue (*Festuca rubra*), though a succulent form of *Plantago coronopus* can do so.

Another fairly widespread community is that of the Armerietum maritimae (see also p. 108), which is generally associated with a soil that is drier than that of the "Plantago sward" and which also has a higher mineral content. In places *Festuca rubra* may become a co-dominant. On St. Kilda, Lundy Island, and also on the Pembrokeshire Islands, this community is highly favoured by the puffins and shearwaters and may often be riddled with their burrows;

indeed these birds are responsible for the hummocky nature of the community.
The sea pink is a plant that is tolerant of salt spray and salt in the soil,
and it also reacts much better to grazing than does fescue, nibbling of the
leaves stimulating growth rather than inhibiting it. The presence of this
community is therefore indicative of heavy grazing associated with excessive
salt spray. Patches of almost pure *Armeria* allied with Cliff sand-spurrey
(*Spergularia rupicola*) will also be found on ledges of cliffs exposed to heavy
spray. On the Cornish cliffs, Hepburn (13) records the sea pink as being most
abundant at the lower levels, where it is associated with Rock samphire
(*Crithmum*), *Spergularia rupicola* and the Sea spleenwort (*Asplenium marinum*),
whilst higher up it occurs with the Sea campion (*Silene maritima*). *Plantago
coronopus* and English stone-crop (*Sedum anglicum*) are two other species to be
found on rock ledges and in clefts at these higher levels.

As Gillham (8) has pointed out, it is clear that there are three main ecological factors leading to dominance of the Armerietum. The first of these is
climatic in that *Armeria* is more resistant to salt spray than all its competitors (except perhaps Sea rocket), and it therefore occurs at the very edges
of cliffs and on ledges all the way down (Belt A, Fig. 10.1). Because it is

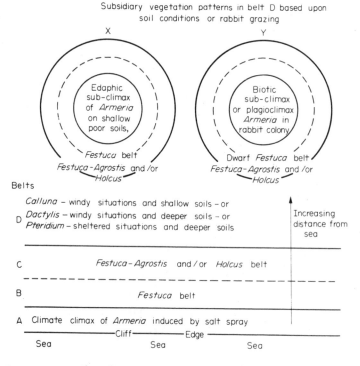

FIG. 10.1. *The three types of Armerietum on Lundy Island in
relation to adjacent communities (after Gillham).*

more resistant to grazing and burrowing under maritime conditions, it dominates bird and rabbit colonies. This community is biotically determined, and
it is therefore a sub-climax, or plagioclimax, which will proceed to a later
stage (Festucetum) (see p. 256) if the grazing is removed (Y, Fig. 10.1).
The third factor is the edaphic one, and because *Armeria* is more tolerant of
shallow, poor soils it dominates exposed eminences where much of the soil has
been eroded away. Should the soil improve, then the *Armeria* would be replaced
by other plants so that again it must be regarded as a sub-climax (X, Fig.
10.1).

In protected areas, Yorkshire fog (*Holcus lanatus*) can take over and form
patches or occupy considerable areas in which it is dominant or is the sole
species. This grass also tends to develop in areas associated with gulls(8).
It persists in spite of a dense rabbit population because it is one of the
species avoided by that mammal. It is, however, intolerant of trampling, and
under such conditions it tends to disappear. It flourishes best in depressions where conditions are the most mesophytic available, and it will occur on
cliffs with Fiorin (*Agrostis stolonifera*) where flushes of fresh water run
down. Algae such as *Hormidium* and *Cladophora* can also occur in this type of
community (5). Another grass community associated with shelter is that of the
Agrostidetum which may be dominated either by Common bent-grass (*Agrostis tenuis*) or *A. stolonifera*, the latter species being encouraged in the presence of
a seagull population. The *Agrostis* sward, which can be regarded as sub-mari-
time grassland, will withstand heavy grazing in protected places or alternatively it will tolerate strong winds if there is little grazing, but when the
two factors are combined it then gives way to other species (Table 10.1).

On the sea cliffs of north Cornwall, as soon as the slope eases the maritime
species are replaced by an *A. setacea* community with stunted herbaceous plants
and in which only Sea pink (*Armeria*), Sea campion (*Silene maritima*), Sea plantain (*Plantago maritima*) and *Spergularia* among the halophytes, can compete.
The *Armeria* zone does not in fact extend much beyond 300 m from the edge of
the cliffs. Both *Armeria* and *Agrostis* do, however, occur clothing the seaward faces of the stone walls which are nearest the cliff edge.

Where there is a heavy bird population, particularly of puffins, a local community dominated by the Sorrels, *Rumex acetosa* or *R. acetosella*, is to be found.
This is a strictly Zooplethismic community and is associated with the high

V. J. CHAPMAN

TABLE 10.1

Effect of Grazing on Agrostidetum tenuis (after Gullham)

Grazing intensity (av. no. rabbit pellets per ½ m^2)	No. of plant species	Percentage of grass cover	Percentage of cover by *Agrostis* and *Festuca*
None	2	100	100
	3	100	96
0- 10	4	100	95
	4	100	75
5-100	21	91	62
	16	75	68
300-500	23	54	50
	24	56	48

guano (bird manure) deposits. The type of vegetation is very similar to the sheep "lair" flora of cliffs described by McLean (14) and Gillham (9). Such places are very rich in nitrogen, the soil is dark and tends to be moist and well pulverised. In these places the plants found are coprophilous (dung "loving") and quick-growing. Characteristic species are Annual poa (*Poa annua*), Chickweed (*Stellaria media*) and Buck's-horn plantain (*Plantago corono-pus*). Chickweed is another species that may become locally dominant in the presence of considerable animal resting populations. Such Stellarieta have been recorded from seal breeding grounds on North Rona (15) and also on the Pembroke island of Middleholm where birds commonly roost (10).

The above represent the communities that can most properly be termed maritime. Others have been described from the off-shore islands, but it is likely that they are really non-halophytic. Included among these is the Molinetum of St. Kilda dominated by Purple moor-grass (*Molinia caerulea*) and the bracken community of the Pembrokeshire Islands. On the cliff faces themselves, cracks with water trickles or small caves are likely to have Sea spleenwort (*Asplenium marinum*) as a dominant associated with mosses and the liverwort *Marchantia*. On the cliffs of Ailsa Craig, where birds congregate, Vevers (23) has reported dwarfed plants of Elder (*Sambucus nigra*) and the Tree mallow (*Lavatera arborea*), together with typical maritima herbs such as *Spergularia*, *Silene* and

Puccinellia maritima. Erodium maritimum (Marine crane's bill) can form pure patches on the tops of cliffs, and *Silene maritima* may do the same where there is shelter on the Pembrokeshire Islands. Here, too, on moderately exposed cliff faces, *Plantago coronopus*, Scentless mayweed (*Matricaria maritima* ssp. *inodora* var. *salina*) or *Holcus lanatus* (Yorkshire fog) are to be found, and with increasing shelter Scurvy-grass (*Cochlearia officinalis*), or Cow parsnip (*Heracleum sphondylium*) or *Agrostis tenuis*. *Holcus, Agrostis stolonifera* and Pennywort (*Hydrocotyle vulgaris*) are species restricted to the fresh water flushes on such cliff faces. On the island of Grassholm, where there is no grazing, Gillham (5) has recorded a Sedetum on rocky areas that are not too exposed, and also small communities dominated either by species of *Atriplex* or *Spergularia*.

On the stacks at St. Cyrus (Kincardineshire) crustaceous lichens form the lowermost zone, the first phanerogams being generally *Armeria* and the grass *Koelaria gracilis*. Rock crevices have *Sedum acre* and *Plantago coronopus*. On higher ledges *Festuca ovina, Silene maritima, Thymus serpyllum* and *Campanula glomerata* are to be found. The summit is essentially a grassland (20).

On the Brittany coast a number of significant papers (1-4) have described the cliff vegetation. On the cretaceous rocks of Cape Blanc-Nez and Havre a community dominated by *Brassica oleracea* commenced at 15 m above H.W.M. and went to the top where it merged with a Mesobrometum. Associated species included *Matricaria maritima* and *Daucus gummifer*. On islets off the north Brittany coast a number of communities have been recognised, the lowest being a *Lavatera arborea* community (Fig. 10.2). The microflora in these communities varies from cliff to cliff and depends on vegetation, substrate and birds. It is most pronounced at the top of the cliffs (Fig. 10.3). Elsewhere on the Brittany coast *Crithmum maritimum* with *Spergularia rupicola* occupies the lowest levels with a higher belt of *Armeria maritima* and *Daucus gummifer*. Additional species include *Silene maritima* and *Plantago coronopus*.

Among the lower plants, lichens are common on the exposed rock of cliff faces. Those that have been recorded as particularly abundant are the yellow *Xanthoria parietina, Ochrolechia parella* and *Ramalina siliquosa*, whilst at the lower levels are to be found the more strictly maritime *Lichina* and *Verrucaria* (see p. 36). In those areas frequented by birds, the fresh water alga *Prasiola* is a common soil-dweller, though it tends to be absent where there is no vegetation so that the soil bakes hard in the summer.

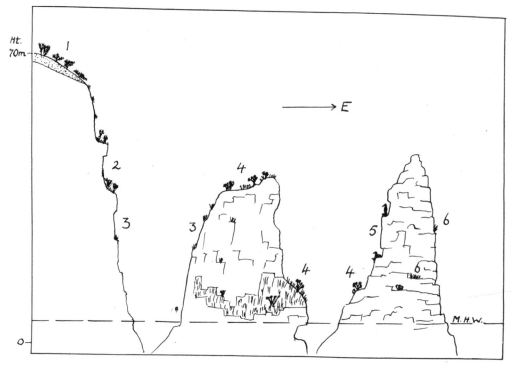

FIG. 10.2. *Distribution of vegetation on the cliffs of Brittany.*
1 = *Ericaceae*; 2 = *Pteridietum*; 3 = Festuca rubra; 4 = Dactylis,
Lavatera *and* Beta *with gull's nests*; 5 = Beta *and* Atriplex *with*
comorant's nests; 6 = Armeria, Crithmum *turfs (after Géhu).*

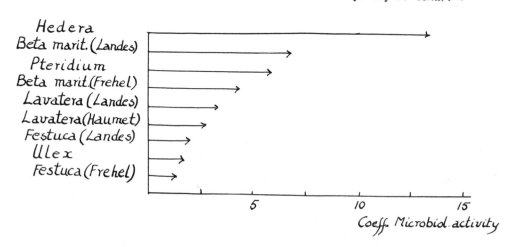

FIG. 10.3. *Microbiological activity in relation to cliff vegetat-*
ion *(after Géhu and Géhu-Franck).*

ENVIRONMENT

As a habitat, coastal cliffs exhibit certain environmental features which undoubtedly play a part in determining the nature of the vegetation. Among
such features are wind and sea spray, the latter affecting not only the exposed parts of the plants but also the salinity of the soil. At very low levels,
splash from storm waves may inhibit growth of many species. The soil is normally shallow and hence is easily subject to drying out, and this not only reduces the moisture but also increases the salt content. The stability of both
soil and vegetation is obviously directly related to the angle of slope. The
geological strata, particularly if rich in chalk, as on the south coast and
in Norfolk, will determine the presence or absence of certain species. The
biotic influence, e.g. birds, rabbits, sheep, is paramount in some areas, and
there is little doubt that the type of community is determined in such places
by the intensity of grazing.

Whilst the nature of the major factors is quite obvious, there is very little
data available. Information about wind intensity and the proportion of on-
shore gales can be obtained from meteorological records, and these serve to
indicate their importance. In the case of the Pembrokeshire Islands, it has
been shown that the greatest damage (caused by wind-carried spray) is derived
from winter gales of over 46 m.p.h. A wet windy spring keeps the soil cool
and also the air temperature, with the result that vegetation growth is re-
tarded as compared with similar plants some little distance inland or under
protection. One would indeed welcome some information on soil temperatures as
compared with adjacent inland soils. Relatively small changes in contours of
the land can bring about considerable variations in wind velocity and direction, and can well determine minor fluctuations in vegetation distribution and
times of flowering (Fig. 10.4). This relationship has been so little studied
that it is well worthy of more attention.

So far as salt in the soil or salt deposit on the leaves is concerned, the
plants of coastal cliffs can be divided into those that are highly salt tolerant, those that are salt tolerant, and those that are not salt tolerant. In
the first group, one finds species such as the Sea pink (*Armeria maritima*),
the Sea plantains (*Plantago maritima, P. coronopus*), Rock samphire (*Crithmum
maritimum*), the Cliff sand-spurrey (*Spergularia rupicola*), the Tree mallow
(*Lavatera arborea*) and plants of the drift-line and shingle that encroach into

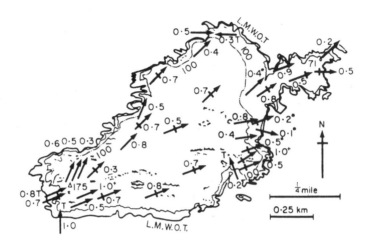

FIG. 10.4. *Map showing variations in direction and speed of a west-south-west wind of 16 m.p.h. (25.9 km.p.h.), i.e. force 4 on Beaufort scale, at the wind indicator on the lighthouse (after Gillham). (Crown Copyright reserved).*

the habitat, e.g. *Beta*, Sea raddish (*Raphanus maritimus*), Golden samphire (*Inula crithmoides*), Babington's orache (*Atriplex glabriuscula*), *Silene maritima*. Species belonging to the second group include Scurvy-grass (*Cochlearia officinalis*) and Danish scurvy-grass (*C. danica*), Dark-green mouse-ear chickweed (*Cerastium tetrandrum*), *Festuca rubra*, *Holcus lanatus* and English stonecrop (*Sedum anglicum*). The third group naturally contains the great majority of plants. Because of the shallow nature of the soil it is often very difficult to secure soil samples and in many cases the roots of the plants descend into rock cracks where there is the minimum of any soil. From such little information as is available it is clear that the salt content varies enormously, and is, of course, dependent upon amount of surf, height above wave splash, normal rainfall, presence of fresh water draining down through cracks in the rock, and protection by crags from rain and splash.

The effect of height in relation to the incidence of spray is well illustrated by figures (Table 10.2) for soils from the St. Kildan islands of North Rona (low cliffs) as compared with Hirta (high cliffs). On the cliffs at the Lizard salt deposition is proportional to wind velocities in excess of 14 m and the zoning of the vegetation is related to salt deposition (16).

For those who have the opportunity there is plenty of scope to obtain further information about the salt habitat of the coastal cliff-dwellers - not only in different communities but also in respect of seasonal variations.

TABLE 10.2

North Rona mg.Cl/100 g. soil		Hirta mg. Cl/100 g. soil		Lizard kg/ha/day	
Festucetum rubrae	82-493	"Plantago sward"	321	Festuceto-Armerietum	2.49-23.67
Armerietum	423	Zooplethismic grassland	149	Festuceto- Dactyletum	1.44-1.70
Rumicetum	257	Molinietum	134	Calluno-Scilletum	0.92-1.15

Biota

Birds and mammals play a very great part in determining the nature of the vegetation and their influence falls under three heads: treading and burrowing,
dunging, and grazing.

Trampling and burrowing may inhibit the growth of vegetation, though not to
the major extent associated with excessive grazing. Over-dunging also eliminates many species and if extreme, results in bare ground. Where there is a
large puffin colony on the cliff top, a bare area is found at the cliff edge
and the few species that occur behind the bare zone have a specialised growth
form (Fig. 10.5). The bare zone is not to be found with shearwater colonies,
but in some roosts where gulls are particularly abundant the plant species are
few, the plants minute and closely adpressed to the ground.

The Sea campion (*Silene maritima*) is apparently very intolerant of trampling,
but on the other hand it is greatly stimulated by guano and so is abundant in
bird colonies, unless there is grazing towards which it is not particularly
tolerant. Where the birds or mammals use recognised paths across the vegetation one finds that the usual plants disappear and are replaced by species such
as *Poa annua*, *Agrostis tenuis* and *Plantago coronopus*, which are able to tolerate trampling.

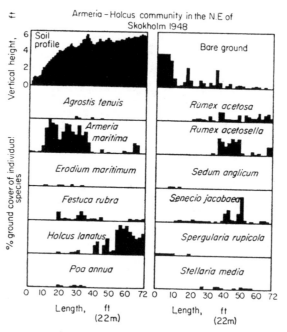

FIG. 10.5. *Belt transect showing the percentage ground cover of the chief species of the puffin colonies and the marginal strip of bare soil at the cliff edge where the birds congregate in large numbers. The profile of the transect is shown top left and the percent bare soil top right. The percent ground cover of the individual species is shown below (after Gillham).*

Puffin, shearwater and rabbit burrows may be very frequent in certain areas. In such cases one can observe secondary successions on the material extruded from the burrows. If the soil is friable and the burrows face the dominant winds (gale winds direction) undercutting of the vegetation takes place, and as a result it is only deep-rooted species such as *Armeria* and the Sorrels (*Rumex acetosa* and *R. acetosella*) that can survive. The presence of numerous burrows must exert an effect upon the soil. Thus it has been shown (10) that they lead to much greater fluctuations in soil moisture content as compared with unburrowed areas. During extended periods of dry weather, the soil above and around burrows is likely to dry out more than it would otherwise be expected to do. It is evident that the presence of burrows enables rain water to penetrate the soil more readily, especially if the soil is of a peaty nature, because peat has a "blotting-paper" action which normally stops much rain water from penetrating to lower levels.

It appears that soil temperatures adjacent to burrows can rise to higher day temperatures and this results in a hastening of growth in the spring. Here then we have a factor that can partially offset high winds and spray that may keep temperatures low (see p. 263). Although it has not been studied in any great detail, it appears that light penetrating into a burrow can bring about an alteration in the direction of growth of underground rhizomes of some species.

Bird dung (guano), much more so than mammal dung, can exert a profound effect upon the vegetation of cliffs. Tree mallow (*Lavatera arborea*) is very resistant to bird pressure and on Breton cliffs (1) is the last major species to be ousted (Fig. 10.2). The flora of guano-rich areas is a restricted flora and for any major region it tends to exhibit a marked uniformity. Minor differences within the basic framework of this coprophilous (dung-rich) community occur because there is a difference in the habitats of the various bird species. Thus in the case of the shearwaters they defaecate in the burrows during the daytime but outside at night. The floors of the burrows as a result become very rich in nutrients. Puffins, on the other hand, defaecate in one of three places: the first is what may be called their "standing ground", the second is at the burrow entrance, and the third is in a specially enlarged portion of the burrow, which is termed the "defaecation chamber", that may be marked above ground by a darker green of some plants. With increasing concentration of the surface dung the normal vegetation is eventually replaced by a Rumicetum (see p. 259), but if it becomes too concentrated even the sorrels cannot survive and bare ground ensues. The stages in transition to the Rumicetum depend upon whether or not there is grazing and we must now turn our attention to this factor.

In the absence of grazing a luxuriant and species-poor Festucetum rubrae develops. In the presence of grazing, and depending upon its intensity, other communities appear determined by the response of species to grazing. A study of the plants found in cliff vegetation shows that they can be classified into:

(a) "Rabbit avoided", e.g. *Holcus lanatus*, *Poa annua*, *Stellaria media*.
(b) "Rabbit resistant", e.g. *Agrostis*, *Festuca*, *Armeria*, *Plantago*.
(c) Non-resistant, e.g. *Beta*, *Crithmum*, *Asplenium marinum*, which are therefore restricted to inaccessible places.

The effect of increased grazing on species-poor submaritime *Festuca* grassland is first to bring about a rise in the number of species as the more resistant halophytes enter. Later there may be a decrease as taller plants such as *Holcus* (rabbit avoided) take over and eliminate others through light competition. The general effect of grazing on maritime vegetation is shown at Y in Fig. 10.1 which illustrates zonation around a large rabbit warren on Lundy Island. The phenomenon in reverse is illustrated in Table 10.3 which shows the change that occurs in a *Plantago coronopus* sward when grazing is removed.

TABLE 10.3

	Heavy grazing Open Plantaginetum with *Ceratodon pureus* (moss)	Medium grazing Closed Agrostidetum + Plantago and *Silene maritima*	Slight grazing Pure closed Agrostidetum
Total no. of species	7	8	3
Percentage cover of grasses (*Agrostis, Festuca, Poa annua*)	8	80	96
Percentage cover *Agrostis*	3	73	92
Percentage cover of herbs	47	19	3
Percentage cover of *Plantago*	41	8	0
Percentage cover of mosses	25	0	0
Percentage bare soil	30	1	1
Av. ht. of sward (cm)	< ½	1	2

Sand dunes, salt marshes and coastal cliffs form habitats in which grazing experiments can be readily carried out. Wire-netting fences placed in strategic localities can yield a wealth of information (Fig. 10.6). When such enclosures were erected on the Island of Skokholm the Armerietum (plagioclimax) gradually gave way to a tall growth of *Festuca rubra* (Fig. 10.7). Height increases in some of the plants can be quite considerable. Thus fescue can increase from ½ cm to 35 cm, sorrel from 2 to 20 cm and buck's-horn plantain from ½ to 35 cm.

Since the sea pink is well fitted to withstand wind and spray, its inability to compete when there is no grazing with a relatively non-aggressive grass

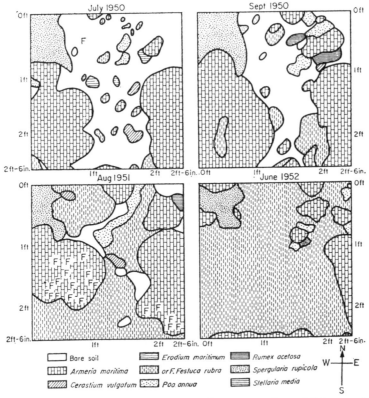

FIG. 10.6. *Four quadrats of the vegetation within a rabbit-proof enclosure on Skokholm Neck to show the change from an open Armerietum to a closed Festucetum 2 years after the cessation of grazing (after Gillham).*

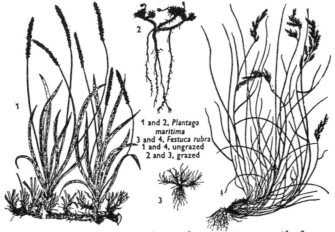

FIG. 10.7. *The effect of grazing on the growth form of* Plantago maritima *and* Festuca rubra *(× 0.22) (after Gillham).*

such as *Festuca rubra* highlights the profound effect of the grazing factor.
In more sheltered localities, *Agrostic tenuis* becomes an aggressive competit-
or, but later it is generally over-run by *Calluna* because the *Agrostis* provides sufficient extra protection to the *Calluna* shoots so that wind damage
to *Calluna* is repaired and the *Agrostis* is ousted through competition for
light.

It has been pointed out by Gillham (7) that the elimination of grazing could
have effects upon other members of the biota. Thus the increased growth of
Yorkshire fog and bracken could well result in restricting wheatears to
cliffs, because the tall vegetation makes unsuitable foraging ground. In the
absence of rabbits, burrows could well collapse and this would reduce or
eliminate those birds, e.g. wheatears and shearwaters (puffins can construct
their own burrows), that are dependent upon ready-made homes.

One major objective of ecological studies on coastal cliffs must be an understanding of the successions and the impact upon the communities of the major
environmental factors of wind, salt spray and the biota. Such objectives
have only been achieved in the British Isles for the Pembrokeshire Islands,
and the hypothetical scheme proposed by Gillham, which effectively summarises
her findings, is reproduced below.

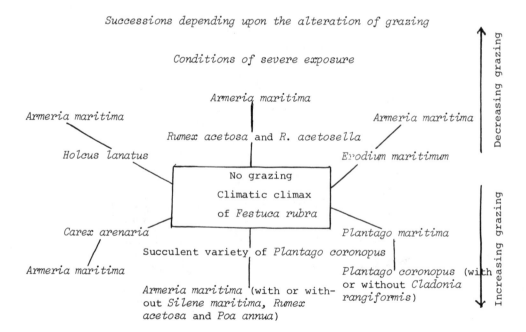

Successions depending upon the alteration of grazing

Hypothetical successions involving the islands as a whole

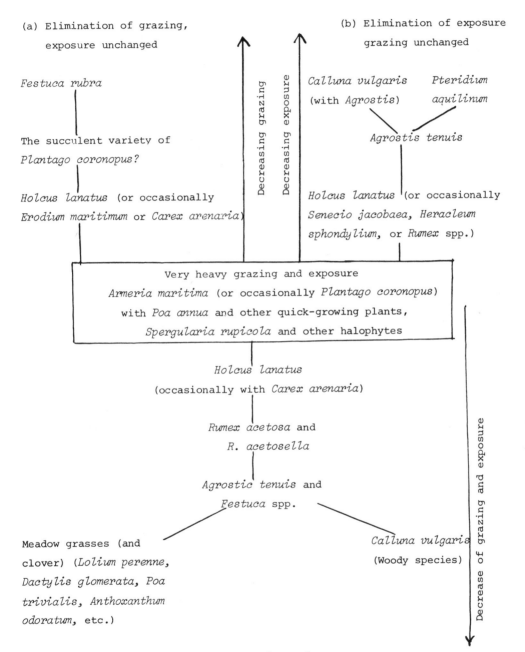

(a) Elimination of grazing,
exposure unchanged

Decreasing grazing

Decreasing exposure

(b) Elimination of exposure
grazing unchanged

Festuca rubra

Calluna vulgaris   *Pteridium*
(with *Agrostis*)   *aquilinum*

The succulent variety of
Plantago coronopus?

Agrostis tenuis

Holcus lanatus (or occasionally
Erodium maritimum or *Carex arenaria*)

Holcus lanatus (or occasionally
*Senecio jacobaea, Heracleum
sphondylium,* or *Rumex* spp.)

Very heavy grazing and exposure
Armeria maritima (or occasionally *Plantago coronopus*)
with *Poa annua* and other quick-growing plants,
Spergularia rupicola and other halophytes

Holcus lanatus
(occasionally with *Carex arenaria*)

Rumex acetosa and
R. acetosella

Agrostic tenuis and
Festuca spp.

Meadow grasses (and
clover) (*Lolium perenne,
Dactylis glomerata, Poa
trivialis, Anthoxanthum
odoratum,* etc.)

Calluna vulgaris
(Woody species)

Decrease of grazing and exposure

(c) Elimination of both grazing and exposure

REFERENCES

1   GÉHU J.M. and GÉHU-FRANCK J., Récherches sur la végétation et le sol de
     la Réserve de l'ile des handes (Ille-et-Vilaine) et de quelques ilots de
     la côte Nord-Bretagne. *Bull. Lab. Mar. Dinard* Fasc. 47, 19-57 (1961).

2   GÉHU J.M., Sur la végétation halophile des Falaises Bretonnes. *Rev. gen.
     Bot.*, 71, 73-78 (1964).

3   GÉHU J.M., Quelques observations sur la Falaise Cretacée du Cap Blanc-
     Nez (P.D.C.) et étude de la végétation de la Paroi abrupti Brassicetum
     oleraceae. *Nov. Ass. Bull. Soc. Roy. Bot. Belg.*, 95, 109-129.

4   GÉHU J.M. and GÉHU-FRANCK J., Premières récherches microbiologiques sur
     le sol de quelques ilots de la côte Nord-Bretonne. *Ann. Inst. Pasteur*,
     105, 218-31 (1963).

5   GILLHAM M.E., An ecological account of the vegetation of Grassholm
     Island, Pembrokeshire. *J. Ecol.*, 41, 84-99 (1953).

6   GILLHAM M.E., Ecology of the Pembrokeshire Islands. III. *J. Ecol.*, 43(2),
     172-205 (1955).

7   GILLHAM M.E., Some possible consequences if rabbits should be extermin-
     ated by myxomatosis on Skokholm Island, Pembrokeshire. *North West Nat.*,
     30-34 (March 1955).

8   GILLHAM M.E., Some effects of the larger animals on the flora of Lundy.
     Trans. Devon. Ass. Adv. Sci. Lit. & Arts., 87, 205-229 (1955).

9   GILLHAM M.E., Ecology of the Pembrokeshire Islands. IV. *J. Ecol.*, 44(1),
     51-82 (1956).

10   GILLHAM M.E., Ecology of the Pembrokeshire Islands. V. *J. Ecol.*, 44(2),
     429-454 (1956).

11   GOODMAN C.T. and GILLHAM M.E., Ecology of the Pembrokeshire Islands. II.
     J. Ecol., 42, 296-327 (1954).

12   HARSHBERGER J.W., Phytogeographical survey of North America. 2nd Repr.
     Ed. Weimar (1958).

13   HEPBURN A., A study of the vegetation of sea cliffs in north Cornwall.
     J. Ecol., 31, 30-39 (1943).

14   MCLEAN R.C., An ungrazed grassland on limestone in Wales with a note on
     plant dominions. *J. Ecol.*, 23, 436-442 (1935).

15   MCVEAN D.N., Flora and vegetation on the islands of St. Kilda and North
     Rona in 1958. *J. Ecol.*, 49(1), 39-54 (1961).

16   MALLOCH A.J.C., Salt spray deposition on the maritime cliffs of the Liz-
     ard Peninsula. *J. Ecol.*, 60(1), 103-112 (1972).

17 PETCH C.P., The vegetation of St. Kilda. *J. Ecol.*, 21, 92-100 (1933).

18 POORE M.E.D. and ROBERTSON V.C., The vegetation of St. Kilda in 1948. *J. Ecol.*, 37(1), 82-97 (1949).

19 PRAEGER R.L., Clare Island survey. X. Phangerogamia and Pteridophyta. *Proc. Roy. Ir. Acad.*, 31, 40 (1911).

20 ROBERTSON E.T., Contributions to the maritime ecology of St. Cyrus, Kincardineshire. I. The Cliffs. *Trans. Proc. Bot. Soc. Edin.*, 35(4), 370-387 (1951).

21 TANSLEY A.G., *The British Islands and their Vegetation.* Cambridge (1939).

22 TANSLEY A.G. and ADAMSON R.S., A preliminary survey of the chalk grass-lands of the Sussex downs. *J. Ecol.*, 14, 1-32 (1926).

23 VEVERS A.G., The land vegetation of Ailsa Craig. *J. Ecol.*, 24(4), 424-445 (1936).

INDEX

Abbotsbury   236

Abundance   7

Acer rubrum   170, 177

Acetabularia crenulatum   224

Achillea millefolium   168

Acrostichum aureum   224, 226

ADAMSON, R.S.   273

Adriatic   22

Aerated layer   130, 131, 132

Aerenchyma   16, 130, 218

Africa   217

Agardhiella tenera   38

Agarum cribrosum   39

Agropyretum junceiforme   158

Agropyron   152, 159, 161

  junceiforme   152, 155, 158, 162,
      178, 189, 208, 237, 244

  pungens   244, 246

  repens   152

Agrostidetum   110, 259

Agrostis   101, 104, 193, 267

  setacea   259

  stolonifera   104, 105, 108, 110,
      136, 193, 246, 259, 261

  tenuis   178, 259, 261, 265, 270

Ailsa Craig   253, 254, 260

Aira   166

  caryophyllea   168

  praecox   168, 257

Alaria   38

  esculenta   31, 67

Alder   213

Alligators   232

Alnus   174

  viridis   254

Alum Bay   94

Amelanchier canadensis   167

Ammophila   159, 160, 161, 166, 167,
      175, 178, 189, 190, 208

  arenaria   158, 162

  arundinacea   161

  breviligulata   158, 163, 189

Ammophiletum   162, 163, 169

Ampelopsis   170

Anas penelope   101

Andropogon   205

Anemometer   13, 184, 186

Angelica sylvestris   254

Anglesey   166, 175, 178, 187, 207

Annual glasswort   135, 246

Annual poa   260

Archangelica atropurpurea   153

  officinalis   105

Arctic   69, 103

Arenaria serpyllifolia   246

Armeria   108, 110, 255, 258, 259, 261,
      266, 277

  maritima   3, 93, 108, 246, 253, 254,
      257, 263

Armerietum   257, 258, 268

  maritimae   257

Arrhenatherum elatine   243

Artemisia   245

  lloydii   161

  maritima   107, 110, 153, 237

Ascophyllum 23, 24, 30, 34, 35, 37, 38, 64, 65, 67, 70, 80

  nodosum 32, 69, 79, 80

    ecad *mackaii* 48, 79

    ecad *scorpioides* 48

Asplenium marinum 253, 258, 260, 267

Assateague 177

Association 11, 22, 36

Associes 11, 46, 103

Aster 108, 123, 143, 245

  subulatus 112, 113

  tenuifolius 114

  tripolium 105, 107, 123, 134, 135

Asteretum 107, 108

Atlantic 31, 37, 38, 39, 94, 101, 104, 144, 161, 163, 166, 170, 248

Athyrium felix-foemina 254

Atmometer 13

Atriplex 153, 154, 237, 261

  arenaria 153, 248

  babingtonii 248

  glabriuscula 153, 248, 264

  hastata 153, 248

  latifolium 152

  littoralis 110, 152, 154

  patula var. *hastata* 110, 112

  sabulosum 152

Autecology 16

Authie 108

Autumnal hawkbit 108

Avicennia 69, 221, 222, 223

  germinans 218, 224, 228, 231

Avrainvillea 40

Ayreland of Bride 239

BAARDSETH, E. 80

Babington's orache 153, 264

Baccharis halimifolia 112, 114

Bacteria 208, 229

Balanus 20, 34, 35

  balanoides 34

BALCHIN, W.G.V. 241

Balearic Isles 22

Baltic Sea 36

Baltrum 90

Bangia 36

Barbula fallax 163

Barchans 156

Barnacle(s) 20, 30, 32, 35, 218, 231

Barnstaple 87, 94, 112

Batis maritima 224

Batophora oerstedii 49, 54, 224

Bay dunes 157

Bay of Fundy 87, 101, 112, 127

Bay of Gdansk 44

Beach heather 167

BEEFTINK, W.G. 107

Berberis 169

Beta 255, 264, 267

  maritima 110, 152, 153, 248

  vulgaris 133

Betula pubescens 174, 175

BIEBL, R. 69, 78

Biomass 40

Birch 16, 213

Bird's-foot trefoil 110, 246

BLACKLER, H. 49

Blackthorn 169

Blakeney 87, 156, 159, 168, 184, 195, 198, 199, 205, 206, 234, 240, 241, 243, 244, 245, 246, 248, 249

Blidingia minima 47, 66, 69

Borrichia frutescens 114, 227

Boston 92

Bostrychia 34, 36, 39, 49, 69, 80, 224

scorpioides 47, 48, 107

Botrychium ternatum 163

BOYCE, S.G. 206

Brachythecium albicans 163, 165

Bramble 169

Brassica oleracea 253, 261

BRAUN-BLANQUET, J. 10

Braunton Burrows 157, 168, 170, 173, 191, 206, 207

BRERETON, A.J. 126

Bridgewater 97, 101

Bristol Channel 18, 99

Brittany 142, 243, 261

Broad buckler-fern 254

Brookweed 110, 173

BROWN, J.C. 209

Bryopsis 49

Bryum capillare 248

pendulum 163

Buck's-horn plantain 108, 153, 173, 246, 257, 260

Burnet rose 169

Caithness 34, 150, 173

Cakile 154

maritima 8, 152, 155

Calamagrostis canadensis 112

California 71

Callithamnion 36

Calluna 166, 193, 208, 270

vulgaris 169

Calluneta 166

Caloglossa 49, 224

leprieurii 62, 81

Calothrix 28, 34, 36, 38

crustacea 27

Calshot 240

Calystegia soldanella 159, 162, 246

Camm(s) 239

Campanula glomerata 261

Camptothecium lutescens 165

Canada 103, 111, 112, 127

Canary Islands 39, 40

Cape Blanc-Nez 261

Cape Hatteras 157

Cape Kennedy 222

Cape Lookout 66

Carex arenaria 162, 166, 168, 169, 177, 178, 208, 246, 248

flacca 169

mackenziei 104

nigra 173

recta 105

salina 104

serotina 193

subspathacea 103

Caribbean 64, 228

Caricetum glareosae 104

subspathaceae 104

Carpinus caroliniana 170

Catapodium marinum 243

Catenella 34, 36, 69, 80, 224

repens 48

Caulerpa 49, 78

cupressoides 49, 224

verticillata 49

Caulacanthus ustulatus 39

Cave(s) 29 et seq.

Cay(s) 218, 226

Cenchrus tribuloides 153, 161, 163

Centroceras clavulatum 49

Cephalosporium 208

Ceramium   36

Cerastium   166

  atrovirens   168

    tetrandrum   254, 257

    vulgatum   265

Ceratodon purpureus   248

Cetraria aculeata   248

Chamaephytes   8

CHAPMAN, V.J.   9, 11, 48, 94, 228

CHAPMAN, D.J.   9, 48

Chara   174

Charante   161

Chenopodiaceae   152

Chesapeake Bay   18, 38, 65, 87

Chesil Beach   234, 236, 239, 241,
      243, 247, 248

Chickweed   162, 260

Chlorococcales   174

Chlorophyceae   29, 48, 78

Chlorophyta   29

Chondrus   32, 38

  crispus   67, 69

Chorda   32, 38

  filum   43

Chordaria   37

Chrysophyceae   64

Chthalamus   20, 35

  stellatus   34, 39

Cicendia filiformis   173

Cirsium   166

Cladonia   165, 167, 248

  furcata   248

  pungens   248

Cladophora   32, 36, 46, 259

  rupestris   36

Clapper rail   144

Clare Island   253

Cliff sand-spurrey   258, 263

Climax   2, 103

Clover   213

Cochlearia   246

  anglica   108, 253

  danica   110, 153, 264

  officinalis   103, 261, 264

Codiaceae   40

Codium   23, 24, 32

Coefficient of community   7

Coefficient of similarity   7

Communal habitat   12

Compensation point   67, 71, 75

Competition   5

Coniothyrium   208

Connecticut   94, 101

Conocarpus   218, 224

  erecta   218, 224

Consociation   11, 22

Consocies   11, 46, 103, 226

Continua(um)   8, 26

Cord grass   8, 47, 69, 99, 107, 145,
      160

Coral root   173

Corallina   32, 36

Corallorhiza trifida   173

Cornwall   255, 259

Corynephorus canescens   162, 166, 169,
      208, 248

Coto Donano   150

Couloir(s)   23, 29

Cow parsnip   261

Crambe maritima   152, 153, 243, 248,
      253

Crataegus monogyna   167, 169

Creek(s)   98, 99, 100, 129, 132

Creeping fescue   108, 166, 208, 224,
      246, 257

Creeping willow   8, 174, 175, 193,
    205
Crested hair-grass   246
Crithmum   255, 258, 267
    maritimum   248, 253, 261, 263
Critical levels   80
Croton   163
    punctatus   153
Cruciferae   152
Cryptopleura variosum   30
Culbin sands   150, 210
Curled dock   153, 244, 247
Cyanophyceae   29
Cyanophyta   29, 37, 38, 39, 48
Cymodocea manatorum   224
Cyperus   177
    grayii   167
Cystoseira   32, 54
    abies-marina   40

Dactylorchis   178
Dakar   217
Danish scurvy-grass   153, 264
Danzig   44
Dark-green mouse-ear chickweed   253,
    257, 264
Darnel poa   246
Darsser Schwelle   36
Daucus gummifer   261
DAVIS, J.H.   221, 224, 225, 226
DE HAAN,   228
Delaware   38, 87, 101, 113
Delesseria   67
Denmark   45, 93, 105, 107, 108, 142
Density   7, 40, 42, 43, 168
Deschampsia flexuosa   169
Desiccation   62, 63
Desmarestia aculeata   43

Desmazeria marina   246
Devon   174
Dianthus gallicus   167
Diatom(s)   37, 170
Dichothrix gypsophila   104
Dictyota   43
Dictyopteris   38
Diotis candidissima   159, 161
Distichlis   97
    spicata   112, 114
Dorset   166, 169, 175, 234, 236, 241
Dover   247
Dovey   95
Drift-line   13, 152, 153, 154, 158,
    263
Dryas octopetala   169
Dryopteris austriaca   254
    thelypteris   177
Dublin   124
Dungeness   156, 241, 247, 248
Dwarf furze   169

Early hair-grass   257
East Anglia   48, 94, 95, 124
Ecesis   4
Echinus esculentus   26, 79
Eel grass   8, 44, 105
EGLER, F.E.   225, 226, 228
Egregia laevigata   67, 70, 75, 80
EHRKE, G.   67
Eire   64, 218, 253, 256
Elbe   87, 107
Elder   169, 260
Eleocharis   105, 226
    palustris   104
    parvula   105
    uniglumis   105

Elymus   161, 246

  arenarius   153, 159, 162, 189

Embryo dune(s)   158

Empetrum nigrum   254

England   99, 150, 245

ENGLEMANN, T.   77

English stone-crop   258, 265

Enteromorpha   34, 35, 38, 46, 49, 54,
     55, 63, 64, 67, 80

  clathrata f. *prostrata*   48

  compressa   45

  intestinalis   36

  nana   47, 66, 69

  prolifera   47

    f. *tubulosa*   47

Ephedra distachya   167

Erica cinerea   169

Erodium cicutarium ssp. *dunense*   162

  maritimum   261

Eryngium   246

  maritimum   159, 162

Essex   48

Estuaries   18, 44, 87, 88, 89, 108,
     217

Eulittoral   20, 21, 28, 34, 38, 39

Euonymus   169

Euphorbia paralias   153, 159, 161,
     162

  peplis   153, 154

  polygonifolia   161, 163

  portlandica   162

Euphrasia   168

Eurhynchium praelongum   165

Europe   31, 36, 37, 44, 48, 55, 67,
     87, 101, 103, 135, 136, 150, 156,
     157

Fair Isle   59, 256

Fanø   107

FELDMANN, J.   9

Fennel   253

Fescue   256

Festuca   110, 256, 268

  dumetorum   161

  ovina   112, 261

  polesica   169

  rubra   3, 105, 107, 108, 168, 177,
     178, 193, 207, 208, 243, 244,
     246, 256, 257, 264, 268, 270

    var. *arenaria*   161, 162, 166

Festucetum   161, 259

  rubrae   104, 108, 237, 256, 257,
     267

Field milk-thistle   245

Finmark   104

Fimbristylis castanea   114, 153

Fiorin   108, 110, 136, 246, 259

Firth of Clyde   253

Firth of Forth   45

Florida   1, 38, 39, 40, 49, 113, 163,
     217, 218, 221, 223, 228, 229,
     230, 231

Foeniculum vulgare   253

Foraminifera   144

Formation   22

Fragaria virginiana   177

France   107, 159

Frankenia laevis   110, 153, 177, 246

Friesia   90

Frequency   7, 23

Freshfield   187

Friesian Islands   87

Fucaceae   20

Fucoxanthin   78

Fucus 28, 30, 37, 38, 44, 45, 70, 75, 80

  ceranoides 36

  distichus 34

    ssp. *anceps* 32

  edentatus 35

  inflatus 34

  serratus 23, 24, 32, 61, 63, 71, 75, 76, 77

  spiralis 34, 35, 36, 62, 65

    f. *nana* 34

    var. *platycarpus* 61, 63, 71

  vesiculosus 23, 24, 32, 34, 37, 63, 65, 66, 67, 69, 126

    ecad *caespitosus* 47, 107, 126

    ecad *filiformis* 48

    ecad *muscoides* 48, 126

    ecad *subecostatus* 48

    ecad *volubilis* 47, 126

Fulmars 254

Fungi 170, 228

Furcellaria 45

Galium arenarium 161

  verum 166, 168, 246

Galway 168

GAUTHIER, B. 112

GÉHU, J.M. 161, 208, 248

Gelidium 38

  arbusculum 39

  cartilagineum 39

General Salt Marsh (Community) 5, 11, 48, 66, 107, 108, 111, 112, 137

Genista littoralis 169

Geophytes 8, 9

Georgia 87, 156

Geranium purpureum 247

Gerardia maritima 112

Germany 107

Gigartina 36

GILLHAM, M.E. 253, 256, 258, 260, 261, 270

GIMINGHAM, C.H. 168, 203, 205

Gironde 153

Glasswort 122, 177

Glaucium flavum 150, 152, 244

Glaux 110, 112, 135, 141

  maritima 105, 108, 112, 135, 173, 237

GODWIN, H. 94

Golden samphire 247, 264

GOODALL, D.W. 7

Gore Point 90

GORHAM, E. 203, 207

Gorse 169

GOSSELINK, J.G. 101

Göteburg 35, 105

Gracilaria confervoides 80

  cornea 49, 224

  verrucosa 38

Grassholm 256, 261

Grateloupia 38

GRAY, T.R.G. 90

Great Britain 27, 61, 87, 94, 107, 114, 142, 146, 169, 174, 187, 210, 256

Great Crosby 187

Greenland 104

GREIG-SMITH, P. 7, 8

GRESSWELL, R.K. 175

Grey dune 165, 166, 168, 170, 237

Groundsel 245

Guano 267

Gulf of Mexico 64

Gulls 254

GUSTAVSSON, V.   29

Hairy hawkbit   173
Halidrys   32
Halimeda   40
  tridens   224
Halimione   48, 69, 101, 141, 237,
      245, 255
  pedunculata   105
  portulacoides   107, 108, 124, 126,
      143, 146, 246
    var. *latifolia*   146
    var. *parvifolia*   110, 146, 177
Halopteris scoparia   40
Halosaccion   38
Hamstead   247
HANLEY, J.A.   249
Hare's foot   201
Harlech   170, 174
HARSHBERGER, J.W.   166
Harveyella   80
Hastate orache   153
Havre   261
Hawthorn   247
Hebrides   64
Helicion pellucidum   79
Helichrysum staechas   167
Hemicryptophyte(s)   8, 9, 114, 171,
      254
HEPBURN, I.   162, 255, 258
Heracleum sphondylium   261
Hildenbrandtia   30
HILL, R.D.   48
HILL, T.G.   249
Himanthalia   32
Hind shore dunes   157
Hippophäe   167, 176, 208
  rhamnoides   8, 169

Hippuris vulgaris   104
Hirta   264
HOEK, C. van den   30
Holcus   261, 268
  lanatus   110, 259, 261, 264, 267
Holland   102, 142, 167
Holmsella pachyderma   80
Holoschoenetum vulgaris   173
Holoschoenus vulgaris   150
Honkenya   154, 158, 159
  peploides   153, 154, 162, 244
Hormidium   259
Hormosira   74
  banksii   58, 67, 71, 80
Horned pond-weed   172
Hudsonia tomentosa   167
Humber   87
Hammocks   222, 224
Hurricane(s)   226, 228
Hurst Castle   240, 247
HYDE, M.B.   76
Hydrobia ulvae   79
Hydrocotyle   173
  vulgaris   261
Hydro-helophytes   8
Hylocomium splendens   165
Hypnum   163, 173
  cupressiforme   165, 248
Hypocotyl   228

Iceland   104
Ilex aquifolius   247
  opaca   170
  vomitoria   170
Individual habitat   12
Inula crithmoides   247, 264
Ipomoea pes-caprae   163
Ireland   168, 245, 256, 257

Irish Sea   34

Iron   15, 206

  sulphide   229

Isle of

  Dun   256

  Harris   205

  Man   43, 239

  Wight   24, 65, 94

Iva oraria   112, 113, 114, 227

Jamaica   229, 230

JENSEN, H.A.P.   248

Juncetum   97, 137

  acuti   173

  baltici   107

  gerardii   104, 107, 110, 112

  maritimi   110, 173

Juncus   3, 11, 173

  acutus   173

  articulatus   193

  balticus   112, 173

  bufonius   155

  gerardi   103, 105, 108, 110, 113,
    136, 177

  marginatus biflorus   177

  maritimus   13, 69, 80, 103, 110,
    133, 173, 193

  roemerianus   103, 113, 114, 143

Juniperus sabina   167, 254

  virginiana   177, 248

KAIN, J.M.   24, 58

KING, C.A.M.   187, 241

Koeleria gracilis   247, 261

Kosteletzyka virginica   114

Labrador   104, 152, 153

Lactuca tatarica   159

  virosa   166

Lady fern   254

Lady's bedstraw   246

Lagoons   217, 226

Laguncularia   223, 226

  racemosa   218, 228

Laminaria   20, 55

  cloustoni   31, 39, 40, 65

  digitata   31, 38, 39, 40, 43, 66

  hyperborea   26, 31, 39, 40, 58, 65,
    66

  longicruris   38, 39

  saccharina   31, 32, 40, 43, 46, 65,
    75, 79

LAMPE, R.H.   76

Lancashire   100, 157, 174, 175

Larger winter-green   175

La Rochelle   153

LA RUE, C.D.   228

Lathyrus maritimus   153, 247

Laurencia   36

  obtusa   32

Lavatera arborea   260, 261, 263, 267

LAWSON, G.W.   40

Least willow   254

Leathesia   36

Lechea maritima   167

Lenticels   218

Leontodon autumnalis   108

  leysseri   173

  taraxacoides   193

Lesser spearwort   110

Lesser twayblade   173

LEVRING, T.   78

LEWIS, J.R.   19, 21, 23, 35

LEWIS, W.V.   241

Lichnia   35, 36, 261

  pygmaea   34

Life form   5, 8, 9, 254

Ligusticum vulgare   167, 169

Ligustrum scoticum   105

Limonium   101, 112, 124, 141

  bellidifolium   110, 177, 246

  binervosum   246

  carolinianum   113, 114, 124

  humile   146

  nashii   112, 113

  vulgare   107, 108, 135, 146, 245,
      256

Limpet(s)   30, 79

Linaria thymifolia   161

Listera cordata   173

Lithothamnion   30

Litter   108, 152, 190, 191, 207

Littorella   193

  uniflora   172

Littorina   20

  neritoides   39

Lobophora variegata   40

Lola   47

Lomentaria   36

  articulata   30

Long Island   248

Long-leaved scurvy-grass   108, 253

Lotus corniculatus   110, 166, 246

Lough Ine   30

Louisiana   223

Low(s)   155, 177, 247

Lundy Isle   257

Lupin   213

Lupinus arboreus   212

Luskentyre   205

Lyme grass   153, 159, 210, 246

Lyngbya   47, 49

  maiuscula   224

Lynn   123

Lythrum lineare   113

Machair   157, 166, 168

McLEAN, R.C.   260

Macrocystis pyrifera   71

McVEAN, D.N.   253

Magnesium   207

Magnolia   222

Maine   38

Manganese   207

Mangrove(s)   1, 3, 4, 13, 14, 15, 16,
      38, 46, 49, 57, 69, 114, 121,
      217 et seq.

MANN, K.H.   38

Marchantia   260

Marine crane's-bill   261

Mariscus   226

  jamaicensis   225

Marram   13, 158, 159, 160, 165, 186,
      189, 208, 210, 211, 212, 213

Marsh arrow-grass   247

Maryland   163, 167

Massachusetts   27, 95, 97, 101, 124

Matricaria maritima spp. *inodora* var.
  salina   253, 261

Matted sea lavender   153, 246

Matthiola incana   161, 253

  sinuata   159

Medicago marina   161

Mediterranean   54

  ball rush   150

Melandrium rubrum   256

Mercury   46

Mertensia   155

  maritima   152, 245

Mesobrometum 261

Metrosideros excelsa 254

Meuse 167

Microcoleus tenerrimus 224

Middleholm 260

Mid-littoral 19, 20, 34, 35, 38

Modiolus 38

Molinia coerulea 260

Molinietum 260

Monostroma 54

  grevillei 36

Monotropha hypopithys 175

Montia lamprosperma 103

Montpellier 23

Mont St. Michel 159

Morecambe Bay 87, 90, 101, 142

Morfa Dyffryn 187

  Harlech 187

MORSS, C.E. 132

Mougeotia 174

Mud rush 108, 136

Mud skippers 232

Muriwai 212

Murrayella periclados 49

MUZIK, T.J. 228

Myrica cerifera 167, 248

  pennsylvanica 177

Mytilus edulis 35

Myxomatosis 16, 169, 254

Myxophyceae 20, 36, 124, 174

Nemalion 36

Neusiedler See 87

Newborough Warren 157, 166, 175,
    178, 187, 195, 198, 203, 207

New Brunswick 163, 170, 177

New England 112, 113, 114, 127,
    137, 163, 218, 254

Newfoundland 48, 152, 153, 254

New Hampshire 94

New Jersey 101, 113, 163, 170, 177

Newlynn 94

New York 101

New Zealand 58, 71, 137, 156, 212.
    254

NIELSEN, N. 95

Nitrogen 15, 142, 206

Nitzschia 174

NORDHAGEN, R. 152

Norfolk 11, 87, 90, 92, 109, 123,
    137, 139, 142, 155, 177, 187,
    207, 210, 240, 246, 247

North America 48, 80, 94

North Carolina 38, 66, 114, 163, 205

North Rona 260, 264

Northam 240

Northern shore-wort 245

NORTON, T.A. 40

Nova Scotia 37, 38, 39, 94

Norway 23, 34, 66, 104, 105, 152

Oarweed(s) 20

Ochrolechia parella 261

Odonthalia dentata 30

ODUM, E.P. 101

Oenanthe lachenalii 110

Oenothera perennis 177

  humifusa 161

Ononis repens 161, 166

Orache 153

Oresund 114

ORRIS, R.K. 38

Oscillatoria 47

Osmunda regalis 177

Ostrea rhizophorae 218

Otago 156

Oxycoccus macrocarpus   174

Oxygen   67, 76, 79, 121, 130, 144,
          161, 231

Oxytropis halleri   169

Padina pavonia   40

Pamlico Sound   87

Pan(s)   99, 100, 143, 144, 218

Pancratium maritimum   161

Panicum amarum   161, 163, 167

  sphaerocarpum   177

  virgatum   114

Parabolic dunes   156, 157

Paracentrotus lividus   79

Parapholis strigosa   108

Parasite(s)   80, 170

Parentucellia viscosa   173

Parnassia palustris   150

Parsley water dropwort   110

Partial habitat   12

Patella   30, 79

  vulgata   30

Pelagophycus porra   70

Peltigera   167

Pelvetia   30, 35, 36

  canaliculata   34, 61, 107, 126

    ecad *libera*   47, 126

    ecad *radicans*   48

Penicillium   208

  nigrans   208

Penicillus   40

Pennywort   261

Periwinkle   20

Perna alata   218

PETCH, C.P.   253

PETIT, M.   161

PFLEGER, F.B.   144

pH   79, 203

Phaeococcus adnatus   66

Phaeophyta   29

Phallus impudicus   170

Phanerophytes   8, 171

Phormidium   47

  corium   36, 104

Phosphate   15

Phosphorus   15, 142, 206

Phragmites   114

  communis   108, 111, 137, 176

Phragmitetum   105, 111, 137

Phyllophora epiphylla   30

Pinus austriaca   213

  corsica   213

  maritima   213

  pinaster   169

  radiata   213

  rigida   170

  taeda   170

Placodium lobatum   248

Plagioclimax   257, 259, 268

Plankton   71

Plantaginetum   48, 66, 256

  maritimi   110, 137, 257

Plantago   112, 143, 267

  coronopus   108, 153, 173, 193, 257,
         258, 260, 261, 263, 265, 268

    var. *pygmaea*   246

  lanceolata   246, 257

  maritima   3, 8, 93, 105, 107, 108,
         110, 135, 245, 254, 256, 257,
         259. 263

  oliganthos   112

Plocamium   43

Pluchea camphorata   8, 114

Plumaria elegans   30

Pneumatophores   49, 69, 218, 220, 221,
         222

Poa annua   260, 265, 267
  pratensis   237
Pohlia annotina   163
Pohutakawa   255
Poland   44
Polygonaceae   152
Polygonum littorale   153
  maritimum   153
  minus   173
  raii   153
Polysiphonia   38, 49
  fastigiata   80
Polytrichum juniperinum   163
  piliferum   163
Pondweed   172
Poole   97, 99
POORE, M.E.D.   11, 253, 257
Pore space   14, 128
Porphyra   36, 38, 74, 76
  atropurpurea   75
  umbilicalis   34
Portland   236
Portugal   110, 152, 161
Potamogeton   172
Potash   15, 142
Potassium   142, 206, 207
Potentilla anserina   153, 155
  egedii   103
  erecta   93, 108
Prasiola   261
Primula scotica   150, 173
Prince Edward Island   37, 38
Prisere   2, 171
Privet   169
'Prop' roots   218
Prunus maritimus   167
  serotina   167, 170
  spinosa   169

Psammosere   171
Pteridium aquilinum   177
Ptilota serrata   39
Puccinellia   101, 112, 245
  americana   111
  distans   105, 110
  maritima   104, 105, 107, 109, 111,
      122, 126, 135, 143, 144, 177,
      237, 246, 248, 256, 261
  paupercula   111
  phryganodes   103, 104
  retroflexa   104
Puccinellietum   108
Puccinellio-Salicornietum   107
Puffins   254, 257, 259, 265, 266,
      267, 270
Purple moor-grass   260
Pyrola   175
  rotundifolia ssp. *maritima*   175
Pyrus angustifolia var. *spinosa*   167

Quadrat(s)   6, 7, 8, 9, 23, 24, 26,
      27, 40
Quebec   104
Quercetum atlanticum   169
Quercus falcata   170

  laurifolia   170
  lyrata   170
  robur   169
  virginiana   167, 170

Rabbit   178, 207, 254, 259, 263, 270,
Ragwort   162, 166, 178, 246
Ramalina siliquosa   261
Ranunculus flammula   110
RANWELL, D.   175, 178, 187
Raphanus maritimus   153, 264

Ray's knotgrass   153

Reaction   5

Red campion   256

Red cedar   170

REDFIELD, A.C.   112

Red mangrove   8, 218

Red pine 170

Red Sea   217

Relative humidity   13

Remanié dunes   155, 189

Restharrow   166

Rhine   167

Rhizoclonium   49

Rhizophora   69, 221, 224, 225, 226,
    227, 229

  mangle   8, 218, 221, 222, 224,
    228, 230, 231

Rhizosphere   208

Rhodochorton   32

  purpureum   30

Rhodomela   80

Rhodophyta   29

Rhodymenia   36, 38

Rhus copallina   167

  toxicodendron   177, 248

Rhynchosinapis monensis   162

Ribes prostratum   254

Ribwort   246, 257

Riccia   173

Rivularia   37

  atra   66

ROBERTSON, V.C.   253, 257

Rock pool(s)   28, 79, 99, 144

Rock samphire   253, 255, 258, 263

Rock sea lavender   246

Romney   89, 92, 124

Rorippa islandica   155

Rosa lucida   163, 167

  rugosa   177

  spinosissima   169

Rose-root   254

ROUND, F.E.   170, 174

Rubus   169

Rumex acetosa   259, 266

  acetosella   163, 246, 259, 266

  crispus   152, 153, 243, 244, 247,
    248

Rumicetum   267

Ruppia maritima   44, 105, 112

Ruppietum   105

Rye   199

Sabal palmetto   226

Saccorhiza polyschides   31, 43

Sagina maritima   110, 257

St. Andrews   166

St. Cyrus   166, 203, 205, 261

St. Kilda   253, 255, 256, 257, 260,
    264

St. Lawrence   87, 103, 112, 163, 167

Salicetum repentis   174, 175

Salicornia   3, 107, 112, 122, 124,
    135, 144, 146

  ambigua   113

  appressa   177

  dolichostachya   146

  europaea   112, 135, 146

  mucronata   113

  prostrata   177

  ramosissima   105

  stricta   105, 112, 124, 134, 135,
    136, 140, 246

  strictissima   105

  virginica   124

Salicornietum   47, 107

Salinity 14, 15, 78, 121, 132, 133,
    134, 135, 136, 137, 141, 144,
    175, 228, 229
SALISBURY, E.J.   150, 154, 186, 199,
    203, 205
Salix 174, 175
  atrocinerea 174, 175
  aurita 174
  cinerea 174
  herbacea 254
  repens 8, 169, 174, 176, 178,
    193, 205
Salsola 158
  kali 152, 154
  soda 153
Salt pan 48, 79, 112
Saltwort 152, 158
Sambucus 169
  nigra 167, 260
Samolus 193
  valerandi 110, 173
Sand couch grass 155, 158, 244
Sand orache 153
Sand sedge 162, 166, 169, 178, 208,
    246, 248
Sandscale 206
Sandwich 209
Sandy Halimionetum 110
Sargassum 38, 40
  natans 224
Scentless mayweed 253, 261
Scheldt 87, 107, 167
SCHOLL, D.W. 217, 229
SCHRAMM, W. 46
Scirpetum maritimi 105, 107
  tabernaemontani 107
Scirpus 136
  acutus 112

americanus 112
maritimus 114, 173
palustris 107
Scolt Head Island 11, 87, 90, 92,
    109, 123, 124, 137, 138, 153,
    156, 159, 163, 170, 195, 234,
    241, 243, 245, 246, 248
Scotland 36, 65, 93, 150, 157, 166,
    168, 245, 254, 256
SCOTT, G.A.M. 236
Scrub dune 169, 170
Scurvy-grass 246, 261, 264
Scytosiphon 37
Scytothamnus 71
Sea arrow-grass 108, 135
  aster 105, 112, 123, 135, 245
  blite 122, 177, 239, 246
  beetroot 152, 153, 253, 255
  buckthorn 8, 169
  campion 153, 245, 246, 247, 253,
    256, 258, 259, 265
  club-rush 173
  convolvulus 246
  couch-grass 244, 246
  hard-grass 108
  heath 153, 177, 246
  holly 246
  kale 152, 153, 253
  knotgrass 153
  lavender 108, 112, 135, 245, 256
  milkwort 108, 135, 173
  pea 153, 247
  pearlwort 257
  pink 93, 108, 246, 253, 255, 257,
    258, 263, 268
  plantain 8, 93, 105, 108, 110,
    135, 245, 256, 257, 259, 263

poa   109, 122, 135, 177, 245, 246,
    256

poppy   152

purslane   69, 108, 124, 126, 177,
    245, 246, 255

radish   153, 264

rocket   8, 152, 155, 158, 258

rush   103, 110, 173

sandwort   153, 158, 244

spleenwort   253, 258, 260

spurge   153, 162

wormwood   110, 153, 245

Sedetum   261

Sedum   162

  acre   237, 243, 244, 246, 261

  anglicum   258, 265

  rosea   254

Senecio jacobaea   162, 166, 178,
    246

  vulgaris   245

Sesuvium portulacastrum   227

Severn   97

SEYBOLD, A.   85

Sharp rush   173

Shearwaters   254, 257, 266, 270

Sheep's sorrel   246

Shore knotgrass   153

Shore orache   152

Shore weed   172

Shrew   207

Shrubby sea blite   48, 69, 136, 153,
    155, 177, 243, 246

Silene maritima   153, 243, 245, 246,
    247, 248, 253, 254, 258, 259,
    260, 261, 264, 265

  thorei   161

SINCLAIR, J.   30

Siphonales   78

Sirocoleum guyanense   224

Skälling   95, 107

Skokholm   255, 268

Slack(s)   1, 155, 157, 170, 171, 172,
    173, 174, 175, 177, 186, 192,
    193, 198, 206, 207, 213

Socies   11, 103

Society   11, 22, 36

SÖDERSTROM, J.   35

Sodium   132, 135, 138, 139, 142, 207

Solanum dulcamara   153, 248

Solidago sempervirens   163, 254

Solway Firth   87, 93, 100, 110

Somerset   101, 150

Sonchus arvensis   245

  oleraceus   245

Sorrel   268

SOUTH, G.R.   48

South Haven   203, 209

Southport   166, 184, 205

Sowthistle   245

Spain   150

Spartina   8, 13, 16, 47, 48, 95, 99,
    108, 111, 112, 135, 141, 163

  alterniflora   97, 108, 111, 112,
    114, 122, 124, 127, 142, 145

  anglica   107

  cynosuroides   112, 114

  juncea   248

  maritima   108

  patens   97, 111, 112, 114, 124, 153

  pectinata   112

  townsendii   4, 69, 107, 108, 145,
    160

Spartinetum   48, 107

Spergularia   259, 260

  marginata   108, 134, 135, 255

  marina   110

media   237

rupicola   258, 261, 263

Spermatochnus   32

Sphacelaria radicans   48

Spit(s)   89, 92, 152, 156, 217, 235,
   240

Splash zone   64

Spongomorpha   38

Spray zone   64

Stabilisation   5

STEERS, J.A.   248

Stellaria   166

   crassifolia   103

   humifusa   103

   media   178, 260, 267

Stellarieta   260

STEPHENSON, A.   19, 20, 23, 32

STEPHENSON, T.A.   19, 20, 23, 32

Stilophora   32

Stinkhorn   170

Stock   253

Strangford Loch   48

Striaria attenuata   48

Stronsay   30, 39

Studland   169, 175

Suaeda   3, 48, 101, 112, 146, 244

   fruticosa   69, 80, 110, 136, 143,
      153, 154, 155, 177, 178, 239,
      243, 246

   maritima   107, 112, 122

      var. *flexilis*   128, 246

      var. *macrocarpa*   128, 177

Subarctic   103

Sublittoral   18, 22, 26, 28, 40, 43,
   46, 48, 67, 71

   fringe   20, 21, 28, 31, 39

Subsere   2

Succession   3, 6, 103, 171, 209, 221,
   226, 257

Successional habitat   12

Succulence   16

Supra-littoral fringe   19, 20, 37, 38,
   39

Sussex   253, 255

Swales   247

Swash zone   64

Sweden   105, 114, 155, 159, 169

Synecology   16

Talbert   248

TANSLEY, A.G.   11, 166, 253, 255

TAYLOR, J.E.   38

Tecoma radicans   170

Temperature   59, 66, 67, 68, 69, 75,
   76, 77, 81, 143, 146, 189, 190,
   231, 267

Teneriffe   39

Terschelling   174, 178

Thalassia testudinum   224

Thalictrum minus ssp. *arenarium*   162,
   166

Thames   87, 102

Therophytes   8, 114, 171, 255

Thyme-leaved sandwort   246

Thymus serpyllum   261

Tide   13, 56

   gauge   13, 56

   pole   13, 56

Tillandsia usneoides   170

Tormentil   93, 108

Tortula ruraliformis   163, 168, 190

Tree lupin   212

Tree mallow   260, 263, 267

Trefoil   213

Tribonema   174

Trifolium   201
  arvense   201
  repens   93, 108, 168
Triglochin   112
  gaspense   112
  maritima   103, 107, 108, 112, 134, 135
  palustris   104, 247
TSCHUDY, R.H.   74
Typha   113, 114

Udotea   78
Ulex europaeus   169
  gallii   169
Ulothrix   36
Ulva   32, 74, 79
  lactuca   38, 55, 67, 69
  linza   36, 75
  thuretii   55
Uniola   161, 163, 205
  paniculatum   158, 161
Urospora   36
U.S.A.   54, 87, 99, 100, 101, 103, 111, 123, 127, 137, 142, 143, 152, 157, 158, 161, 163, 165, 167, 170, 171, 177, 222
Usnea   170

Vaccinium atrococcum   170
  corymbosum   177
  pennsylvanicum   167
Valonia   39
VAN DE MAAREL, E.   203
Vaucheria   174
  sphaerospora   46
  thuretii   47
Vendee   161

Verrucaria   20, 261
  marina   36
  maura   36, 248
VEVERS, A.G.   260
Viburnum pauciflorum   254
Vicia cracca   161, 163
Viola tricolor ssp. *curtisii*   162
Virginia   100, 113, 163
Vitis   170
Viviparous seedlings   221, 228
Vole   207
Volvocales   174
Voorne   150
Vulpa membranacea   168

Wadden   167
Wales   48, 150, 155
Wall-pepper   162, 244, 246
Walney Isle   166, 169
Wash, The   87
Water table   14, 15, 126, 130, 131, 132, 192, 193, 195, 197, 198, 205, 230, 249
WATSON, J.G.   228
Wavy hair-grass   169
WESTHOFF, V.   150, 203
Wheatears   270
White clover   93, 108
White Sea   103
White mangrove   218
WHITTAKER, R.H.   11
WIEHE, P.O.   121
Wild angelica   254
  cabbage   253
Wigeon   101
Wind rose   184
Winterton Ness   195, 240, 248
Woody nightshade   153

Xanthium canadense   163

  strumarium   163

Xanthoria parietina   261

YAPP, R.H.   99

Yellow Bartsia   173

  bird's nest   175

  dune   159, 161, 162, 163, 167,
      199, 237

  horned poppy   244

Yorkshire fog   110, 259, 261, 270

Yucca   163

Zannichellia palustris   172

Zonation   6, 46, 246

Zostera   44, 45, 46, 105, 107, 112,
      224

  marina   8, 104

  nana   104

  noltii   104

Zosteretum   103, 104

Zuyder Zee   102